Jonathan M. Platter
Divine Simplicity and the Triune Identity

Theologische Bibliothek
Töpelmann

—

Edited by
Bruce McCormack, Friederike Nüssel
and Christoph Schwöbel

Volume 195

Jonathan M. Platter

Divine Simplicity and the Triune Identity

A Critical Dialogue with the Theological Metaphysics of Robert W. Jenson

DE GRUYTER

ISBN 978-3-11-221611-8
e-ISBN (PDF) 978-3-11-073596-3
e-ISBN (EPUB) 978-3-11-073601-4
ISSN 0563-4288

Library of Congress Control Number: 2021936773

Bibliographic information published by the Deutsche Nationalbibliothek
The Deutsche Nationalbibliothek lists this publication in the Deutsche Nationalbibliografie;
Detailed bibliographic data are available in the Internet at http://dnb.dnb.de.

© 2025 Walter de Gruyter GmbH, Berlin/Boston
Dieser Band ist text- und seitenidentisch mit der 2021 erschienenen gebundenen Ausgabe.
Druck und Bindung: CPI books GmbH, Leck
www.degruyter.com

Inhalt

Acknowledgements —— IX

Abbreviations —— XI

Introduction —— 1

Part I Conceiving divine simplicity

1   Divine simplicity: orientation to current discussions —— 9
1.1   Introduction —— 9
1.2   Simplicity as a regulative category —— 10
1.3   Simplicity as a metaphysical category —— 11
1.4   The theological deployment of simplicity —— 14
1.4.1 Simplicity and the Creator–creature distinction —— 14
1.4.2 Simplicity and the multiplicity of divine names —— 18
1.4.3 Simplicity and Trinity —— 23
1.5   Conclusion —— 29

2   Simplicity in Christian doctrine: Gregory of Nyssa, Augustine, and Thomas Aquinas —— 31
2.1   Introduction —— 31
2.2   Gregory of Nyssa on the *adiastēmic* plenitude of the simple God —— 34
2.2.1 *Creatio ex nihilo* as a regulative principle in discerning the divine —— 34
2.2.2 Propria and perfections —— 37
2.2.3 Infinity, simplicity, and *diastēma* —— 41
2.3   Augustine on the self-same (*idipsum*) triune God —— 45
2.3.1 Augustine's exposition of divine simplicity —— 46
2.3.2 Predication and divine simplicity —— 48
2.3.3 Simplicity and Trinity —— 49
2.4   Thomas Aquinas and the pure actuality of the simple God —— 54
2.4.1 Simplicity, apophasis, and creation as causal relation —— 55
2.4.2 Prior unity, participation, and the one and the many —— 61
2.4.3 Simplicity and Trinity —— 63
2.5   Simplicity, prior unity, and the Creator–creature distinction —— 67

2.6 Conclusion —— 71

Part II Divine simplicity in the revisionary metaphysics of Robert W. Jenson

3   **The contemporary crisis of divine simplicity —— 75**
3.1   Introduction —— 75
3.2   Scripture, metaphysics, and the problem(s) with divine simplicity —— 76
3.3   Robert Jenson on the task of metaphysics —— 82
3.3.1 Situating Jenson —— 82
3.3.2 Scripture and revisionary metaphysics —— 83
3.4   Promise: developing a Christian revisionary metaphysics —— 89
3.5   Jesus Christ and created being —— 93
3.5.1 Election and predestination: Barth and Jenson's revisionary metaphysics —— 93
3.5.2 Being and the horizon of the future: Heidegger and Jenson's revisionary metaphysics —— 94
3.5.3 Being human: Christ and the communal concept of 'nature' —— 97
3.6   Dramatic unity —— 99
3.7   Conclusion —— 103

4   **Simplicity and Trinity in Robert Jenson's theology —— 104**
4.1   Introduction —— 104
4.2   Divine simplicity as lively event —— 106
4.2.1 Divine persons and divine temporal infinity —— 107
4.2.2 Identity of essence and existence —— 112
4.2.3 Impassibility and God's being as lively event —— 114
4.3   Simplicity and Trinity —— 118
4.3.1 Subsistent relations —— 118
4.3.2 Jesus in the Trinity: the body of God —— 122
4.3.3 The Holy Spirit in the Trinity: the simple event of futurity —— 125
4.4   Divine simplicity and divine names —— 130
4.5   Conclusion —— 134

Part III Toward a dramatic theology of divine simplicity

5 Divine simplicity and the triune identity — 139
5.1 Introduction — 139
5.2 Metaphysics, divine simplicity, and dramatic unity — 141
5.3 Jenson on divine simplicity — 145
5.4 Critical engagements — 150
5.4.1 Divine simplicity and the names of God — 151
5.4.2 Divine simplicity and the question of God's availability — 159
5.4.3 Divine simplicity and the relations of God — 170
5.5 Conclusion — 181

6 Conclusion — 183

Bibliography — 188

Index of Names — 206

Index of Subjects — 209

Acknowledgements

Even when the experience of writing consists of largely solitary effort, striving to bring one's thoughts to relatively coherent expression, what remains on the page is nonetheless a calescence of the history, relationships, stories, discussions, debates, proof-reads, and rewrites that enabled those thoughts and checked them. The list of people to thank is consequently potentially endless and extends beyond what I will likely ever fully recognize.

Several communities and individuals gave generously to offset relocation and living costs when my wife Janette and I were preparing to move to Cambridge: friends and members of the Cummings, Parker, Platter, Snowbarger, and Stroman families generously gave money and other gifts; we also received support through prayer and donations from Rogers First Church of the Nazarene and Duncanville Trinity Church of the Nazarene. With the birth of our son Julian, friends from the community at Tyndale House and St. Mark's Church, Newnham, enveloped us with familial love and warmth, generously providing the emotional and practical care that we needed as first-time parents in a new place. Several people spent time with Julian when I needed extra time to work or to meet with my supervisor: especially Rachel-Anne Rose ('Ra-Ra'), Erin and the Howard family, Katie and the Hixson family, Niamh Colbrook, Jesse and Iane Grenz ('Tio and Tia'), and Sanjung and Daniel Eng. It is a gift to have such a host of people who love and care for our son.

Several teachers, from both undergraduate and postgraduate studies, have continued to shape my thinking, either through continued conversations or through impressing on my mind questions and convictions with which I have continued to grapple: Joseph Coleson, Timothy Crutcher, Steve Green, Andy Johnson, Steve McCormick, Brint Montgomery, and Thomas Noble. The community of families and scholars at Tyndale House provided a rich environment in which to live and work during 2016–2018; thanks to principal Peter Williams for welcoming a systematic theologian like me to live amongst biblical scholars for a couple of years. Nazarene Theological College, Manchester, has welcomed me on several occasions; thanks especially to Steve Wright for trusting me to teach some courses on his behalf and to Geordan Hammond for taking the risk of co-teaching a masters seminar with a novice academic. For conversations during the time of research and writing: Richard Bauckham, Jeremy Begbie, Niamh Colbrook, Andrew Davison, Bradley Green, Daniel De Haan, Tim Hahn, Pui Ip, Veli-Matti Kärkkäinen, Maureen and Brian Langdoc, James Orr, Joanna and Luke Tarassenko, and Stephen John Wright. Frequent conversations with Jesse Grenz and Austin Stevenson have especially helped me to think about my research within the broader context of Christian theology. And for reading and commenting on earlier drafts: Alex Abecina, Phillip Cary, Matthew Codd, Douglas Hedley, Jacob Lett, Janet Soskice, and Austin Stevenson; their careful reading helped clarify my thinking and writing, and in one case even prevented an embarrassing error. Matthew Codd not only read most of my work and discussed it with me but is largely to thank (or blame) for my continued engagement with Robert Jenson. Jacob Lett has been a constant dialogue partner and has shaped my thinking in significant ways through our regular video chats and exchange of drafts. Simeon Zahl and Christoph Schwöbel served as the internal and external examiners (respectively) for the PhD thesis, and their critical engagement not only helped me increase clarity at several points but also raised some questions that have helped me think about the direction my work might go next. I am especially grateful for the consistent, thorough, and judicious guidance of my supervisor Ian McFarland, who helped me to write more clearly, to keep writing when I was not sure what the next steps would be, and to recognize when I was making progress. For remaining errors and lack of clarity, I alone am responsible.

I would also like to thank our families: my siblings Cori, David, and Joshua, along with their spouses, for encouraging me and for attending to my development as a person and not just an academic; my parents Paul and Joan, for endlessly expressing love, joy, and pride; and Janette's parents, Perry and Dallis, and other members of the Parker and Cummings families, for supporting us and for their consistent affirmations. I'm thankful to Julian, my son, for the focus and expansiveness of his imagination; it's been a constant joy to be invited into his world. And to my wife Janette, who has worked full-time—sometimes multiple jobs—to support our family during my research. She encouraged me to find rhythms of work and rest, prodded me to participate in seminars and academic events when I might have defaulted to staying home, and continues to display a confidence in me that far outstrips my own. I keep trying—to no avail—to catch up with her foresight, tenacity, inventiveness, and energy. If my work displays any of these virtues, it is thanks to their excess in her.

During the last phase of writing, both of my paternal grandparents died, my maternal grandparents having died before I finished high school. Both sets of grandparents have been models for me of Christian love, generosity, and faithfulness. I cannot image having completed a project like this one apart from their influence, and so I dedicate it to their memory.

Cambridge, UK
Lent 2021

Abbreviations

Athanasius

c. Ar. *Orationes Contra Arianos* (Orations Against the Arians). Edited by Philip Schaff and Henry Wace. Nicene and Post-Nicene Fathers of the Christian Church, Second Series, Vol. IV. Edinburgh: T&T Clark, 1892.

Augustine

Civ. *De Civitate Dei* (The City of God). Translated by William Babcock. 2 vols. New York: New City, 2013.
Trin. *De Trinitate* (The Trinity). Translated by Edmund Hill. Hyde Park, NY: New City, 1991.
De Rel. *De Vera Religione* (True Religion). Translated by Edmund Hill. In *On Christian Belief*, ed. Boniface Ramsey. Hyde Park, NY: New City, 2005.
En. Ps. *Enarrationes in Psalmos* (Expositions on the Psalms). Edited by Boniface Ramsey and John E. Rotelle. Translated by Maria Boulding. 6 vols. Hyde Park, NY: New City, 2000–2004.
In Ioh. *In Iohannis Evangelium Tractatus* (Homilies on the Gospel of John). Edited by Alan Fitzgerald. Translated by Edmund Hill. Hyde Park, NY: New City, 2009.
Conf. *Confessiones* (The Confessions). Translated by Maria Boulding. Hyde Park, NY: New City, 1997.

Latin quotations are from *S. Aurelii Augustini Opera Omnia*, ed. Franco Monteverde, online at http://augustinus.it.

Dionysius the Aereopagite

DN *The Divine Names*. Translated by Colm Luibheid. In The Complete Works. Mahwah, NJ: Paulist, 1987.
MT *The Mystical Theology*. Translated by Colm Luibheid. In The Complete Works. Mahwah, NJ: Paulist, 1987.

Gregory of Nyssa

Eun. *Contra Eunomium I–III*. Translated by Stuart George Hall. 3 vols, with Supporting Studies. Leiden: Brill, 2007–2018. Full details for each volume are provided in the bibliography, according to editors: Brugarolas, Karfíková et al, and Leemans et al, respectively.
All English quotations of *Contra Eunomium* are taken from Hall's translation, though for ease of reference I also provide page numbers for $NPNF^2$.
GNO *Gregorii Nysseni Opera*. Edited by Wernerus Jaeger et al. Leiden: Brill, 1960–.
In Eccl. *Homilies on Ecclesiastes*. Translated by Stuart George Hall and Rachel Moriarty. Berlin: Walter de Gruyter, 1993.

Cat. *Catechetical Discourse.* Translated by Ignatius Green. Yonkers, NY: St. Vladimir's Seminary Press, 2019.

Irenaeus of Lyons

AH *Adversus Haereses* (Against Heresies). Edited by Alexander Roberts and James Donaldson. Ante-Nicene Fathers of the Church, Vol. I. Edinburgh: T&T Clark, 1885

Robert W. Jenson

A&O *Alpha and Omega:* A Study in the Theology of Karl Barth. New York: Thomas Nelson & Sons, 1963.
AT *America's Theologian:* A Recommendation of Jonathan Edwards. Oxford: Oxford University Press, 1988.
CC *Canon and Creed.* Louisville: Westminster John Knox, 2010.
GaG *God After God:* The God of the Past and the God of the Future, Seen in the Work of Karl Barth. New York: Bobbs-Merrill, 1969.
KNTHF *The Knowledge of Things Hoped For:* The Sense of Theological Discourse. Oxford: Oxford University Press, 1969.
OTH *On Thinking the Human:* Resolutions of Difficult Notions. Grand Rapids: Wm. B. Eerdmans, 2003.
RAI *A Religion Against Itself.* Richmond: John Knox, 1967.
S&P *Story and Promise:* A Brief Theology of the Gospel About Jesus. Philadelphia: Fortress, 1973.
ST *Systematic Theology,* 2 Vols. Oxford: Oxford University Press, 1997–1999.
TI *The Triune Identity:* God According to the Gospel. Philadelphia: Fortress, 1982.
UG *Unbaptized God:* The Basic Flaw in Ecumenical Theology. Minneapolis: Augsburg Fortress, 1992.
VW *Visible Words:* The Interpretation and Practice of Christian Sacraments. Philadelphia: Fortress, 1978.

Plotinus

Enn. *The Enneads.* Edited by Lloyd P. Gerson. Translated by George Boys-Stones, John M. Dillon, Lloyd P. Gerson, R. A. H. King, Andrew Smith, and James Wilberding. Cambridge: Cambridge University Press, 2018.
Enneads I–VI: With an English Translation by A. H. Armstrong. 7 vols. Loeb Classical Library. Cambridge, MA: Harvard University Press, 1969–1988.

Thomas Aquinas

Comp. *Compendium of Theology.* Translated by Richard J. Regan. Oxford: Oxford University Press, 2009.

Pot.	*De potentia Dei* (The Power of God). Translated by Richard J. Regan. Oxford: Oxford University Press, 2012.
In div. nom.	*In librum Beati Dionysii De divinis nominibus expositio* (Commentary on Pseudo-Dionysius' *The Divine Names*). In *Corpus Thomisticum: S. Thomae de Aquino Opera Omnia*, ed. Enrique Alarcón, online at www.corpusthomisticum.org, 2000.
ScG	*Summa Contra Gentiles*. Edited by Joseph Kenny. Translated by Anton C. Pegis, James F. Anderson, Vernon J. Bourke, and Charles J. O'Neil. Notre Dame: University of Notre Dame Press, 1975.
STh	*Summa Theologiæ*. Edited by Thomas Gilby. Translated by The English Dominican Friars. Blackfriars Edition. 60 vols. London: Eyre & Spottiswoode, 1963–1981.
In Ioann.	*Super Evangelium S. Ioannis Lectura* (Commentary on the Gospel of John). Edited by Daniel Keating and Matthew Levering. Translated by Fabian Larcher and James A. Weisheipl. 3 vols. Washington, DC: Catholic University of America Press, 2010.

Other

DS	*Enchiridion Symbolorum: A Compendium of Creeds, Definitions, and Declarations of the Catholic Church,* Latin text online at http://catho.org/9.php?d=g1
NPNF[2]	*Nicene and Post-Nicene Fathers of the Christian Church, Second Series*. 14 volumes. Edited by Philip Schaff and Henry Wace. Edinburgh: T&T Clark, 1886–1900.

Unless stated otherwise, quotations from the Bible are from the New Revised Standard Version.

Introduction

'God is one being in three persons'. So goes a standard description of the Christian doctrine of the Trinity. After several decades of vigorous defence and renewed attention to the affirmation of 'three persons', the sense of 'one being' has come to a new point of critical reflection. The doctrine of divine simplicity, which holds that God has no parts, is one way to express God's unity, and in the past it enjoyed near unanimity in Christian theology. In the previous generation of theologians, however, many voiced a desire to set the question of the unity of God *after* discussion of God's threeness, explicitly rejecting what was seen as the scholastic over-emphasis on God's oneness and simplicity to the detriment of the three persons.[1] If the recent number of publications on divine simplicity is any indication, then we might wonder if this reordering – three *then* one – is taking place on a broader, historical scale: following decades of fruitful reflection on God's tri-personhood, theologians and philosophers of religion are now returning more directly to God's unity, simplicity in particular.[2] My argument joins this growing body of literature on the positive contribution of divine simplicity to Christian theology, but I attempt a more sympathetic engagement with the 'trinitarian revival' by way of dialogue with the theology of Robert W. Jenson, whose relation to divine simplicity is controversial.[3]

The question of divine unity pertains to the core of Christian faith. On the one hand, we are pushed to ask how Father, Son, and Spirit are not three Gods but one. But on the other hand, the very possibility of the coherence of history and of humanity hinges on their coherence with reality's origin, persistence, and future. These are, as Robert Jenson never tired of pointing out, two sides of the same coin: does what happened in Jesus cohere with what happened at Is-

---

[1] Rahner, *Trinity*; and Lacugna, *God For Us*. Coakley distinguishes 'three waves' of trinitarian revival – Rahner in the first wave with Barth and Lossky; Lacugna in the second with Gunton, Jenson, Moltmann, Pannenberg, and Zizoulas (Coakley, '"Relational Ontology", Trinity, and Science', 185–94). Her 'third wave' includes theologians who have retrieved simplicity and questioned the East/West antinomy in trinitarian theology, like Lewis Ayres, Michel René Barnes, John Behr, herself, Kallistos Ware, and Rowan Williams (192n26).
[2] E.g., Barrett, *Divine Simplicity*; Dolezal, *God without Parts*; Duby, *Divine Simplicity*; Hart, *Experience of God*; Hinlicky, *Divine Simplicity*; Sonderegger, *Systematic Theology 1*. As well as numerous essays, including a special issue in *Modern Theology* (35, no. 3 [July 2019]).
[3] For instance, Sonderegger frames her own project's priority of 'unicity' and simplicity in direct opposition to Jenson's theology (*Systematic Theology 1*, 5–9). But on the other hand one of the most significant monographs on Jenson's theology dedicates a chapter to arguing that Jenson upholds simplicity (Wright, *Dogmatic Aesthetics*, 53–99).

https://doi.org/10.1515/9783110735963-003

rael's exodus? Are these events of the same God? Is history's creator also its redeemer? Jesus prays in the garden, just before his death, that all who believe would be one, and he expresses the oneness of the Christian community by reference to and dependence on the oneness shared between himself and the Father: just as he and the Father are one, Jesus prays that all who believe would be one in them (Jn. 17:20–23). 'May they also be in us… The glory that you have given me I have given them, so that they may be one, as we are one, I in them and you in me, that they may become completely one' (Jn. 17:21b–23). St. Paul echoes Jesus' prayer when in Romans 15:5–6 he connects the harmony within the church to God's own 'steadfastness', a present harmony that anticipates the day when all will glorify God 'with one voice'. We may not know the extent to which the unity of the Christian community displays the character of God's unity, but Paul and Jesus both convey the conviction that Christian unity is derived from God's unity and is manifest by virtue of God's joining with humanity.

This implies that from a Christian perspective, the possibility of human reconciliation is not primarily predicated on the horizon of human imagination and powers but more fundamentally on who God is. While there are legitimate concerns with the procedures some trinitarian theologies have followed for connecting God's unity-in-relation to human political programs,[4] we should not doubt that our understanding of God's unity shapes what we think is possible and desirable for human unity.[5] Consequently, God's unity, in this book considered through the concept of simplicity, is relevant to but not commensurable with the kind of unity experienced among finite creatures.

---

[4] In response to social trinitarian arguments that human society should be modelled on the Trinity's perfect, egalitarian perichoresis (i.e., Boff, *Trinity and Society*; Volf, *After Our Likeness*), some have argued that this inevitably projects human ideals onto God in order to justify them, without attending to the radical discontinuity between intratrinitarian relations and human relations (esp., Kilby, 'Perichoresis and Projection', 432–45; Tanner, *Christ the Key*, 207–46).

[5] Consider Augustine's interpretation of Psalm 121.3 (Vulgate), where Jerusalem is being made into a genuine, unified city by virtue of participation in God's self-same (*idipsum*) simplicity (Augustine, *En. Ps.*, 121.5). Aquinas distinguishes created unity from God's unity by noting that created unity obtains *as an ordering* of the whole universe (and is, therefore, a configuration of multiple elements and constituents) and is the *object* of God's knowledge, which directs creation to its perfection (*STh*, I.15.2, *responsio*). And yet, for Aquinas, creation's unity is no doubt attendant on the fact that all finite natures are themselves ways in which the simple, indivisible divine essence is participable, so that all of created reality is oriented to its own perfection of created unity as also perfect participation in the God who is the infinite and simple convergence of all perfections.

These complications about 'unity' reveal both the multifaceted nature of our inquiries about it and suggest that we do not come to the question of divine unity already knowing what will satisfy the quest. 'Unity' as a concept is embedded in a nexus of practical and theoretical concerns, and this is particularly true for the 'unity' of the Holy Trinity and the doctrine of divine simplicity. Consequently, throughout these chapters, I draw attention not only to the doctrinal formulations and functions of divine simplicity in the various thinkers I engage, but I also reflect on the kinds of unity their versions of divine simplicity satisfy. For when analyzing or advancing a form of divine simplicity, we do not start with a given, univocal concept of 'unity' and simply decide how extreme the concept becomes when applied to God. Rather, we have to negotiate the very limits of our language and imaginations in order to think the relation and difference between God and creatures, which is to say that the concept of unity should function non-contrastively and analogically when we use it of God.

To this end, I sympathetically engage what I call Jenson's rule of dramatic unity in order to allow for the ways that the concept of unity itself has varied resonances and functions at different orders of reflection. This holds for the use of the category across the Creator–creature distinction and for the various contexts within which we speak of God. And from this perspective, I aim toward a flexible doctrine of divine simplicity without developing a revisionist doctrine of God.

It is necessary not only to retrieve and develop accounts of God's unity, like divine simplicity, but also to do so in dialogue with recent theologians who have broadened the range of metaphysical and conceptual options on offer for the Christian doctrine of God. For if a retrieval of divine simplicity – as one dimension of an account of God's unity – is to serve our identification of God as Trinity, then we would benefit from considering how divine simplicity does not only reappear by jumping over the recent trinitarian revival but can in fact be sustained through sympathetic engagement with it. This is not to say that the current revival of interest in divine simplicity should have nothing critical to say to particular arguments and claims within the trinitarian revival. But as various advocates of divine simplicity have rightly noted, in order to properly evaluate this ancient doctrine, we must attend to the metaphysics within which it is articulated; and where there are distinct metaphysical perspectives at play, attention should be directed to both sides.[6]

My argument enters into the debates surrounding divine simplicity and the Trinity particularly by recognizing the varying metaphysics that attend different

---

6 Cf. Mascall, *He Who Is*, 25–39; White, 'Simplicity and Trinity', 71–82.

articulations. My ultimate aim is to develop an initial sketch of divine simplicity in trinitarian perspective. On the way toward that end, I engage in a sympathetic dialogue with earlier articulations of simplicity and Trinity – Gregory of Nyssa, Augustine, and Aquinas – as a background to deeper engagement with one theologian of the trinitarian revival, Robert Jenson.

* * * * *

This work is divided into three parts. The first part analyses various criticisms, debates, and constructive articulations of divine simplicity. In the first chapter, I situate the doctrine of divine simplicity in contemporary theology and philosophy of religion. This discussion highlights the diversity of issues and approaches that have emerged in relation to the doctrine and lays out some of the central categories needed to understand different perspectives on simplicity within medieval theology as well as current philosophy. In the latter half of the chapter, I present three theological deployments of simplicity: expressing the distinction between God and creation, the multiplicity of divine names, and the Trinity.

Chapter two focuses on Gregory of Nyssa, Augustine, and Thomas Aquinas, assessing how they use divine simplicity in relation to the three theological deployments identified in chapter one. My reading of these three theologians highlights the potential for overlap in their thought, while also acknowledging differences both in form and content. Throughout this chapter, I consider what kind of 'unity' each thinker develops in their articulation of God's unique reality and discuss to what extent their conception of unity regulates their expression of divine simplicity. Two rules emerge: the *rule of prior unity* and the *strict Creator–creature distinction*. I argue that both are concerned with what kind of unity we understand in the case of God, and that they can be used together for Christian theology. However, for all three theologians the Creator–creature distinction remains primary.

Part Two turns to our present theological context and initiates the dialogue with Robert Jenson. In chapter three, I first raise the question of why divine simplicity is questionable in a new way for recent generations of theologians. I argue that the main factor is an increasing dichotomy between scriptural thinking and philosophical/metaphysical reasoning, so that the more philosophically entrenched a doctrine appears, the less biblical it is taken to be. This suggests that continuing to speak of God as simple requires carefully negotiating the relationship between scripture and metaphysics. I introduce Robert Jenson's theological metaphysics as a particular response to this dilemma. Jenson's way of handling the exigencies of metaphysical reflection in interpreting scripture turns on the *unity* of the scriptural narrative in relation to the *unity* of scripture's primary author, God. Consequently, in Jenson the enduring themes of my argument up to this point converge: the question of divine unity is implicated in the basic categories by which we interpret the world we inhabit (metaphysics), regulated by the narratives that shape our imaginations (scripture), and concerns the dramatic involvement of God with creatures (the possibility of creation's/humanity's unity in relation to the unique unity of the Creator).

However, Jenson's theology is rarely seen as an ally for those committed to divine simplicity. Consequently, in chapter four I offer a reconstructed doctrine of divine simplicity from within Jenson's theology. This is a creative redescription that operates primarily in an analytical-descriptive mode. I argue for a way of reading Jenson's trinitarian theology that is commensurable with divine simplicity, which shifts the center of balance in debates between 'classical theism' – those who defend the traditional metaphysical conception of God as simple, etc. – and recent trinitarian theology. For if someone like Jenson, who often raised strong criticisms of divine simplicity, can be shown to rely on its logic in important respects, then perhaps there need not be so great an opposition between classical theism and the trinitarian revival as some have charged.[7] Further, my reading of Jenson provides clarification and defence of some of the more controversial points of his theology, especially his historicist metaphysics and the perceived threats this brings in his doctrine of God.

This enables dialogue on some finer points, which is the content of chapter five, the third part. Here, I defend a version of the *rule of dramatic unity* while clarifying why it need not involve a reduction of God's transcendence, being concerned instead with the diversity of contexts within which we speak of God and with theology's self-involving character. Although I have argued that Jenson's theology is largely compatible with divine simplicity, in this chapter I raise three critical questions where divine simplicity enables further development on Jenson's thought; I argue that Jenson's position on these points is ambiguous or problematic; and I develop constructive proposals to address these shortcomings. My three critical questions concern the three deployments of divine simplicity identified in chapter one (viz., Creator–creature distinction, multiple divine names, and the triune relations), and through them I engage some of the more polemical edges of Jenson's theology. Consequently, I develop Jenson's doctrine of God in ways that contribute to an ecumenical and trinitarian conception of divine simplicity.

---

7 E.g., Ayres, *Nicaea and Its Legacy*, 404–14; and Holmes, *Holy Trinity*, 182–200.

In this way, I advance a defence of divine simplicity for Christian theology, by way of exposition and critical engagement with Jenson, a contemporary theologian who has voiced significant criticisms of divine simplicity and the role it has played in Western trinitarian thought. I defend the primary thesis that divine simplicity is an asset to trinitarian theology in part by making explicit the underlying logic of divine simplicity in Jenson's own thought and by showing how a generous doctrine of divine simplicity can actually benefit a trinitarian theology that is broadly sympathetic to Jenson's constructive work. If this argument successfully diffuses some of the polemics between Jenson's thought and more classically oriented theologians, then it might also contribute to a broader rapprochement between advocates of divine simplicity and theologians sympathetic to the 20th century trinitarian revival.

Part I **Conceiving divine simplicity**

1 Divine simplicity: orientation to current discussions

1.1 Introduction

The doctrine of divine simplicity has become contentious and often hotly debated. Consequently, it is important to become familiar with some of the main contours of the doctrine and the debates connected with it. While varying in formulation, its minimal claim is that God is not composed of any more basic constituents – or, according to St. Augustine, God *is* all that God *has*.[1] Many theologians reject simplicity entirely, often with a diagnosis of either incoherence or incompatibility with Christian theology and scripture. Yet others have claimed that simplicity is necessary for the coherence of the Christian conception of God. So David Bentley Hart has averred, 'any denial of divine simplicity is equivalent to a denial of God's reality', and even more pointedly, 'a denial of divine simplicity is tantamount to atheism'.[2] No small contributing factor in these oppositions is a lack of consensus on the role of metaphysics in theology, though even here the disagreements are multifaceted.[3] When rejection of divine simplicity is voiced by process theists, for example, it is not as a result of the rejection of metaphysics but rather as a corollary of their metaphysical commitments.[4] While many defenders of simplicity are also committed to 'classical' metaphysics (Hart being a ready example), others would prefer to remain agnostic towards issues metaphysical, while yet others would reformulate simplicity in explicit rejection of its metaphysical form.[5] Consequently, there are two broad concerns to be ad-

---

[1] Augustine, *Civ.*, XI.10.
[2] Hart, *Experience of God*, 134, 128.
[3] So, for instance, two recent defenders of simplicity, each of which is attentive to metaphysical issues, also seem to disagree about general metaphysical questions. Steven J. Duby, for instance, deploys Thomist-Aristotelian metaphysics unapologetically to defend a dogmatic and exegetical account of simplicity (*Divine Simplicity*). Andrew Radde-Gallwitz defends the more Neoplatonic approach of the Cappodocian brothers in *Basil, Gregory, and Divine Simplicity*. In his review of Duby's book, Radde-Gallwitz wonders whether Duby has conflated the broader metaphysical articulation of divine simplicity with that of high scholasticism ('Review of Duby, *Divine Simplicity*').
[4] Consider: 'Whitehead repudiates ontological simplicity in favor of a differential pluralism of becoming. For him this process of becoming explicitly replaced the *creatio ex nihilo* with an unbounded process of creativity' (Keller, *Face of the Deep*, 164; also 63, 175–82).
[5] Dolezal and Duby defend a broadly classical approach to simplicity, relying on scholastic metaphysics (respectively: *God without Parts*; *Divine Simplicity*). Jordan Barrett (*Divine Simplicity*),

dressed in understanding the doctrine of divine simplicity: (2.2) its regulative function in speech about God, and (2.3) the use of metaphysics in its formulation. After introducing these two concerns, I will then turn to (2.4) three central theological uses to which simplicity is put: the Creator–creature distinction, multiplicity of divine names, and the doctrine of the Trinity. These three theological uses will guide my interpretations and arguments in the following chapters.

1.2 Simplicity as a regulative category

Divine simplicity has a regulative function in theology; consequently, David Burrell calls it a 'formal feature' of divinity.[6] In this role, simplicity governs or regulates the apprehension, interpretation, and formulation of speech about God. By using simplicity as a 'formal feature', any implicit or explicit attribution of composition in God is precluded – our speech about God simply does not have direct purchase on the ontological constitution of God. Because created things *are* composite, simplicity as a formal feature serves as a reminder not to think of God in creaturely terms. While attention to the regulative function need not exclude a metaphysical or descriptive function of simplicity, it is helpful to appreciate its distinct role. This can be seen in Paul Hinlicky, who advances a purely regulative, 'rule-based' understanding of divine simplicity.[7]

For Hinlicky, divine simplicity has two regulative functions when purged of its 'protological' orientation. First, it serves to free theology from idolatry by governing our language according to the *Shema*, understood as an *ethical* injunction to remain faithful to the one singular God with whom we have a covenant relation (rather than the other gods we might encounter).[8] Second, simplicity functions as a rule of eschatological confirmation and union. This function is regulative because it primarily works to shape the kind of faith and speech that is appropriate in response to God's promises. In a world of competing deities –

---

without rejecting the metaphysical approach, develops a constructive account from the Biblical practice of divine naming. For a recent attempt in systematic theology to revitalise a regulative and metaphysical conception of simplicity through careful reading of scripture and an eye to theology in the doxological mode, see Sonderegger, *Systematic Theology 1*. Hunsinger prefers to remain agnostic about metaphysics (*Reading Barth with Charity*, 178–80). And, for an example that is not 'metaphysical', cf. Hinlicky, *Divine Simplicity*.

6 Burrell, *Aquinas*, 5–6, 16–21; Burrell, *Knowing the Unknowable God*, 46–47.
7 *Divine Simplicity*; which is the development of a thread of the argument in his earlier book, *Divine Complexity*, x–xi, 3–4, 173–84.
8 *Divine Simplicity*, xix.

competing objects of trust and faith – God has promised eschatological participation in the triune life. Consequently, proper faith – regulated by divine simplicity – is exclusively oriented toward eschatological fulfilment. For Hinlicky, then, simplicity does not describe the plenitude of divine being self-subsisting as the identity of essence and existence, as a more metaphysical rendering might conclude. Instead, it is fundamentally a rule for situating faith between promise and fulfilment and accepting the instability of the present, wherein one's theological claims are not brute givens but are tentative proposals for directing one's life and mind to the eschatological consummation of all things in the 'Beloved Community'.[9] Although Hinlicky himself concedes that this rule-version of simplicity has ontological implications, he prefers not to develop the doctrine in a metaphysically robust manner and, consequently, refers to his version as 'weak simplicity'. Hinlicky's approach is one example of the regulative function of simplicity, developed explicitly in distinction from metaphysical formulations. While the two need not be opposed, Hinlicky's example helps to demonstrate the difference between them. Simplicity is regulative insofar as it governs the grammar of speech about God, ensuring that God is spoken of differently than creaturely beings (avoiding idolatry) and as the one on whom our faith exclusively rests (eschatological union).

1.3 Simplicity as a metaphysical category

In contrast to Hinlicky's approach, traditional doctrines of simplicity have explicitly developed the doctrine's metaphysical function. Central to metaphysical approaches is the metaphysics of composition, for what it means to say that God is metaphysically simple depends on the kinds of composition one is denying. Creatures can be simple in the sense of having no component parts, like electrons or quarks are simples, while still being *metaphysically* composite by virtue of having properties distinct from their being, an essence distinct from existence, and by being defined by genus and differentia.[10] For Thomas Aquinas, the dis-

---

[9] *Divine Simplicity*, 144–47, 152, 160–61, 173–90, 202–9.
[10] Even electrons and quarks are composed of genus and differentia: for an electron is in the genus 'subatomic particle' (or more specifically, 'lepton') differentiated by having negative energy; and quarks come in six 'flavours', so that 'quark' is a genus and 'flavour' its differentia. Oliver Crisp's model of simplicity takes simples like electrons or quarks as useful analogues for God's simplicity ('Parsimonious Model of Simplicity', 558–73), though most uses of divine simplicity that I draw on stress the radical *discontinuity* between divine simplicity and creaturely instances of simplicity.

tinction of essence and existence is one of the most metaphysically basic forms of composition.[11] In creatures there is a real distinction between essence and existence, between 'what something is' and 'that it is'. In Aquinas' view, existence is ontologically prior to essence in created beings, in the sense that existence is an *activity*, the self-communicative act by virtue of which an essence stands out from nonbeing.[12] The priority of existence signals that a creature's essence does not account for its own existence – a creature does not cause itself to be – and yet insofar as a creature does exist there is a real unity of essence and existence and not a simple mereological sum of the two. This unity-in-distinction of essence and existence (or 'polarity', as Hans Urs von Balthasar calls it) both reflects the connection of creatures to their Creator *and* marks their distinction from the Creator.[13] The *unity* of essence and existence in creatures is a reflection of the perfect identity of essence and existence in God, while the *real distinction* of essence and existence marks creation's dependence on God as the self-subsisting source and plenitude of existence (*ipsum esse subsistens*). Hence, the affirmation of divine simplicity in terms of the identity of essence and existence requires metaphysical explication insofar as it depends on an interpretation of creaturely being.

The metaphysical explication of divine simplicity relies on the categories of essence and existence, but both terms have changed meaning over time. Consequently, what Aquinas, for instance, meant by them is significantly different from what many modern philosophers and metaphysicians take them to mean. It is important to clarify these differences in order to navigate the debates of the last fifty years. This is especially evident in the metaphysics of analytic philosophers.[14] Relying on the modal logic of possible worlds, the most common use of 'essence' in analytic philosophy, deriving from Saul Kripke's theory of modality, is to name a set of properties a being possesses in every possible world in

---

11 Burrell argues that because of how fundamental this metaphysical pair is, Thomas uses it to express 'the distinction' between God and creation (*Knowing the Unknowable God*, 14–18, 24–34).
12 For example, cf. *ScG*, I.43, II.69, III.69; *Pot.*, q. 2, art. 1. For interpretation, cf. Clarke, 'Action as Self-Revelation'; 'Limitation of Act by Potency'; Rolnick, *Analogical Possibilities*, 53–58. The 'prior' in this sentence is part of what funds criticisms like that of Hinlicky, whereby he charges proponents of 'strong' simplicity with importing a Hellenistic 'protological' doctrine of God (*Divine Simplicity*, xvii–xxiii, 43–4, 106–11, 157).
13 *Theo-Logic*, 1:105: 'Polarity means that the poles, even as they are in tension, exist strictly through each other. ... The two poles coinhere in an intimate unity that constitutes the irresolvable mystery of created being'.
14 There are important exceptions within analytic philosophy. E.g., Oderberg, *Real Essentialism*; and Feser, *Scholastic Metaphysics*.

which they exist, whereas those properties a being possesses in some but not all of the worlds in which they exist are 'accidental' or 'non-essential'.[15] For ancient and medieval philosophers, however, essences were understood as the 'active' principle of a being – relative to their matter, properties, and accidents – which is *expressed* through properties but is not identical to those properties. The essence of a being, for these earlier thinkers, is the definition of the being according to genus and differentia (i.e., a human essence is an *animal* (genus) that is *rational* (difference)).[16] The essential definition makes the being and its action intelligible by enabling one to recognize the form of the individual being.

'Existence', with some exceptions, has tended to be reduced to a quantifier in analytic philosophy, following Bertrand Russell and Gottlob Frege, which is a view in metaontology known as the redundancy theory of existence.[17] According to Frege, 'existence' is not a real predicate, and any sentence which appears to use it as a predicate can without remainder be paraphrased or analyzed without it.[18] Consequently, such sentences are transformed into propositions of the form $(\exists x)(x=E)$, which means, *it is the case that there is some object x such that x is identical to E (or has E as its essence or properties)*. The existential quantifier, $\exists$, simply modifies the proposition $(x=E)$, which consequently does not itself contain reference to existence.[19] On this view of existence, it is practically meaningless to assert that God's essence and existence are identical, which can be seen in Christopher Hughes' criticism of divine simplicity. Hughes charges that if God is identical with God's existence, then God is just divine existence existing, but without 'being the existence of anything ... [which] is like supposing that something could be a shape, without being the shape of anything but that shape ... a merely existent substance is too thin to be possible'.[20] For Hughes, Aquinas's claim that essence and existence are identical in God is like saying God is a quantifier that quantifies nothing but itself.

---

15 Kripke, *Naming and Necessity*, 97–127.
16 Cf. Wuellner, *Dictionary of Scholastic Philosophy*, 42.
17 Cf. Berto and Plebani, *Ontology and Metaontology*, 14–52.
18 Frege, 'Dialogue with Pünjer over Existence'.
19 For criticism of this view and an alternative that attempts to reformulate Aquinas' own approach, see Miller, *Fullness of Being*; and Braine, *Reality of Time and Existence of God*, 92–120. For defence of the Fregean view, see Peter van Inwagen's 'Meta-Ontology', and 'Being, existence, and ontological commitment'.
20 Hughes, *Complex Theory of a Simple God*, 21. Jay Wesley Richards attempts a mediating position between the critical analytic philosophers and classical metaphysical tradition. However, while he notes the differences in concepts of 'essence', I do not think he sufficiently attends to the differences in concepts of 'existence'; cf. Richards, *Untamed God*, 219–22.

As will be discussed below and in the next chapter, Aquinas understands existence in a very different way.[21] Drawing on Aristotle's priority of act over potency and Plato's participatory metaphysics, Aquinas articulates existence as the *activity* by virtue of which a being, its essence, and all its properties are actual. In God, for Aquinas, the *activity* of existence is unbounded by essence, for God's essence *is* 'to be', and consequently all finite beings have existence by participating in God's infinite act of being.[22]

1.4 The theological deployment of simplicity

The difference between God and creation, which I suggested is central both to the regulative and metaphysical functions of simplicity, is the first theological deployment of simplicity that I consider. Not only is the Creator–creature distinction the most immediate theological use of divine simplicity, it also shapes how the other two theological deployments are approached and articulated. Consequently, I turn to it presently. In the sections that follow, I briefly introduce the other two theological uses: *multiplicity of divine names*, and *Trinity*. In the next chapter, I discuss how Gregory of Nyssa, Augustine, and Aquinas approach all three uses of simplicity.

1.4.1 Simplicity and the Creator–creature distinction

The difference between Creator and creation is *sui generis* – no other difference can serve as an adequate analogue. Consequently, expressing this difference puts strain on our language and provides immediate motivation for apophaticism, insofar as it might appear that our language simply fails when used of that which is radically other.[23] As we will see in the next chapter, Gregory, Augus-

---

21 Cf. Clarke, 'Action as Self-Revelation', 46–52.
22 Cf. Wuellner, *Dictionary of Scholastic Philosophy*, 13–15. This claim will be qualified somewhat in the next chapter when discussing *esse commune*. Consider also: '[God] is the active power, activity, or actuality which … grounds or energises all created actuality or activity. To express the point with a flourish of rhetoric, we might say that God is the actuality which gives actuality and the character of being an actuality to every other actuality' (Braine, *Reality of Time and Existence of God*, 311). Braine suggests that an apt metaphor for God along these lines is that of a furnace (133).
23 For some critics of simplicity, this creates an insurmountable conundrum. Barry Smith, on the one hand, thinks that simplicity fails to follow through on the demands of apophatic reserve (*Oneness and Simplicity*, 114–19, 126–29), whereas Ryan Mullins, on the other hand, finds apo-

tine, and Aquinas are each sensitive to the strain God-talk puts on language, and their uses of divine simplicity are part of how they regulate theological language to express the Creator–creature distinction. Each of them finds ways to persevere in positive, cataphatic use of language for God, while insisting that all God-talk is apophatically conditioned.[24]

The place of simplicity in the logic of Christian belief can be seen in the early Christian development of the doctrine of *creatio ex nihilo*. For *ex nihilo* is primarily the affirmation that nothing conditions God in the act of creation.[25] This interplay can be seen in the way that both Irenaeus of Lyons and Pseudo-Dionysius the Areopagite develop *ex nihilo* and simplicity. Irenaeus distinguishes between that which contains and that which is contained: God 'contains all things, but He Himself can be contained by no one'.[26] Contrary to the Gnostics, Irenaeus argues that God cannot be contained and therefore is completely unbounded: 'there is one Being who contains all things, and formed in His own territory all those things which have been created'.[27] The difference this suggests between God and creatures leads Irenaeus to conclude to God's simplicity, saying that God is:

---

phaticism so obviously problematic that simplicity is compromised by association ('Analytic Response to Holmes').

24 In contrast to Smith and Mullins, in the previous note, Coakley expresses well the richer classical understanding of apophasis: 'Apophatic theology, in its proper sense then, can never be mere verbal play, deferral of meaning, or the simple addition of negatives to positive ("cataphatic") claims. Nor on the other hand, can it be satisfied with the dogmatic "liberal" denial that God in Godself can be known at all: it is not "mysterious" in this sense'; Coakley, *God, Sexuality, Self*, 46. Coakley's account makes it clear that Colin Gunton also frames his critique of the tradition of negative theology in too stark a contrast (*Act and Being*, 36). For an account of apophaticism and an alternative approach that roots reference to God in human transformation, see Ticciati, *New Apophaticism*, 23–52, 217–46.

25 Cf. McFarland, *From Nothing*, 87–91, 98–100. He takes *ex nihilo* as entailing, '(1) that creation is grounded in nothing but God, (2) that the doctrine of creation implies the existence of nothing apart from God, and (3) that in creation nothing limits God' (87). For a more explicit connection between *ex nihilo* and divine simplicity, see Oliver, *Creation*, 43–53; and Levering, *Engaging the Doctrine of Creation*, 73–108. From a different angle, Sonderegger (*Systematic Theology 1*, 84–5) understands simplicity in the context of the theology of creation under her unique category of 'compatibilism' – i.e., that God, while radically other, is intimately and inexhaustibly *compatible* with creation.

26 Irenaeus, *AH*, II.30.9. Similarly, see Gregory of Nyssa, *Life of Moses*, II.236–38.

27 *AH*, II.1.5. It should be noted that Irenaeus' christological and Platonic development of this container language avoids spatializing the relation of God and creation – it is in fact explicitly in rejection of such spatialization (cf. *AH*, IV.3.1, IV.20.1). Newton, by contrast, identified God as 'container' with absolute space, which then meant that God could not become incarnate on pains of directly contradicting the container/contained distinction; cf. Torrance, *Space, Time and Incarnation*, 39.

simple, uncompounded Being, without diverse members, and altogether like, and equal to himself, since He is wholly understanding, and wholly spirit, and wholly thought, and wholly intelligence, and wholly reason, and wholly hearing, and wholly seeing, and wholly light, and the whole source of all that is good.[28]

Dionysius makes a similar distinction between the unparticipating God and creatures as participating.[29] God possesses all 'ideas' or forms of creaturely beings in the unity of God's super-essential (ὑπερούσιον) being. Rather than receiving form by participating in an abstract universal, creatures possess form by participation in God. A creature is good, for instance, by participating in God, who is goodness itself. Consequently, God and creation are distinguished by the relation of participation: creatures, by virtue of having properties predicatively, are composed of properties that are themselves distinct from the subject in whom they inhere, whereas God is identical to the participated perfection or 'property'. Consequently, the participation relation culminates in affirming God as the simple possession of the goodness (i.e., perfections or properties) shared to creaturely being.[30]

Simplicity for Dionysius, then, is God's prior 'superessential' plenitude, by virtue of which finite being receives perfections such as goodness by participation. The contained/uncontained and participating/unparticipating distinctions between creation and God lead to the apprehension of a further distinction between composition and boundedness in creaturely being and the boundless simplicity of God's own being. Creaturely participation displays God's superessential being, but only by 'naming' what is 'in fact nothing other than certain activities apparent to us, activities which deify, cause being, bear life, and give wisdom'.[31] Because the participation relation not only distinguishes the mode of predication but also denotes a causal relation, it specifies how creaturely participation obtains through ontological dependency on God the Creator. So whatever creatures

---

28 *AH*, II.13.3. Cf. Behr, 'Synchronic and Diachronic Harmony'. Behr is critical of Eric Osborn's interpretation in *Irenaeus*, 27–43, arguing that Osborn distinguishes too sharply an antecedent 'theism' from Irenaeus' exegetical account of simplicity by attention to the divine economy. Nonetheless, much of Osborn's account is still quite helpful in situating Irenaeus within his Platonic context.
29 *DN*, II.5, 644 A; XI.6, 956 A. Dionysius' philosophical language here is likely due to Proclus; cf. Perl, *Theophany*, 44–45.
30 *DN*, I.7, 596D–597 A.
31 *DN*, II.7, 645 A. For broader discussion of the theme of participation in the theology of creation, see Oliver, *Creation*, 46–48.

have by participation, God has by identity and through the creative act chooses to share with other, finite beings.³²

If one begins from a theological commitment to *creatio ex nihilo*, then with Burrell we might understand divine simplicity to express the grammar of divinity. Analogy comes in at this point, for the active judgment concerning the existence of things is also a judgment about fittingness or proportionality between things. According to Aristotle, the intellect is that which apprehends the intelligible (viz., the real) *in* the sensible (appearances or surfaces), and the task of *judgment* is to make known to oneself what is knowable in itself.³³ As argued in *Posterior Analytics*, 'what' a thing is – its intelligible reality – does not specify 'that' it is.³⁴ Plotinus draws the further conclusion that when the mind apprehends a being to be genuinely *there*, its being there ('what' it is in its intelligibility) is in fact existentially dependent on some other 'being' ('that' it is), who does not receive existence but gives it.³⁵ These two kinds of being – giving being and received being – are not univocal, though there is a fittingness or analogy between them that is ascertained in an act of judgment. This fittingness is a '*pros hen*', or attributive, analogy, because giving being has primarily what received being has derivatively or secondarily. What this judgment discerns is not a discrete being that extrinsically causes other discrete beings to come into existence; rather it discerns the very *act of existence*, which cannot be divided or reduced to one among many because this act is at once the fullness of existence itself and the activity which is immanent in all things bringing them forth in actuality.³⁶ It is because this judgment does not discern a discrete being that an attempted deduction to a simple being as the explanation of finite being is potentially misleading: such an argument, apart from a 'conversion' of one's judgment whereby one sees existence as an *active principle*, could be taken as concluding to a bounded entity alongside, even while more causally powerful than, the series of finite beings.³⁷ But divine simplicity becomes more tractable

---

32 Cf. also Przywara, 'Scope of Analogy', 362; and Mascall, *Existence and Analogy*, 109–21.
33 Aristotle, *Metaphysics*, Z.3.1029a35–b8. See also Perl, *Thinking Being*, 84–85.
34 Aristotle, *Posterior Analytics*, II.7, 92b5–11.
35 *Enn.*, 2018, V.1 [10].7.23–7, 3 [13].13.1–5, 3 [13].15.33. See Perl, *Thinking Being*, 117, 120–24.
36 *Enn.*, 2018, VI.9 [9].3.36–41. In a similar vein, Barth argues that God cannot be included within a genus, for this ultimately would be to conceive of God as a cause *within* the plane of finite beings (which turns out, somewhat ironically, to fuel Barth's rejection of the *analogia entis*); cf. Barth, *KD*, II/1, 91–92, 504: 'Gott aber ist Exemplar außerhalb jedes Genus'. References to the English edition will be given in brackets [*CD*, II/1, 83–84, 447]. For a discussion of Barth here, see Franks, 'Simplicity of Living God', 294.
37 This is the conviction behind Dionysius' Neoplatonic appellation of 'beyond being' for God, by which he means that God is not *a being* (cf. *DN*, IV.1–3, 693 A–697 A; and *MT*, I.2, 1000B; V,

when conceived so that God is understood as the transcendent *and* immanent (or non-contrastively transcendent) act of existence itself, and thus as ontologically distinct from created beings.[38]

Recently, the role of divine simplicity in relation to the doctrine of creation has become a matter of intense debate centering on whether God's act of creation can rightfully be called 'free' if God is simple and whether divine simplicity entails a 'modal collapse' – i.e., that God's necessity and simplicity results in a single, all-encompassing necessary act of creating in which every created fact and reality is determined (because each is necessary and so not one possibility among many). These debates, mostly exercising analytic philosophers of religion, are beyond the scope of the present work and are by no means settled, with powerful arguments for and against.[39] However, they serve nonetheless to remind us of the centrality of the Creator–creature relation to divine simplicity. Divine simplicity is first and foremost about how to negotiate the difference between God and creation and what implications this has for the practice of theology.

1.4.2 Simplicity and the multiplicity of divine names

Another implication of divine simplicity, and one of the most easily recognized conceptual difficulties it brings, concerns the multiplicity of attributes and names used for God. If God is absolutely simple, with no genuine distinctions, then what do the several predicates we use of God actually express? If each pred-

---

1048B); for commentary, see Perl, *Theophany*, 10–16. Infinity as the quantitatively maximal instance in the series of finite things is also the content of Hegel's notion of 'bad infinity'; cf. Adams, *Eclipse of Grace*, 193; and Beiser, *Hegel*, 44–45.

[38] On 'non-contrastive transcendence', see Tanner, *God and Creation*. See also Franks, 'Simplicity of Living God'; and Przywara, 'Time, Space, Eternity', 589: 'The essentially supraspatial and supratemporal God pervades the intraspatial and intratemporal realm of the creature so thoroughly that, in relation to space, he is the one who is "both interior to all things, because all things are in him, and exterior to all things, because he is beyond all things"' (quoting St. Augustine, *De Gen. ad Litt.*, VIII, xxvi, 48).

[39] Important contributions on freedom and simplicity include (in order of publication): Stump and Kretzmann, 'Absolute Simplicity'; Hasker, 'Simplicity and Freedom'; O'Connor, 'Simplicity and Creation'; Grant, 'Aquinas, Simplicity, and Freedom'; Brower, 'Making Sense of Divine Simplicity'; Dolezal, *God without Parts*, 188–212; Duby, 'Simplicity, Freedom, and Contingency'; and Leftow, 'Simplicity and Freedom'. On the modal collapse argument, see Mullins, 'Simply Impossible', 194–99; Lenow, 'Shoring Up Divine Simplicity'; Tomaszewski, 'Collapsing the Modal Collapse Argument'.

icate actually refers to the self-same reality (viz., the divine nature) how do they continue to have distinct semantic content? Further, has God been reduced in this way to an abstract object rather than a living being? In recent debates about divine simplicity and the divine names, these questions are often at the forefront. However, based on the discussion of God's relation to creation in the previous section, it is not hard to see that the issues have not always been framed this way. The difference could be characterized by referring to the earlier approach as the question of 'divine names' and referring to the recent debates as the question of 'divine properties'. In the former, the question concerns what kind of practice we are engaged in when we use names derived from God's refracted, manifold effects within creation to speak of God. In the latter, the question concerns how putative properties of God hang together in the divine being.[40]

Dionysius is representative of this earlier 'divine names' tradition when he connects God as simple with the diverse names or perfections that we develop for God from creaturely perfections. All finite beings *receive* intelligibility by the excess (ὑπερβολή) of generosity in God, who gives and illuminates all being.[41] Because the diverse forms or perfections by which all beings are intelligible are received and illuminated by God, and because God is not distinct from any divine perfection as the unparticipating source of participable forms, God possesses *all* perfections found in creation in a superlative (ὑπερούσιον) mode. God is the simple and perfect plenitude of all perfections, identical in God's own self but multiple in the finite participations in which these perfections are manifest.[42] As Fran O'Rourke expresses Dionysius' position, divine simplicity is the 'fullness of Being – the plenary presence of the perfection of all reality in God'.[43]

God's act of participable creativity refracts the simple divine being into the manifold of finite perfections. Consequently, by virtue of *being* the activity by which finite beings bear forth their multiple perfections, God is positively *identified* by these multiple perfections and can be named according to them without

---

[40] Janet Soskice, in 'Naming God', 241–54, draws this distinction and shows what differences it generates through a comparison of Aquinas and Locke. Hart elaborates: 'The difference ... is nothing less than the difference between two ontologies: between a metaphysics of participation, according to which all things are embraced in being as in the supereminent source of all their transcendental perfections, and a "univocal" ontology, which understands being as nothing but the bare category of existence, under which all substances (God no less than creatures) are severally placed' ('The Offering of Names', 2).
[41] *DN*, IV.10, 708AB; IV.14, 712 A–713 A. So Irenaeus: God is 'the whole source of all that is good' (*AH*, II.13.3).
[42] *DN*, II.7, 645 A.
[43] O'Rourke, *Dionysius and Aquinas*, 69. Also: Perl, *Theophany*, 13–16.

being identical to the perfections in their finite instantiations. As Dionysius writes:

> as Cause of all and as transcending all, he is rightly nameless and yet has the names of everything that is. ... He is 'all in all', as scripture affirms, and certainly he is to be praised as being for all things the creator and originator ... and all this in the one single, irrepressible, and supreme act. For the unnamed goodness is not just the cause of cohesion or life or perfection so that it is from this or that providential gesture that it earns a name, but it actually contains everything beforehand within itself – and this in a simple and boundless manner – and it is thus by virtue of the unlimited goodness of its single all-creative Providence. Hence the songs of praise and the names for it are fittingly derived from the sum total of creation.[44]

So, God does in fact possess the diversity found in creaturely beings, but simply and pre-eminently, in a manner radically transcending the participating mode by which creatures possess these perfections. Consequently, while the 'divine names' approach does not conceive a problem in terms of multiple divine properties *per se*, it is concerned with expressing the conviction that the multiplicity resulting from God's creative act is somehow already possessed by the simple divine essence without entailing a comparable composition within God.

In recent debates in philosophy of religion, the issue is transmuted into the question of 'divine properties', how it is that a purportedly simple being can have several properties. Indeed, many philosophers and theologians have concluded that the attempt to reconcile multiple divine perfections or attributes with divine simplicity is destined for incoherence or theological inadequacy. Alvin Plantinga, in his Aquinas Lecture entitled *Does God Have a Nature?*, raised what has become a standard criticism:

> if God is identical with each of his properties, then since each of his properties is a property, he is a property – a self-exemplifying property. ... No property could have created the world; no property could be omniscient, or indeed, know anything at all. If God is a property, then he isn't a person but a mere abstract object; he has no knowledge, awareness, power, love or life. So taken, the simplicity doctrine seems to be an utter mistake.[45]

Plantinga argues that if God is identical to the divine properties, then because God's properties are, as properties, abstract objects, God is an abstract object. The conclusion follows by the transitivity of identity, which states: if x is identical to y, and y is identical to z, then x is identical to z. So, if God is identical to God's properties, and properties are abstract objects, then God is an abstract ob-

---

[44] *DN*, I.7, 596C–597 A (translation slightly altered).
[45] Plantinga, *Does God Have a Nature?*, 47.

ject. Plantinga then considers the additional implication that all God's properties would be identical to one another.⁴⁶ The conclusion would seem to follow that there is no difference in sense between saying 'God is good' and 'God is holy', even though the words 'good' and 'holy' each bear different meanings in ordinary usage.⁴⁷ This conclusion empties theological language of all content, preventing any genuine speech about God.⁴⁸

When divine simplicity is analyzed according to the problem of 'divine properties', two challenges arise: first, God is reduced to the ontological status of an abstract object through identification with properties, and, second, the identity of all God's attributes means that there can exist no real distinction between the various properties attributed to God. Several responses to these two issues have been presented. These responses could be characterized under three broad types: 1) God does in fact have multiple properties; 2) all God's properties are reducible to one so that God only has one 'super property' or 'rich property'; 3) God has no properties.⁴⁹ Not surprisingly, many proponents of the first option dismiss divine simplicity as a contradiction of God's multiple attributes.⁵⁰

Some, however, have attempted to revise divine simplicity in order to make it compatible with a real multiplicity of properties. Keith Yandell (and William Hasker) have distinguished between 'parts' broadly speaking and 'proper parts', so that not all kinds of 'parts' are problematic for simplicity.⁵¹ A 'proper part' would be a part separable from God and on which God depends. It could be said, then, that God is complex by virtue of consisting of multiple properties (and persons) and yet is still simple in a qualified sense to the extent that God is not composed of 'proper parts'.⁵² Andrew Radde-Gallwitz provides another way to revise divine simplicity through a reading of Basil of Caesarea and Gregory of Nyssa, the fourth-century Cappadocian brothers. He sets his complex account

---

46 As both Augustine and Aquinas affirm: Augustine, *Trin.*, VI.8; and Aquinas, *STh*, I.3.3 ad 1; I.13.5, responsio.
47 Cf. Gale, *Nature and Existence of God*, 20–24; Hughes, *Complex Theory of a Simple God*, 62–63; Morreall, 'Simplicity and Properties'; Plantinga, *Does God Have a Nature?*, 47–50.
48 Wolterstorff, 'Divine Simplicity', 109.
49 Isaak Dorner finds instances of these three possibilities to various degrees (*Divine Immutability*, article 2). Daniel Bennett also identifies these three options, offering a playful account of their results. He concludes that in the case of God whatever a predicate expresses should be taken not as 'properties' but as 'concreta' ('Divine Simplicity', 634–35).
50 Cf. Hasker, *Metaphysics and Tri-Personal God*, 60–61; Mullins, 'Simply Impossible', 201–3; Plantinga, *Does God Have a Nature?*, 132–46; Ward, *Christ and Cosmos*, 14–17.
51 Yandell, 'An Essay'; for further discussion, cf. McCall, *Which Trinity?*, 37–39. Hasker, *Metaphysics and Tri-Personal God*.
52 For a similar, though more explicitly Scotist approach, cf. McCall, 'Trinity Doctrine'.

in opposition to the 'identity-thesis' – i.e., that all God's attributes are strictly identical. Shifting from metaphysics to epistemology, Radde-Gallwitz argues that the Cappadocian brothers reject definitional knowledge of the divine essence but conceive of *propria* by which God can be identified or recognized without constituting definitional knowledge. *Propria* are 'properties co-extensive with and intrinsic to the divine essence, but not individually definitive'.[53] He concludes that the Cappadocians represent an alternative to the strict identity of divine attributes by distinguishing the mode of knowledge and a unique kind of divine properties identified through this knowledge; consequently, persons can have genuine knowledge of multiple divine perfections without the implication of an essential complexity in God.

The second type of response to the problem of multiple attributes argues that all the divine attributes are identical to one another, forming a single 'rich property' of which God is the sole instance. William Mann argues that in this respect God is similar to human persons, who also have 'rich properties', namely a 'conjunctive property which includes all and only the essential and accidental properties of some individual thing'.[54] However, for God this property is self-instantiating, which allows Mann to affirm divine aseity. Because God is identical to a self-instantiating rich property, God is not an abstract object (because God's 'rich property' is not an abstract object).[55] Mann hopes to avoid rendering synonymous different divine predicates, for they actually name properties constitutive of God's single rich property.

Finally, there are recent proposals that follow the third option listed above and claim God has no properties. This move could be seen as approximating the earlier 'divine names' tradition, and its proponents draw on Aquinas.[56] James Dolezal questions the 'property account', claiming that talk of properties

---

53 Radde-Gallwitz, *Basil, Gregory, and Divine Simplicity*, 107. More recently, Radde-Gallwitz has revised his account and suggests that Gregory does not provide an account of *propria* as distinct properties inhering in the divine essence, but rather that *propria* are *epinoiai*, conceptualizations that do not come loaded with a particular metaphysical account of properties by virtue of which the conceptualizations are true. The divine essence alone accounts for the truth of the names (viz., *propria* and *epinoiai*) ('Gregory of Nyssa and Divine Simplicity', esp. 455–56), which potentially aligns more closely with the third 'property-less' group.
54 William E. Mann, 'Divine Simplicity', *RS* 18, no. 4 (December 1982): 467.
55 Mann reviews this claim, defending it from the criticisms of Thomas Morris, in 'Simplicity and Properties: A Reply to Morris', *RS* 22, no. 3–4 (September 1986): 344–46; in response to Thomas V. Morris, 'On God and Mann: A View of Divine Simplicity', *RS* 21, no. 3 (September 1985): 299–318.
56 Cf. *ScG*, I.31, 34; *STh*, I.13.5, *responsio*; I.13.6.

is problematic in the case of God[57] and, following Jeffrey Brower and others, develops a 'truth-maker' account of divine simplicity, according to which God is not properly conceived as identical to God's *properties* but as the 'truth-maker' for all divine predicates.[58] Whereas in creatures, a property actually possessed by the subject is what makes predications true (viz., the property is the 'truth-maker' for the predication), in God's case God is the only truth-maker for all true predications of God. Truth-maker theory is one way to express a property-less account of God, which most fundamentally claims that because God is pure act (as the identity of existence and essence), there is no potency in God, and consequently God cannot receive properties as actualizations or determinations of something otherwise unactualized.[59]

1.4.3 Simplicity and Trinity

Although on the face of it simplicity and Trinity seem incompatible, simplicity was instrumental in the development of 'pro-Nicene' trinitarian theology.[60] The driving question can be put simply: are the three persons 'parts' of God? If the question is answered in the affirmative, then God would be composed of three persons and consequently not simple; if answered negatively, a further question arises: how are the three persons not then identical to one another?

Defending and deploying the doctrine of divine simplicity for the doctrine of the Trinity will require clarifying how the persons are not properly conceived as 'parts' of God. I will discuss this in dialogue with Gregory of Nyssa, Augustine,

---

57 Dolezal, *God without Parts*, 125–26.
58 *God without Parts*, 125–26, drawing on Brower, 'Making Sense of Divine Simplicity'. Dolezal includes Brian Leftow as a proponent of the truthmaker account of divine simplicity. However, Leftow has since made explicit his rejection of truthmaker accounts; 'Simplicity and Freedom', 46–47.
59 Consider also Duby, *Divine Simplicity*, esp. 91–108. It is not entirely clear if Duby would consider his a 'property-less' account, especially given his continued use of the language of attributes. Still, his account is closer to the classical 'divine names' approach than to the later 'divine properties' approach.
60 Consider, for example: 'Confessing that the Spirit belongs to the divine nature, we recognize ... absolutely no variation in it, such that the divine and transcendent nature would be divided from itself through a kind of increase or decrease and would differ from itself as greater and lesser. It is believed to be simple, uniform, and non-composite, and no intertwining or composition from dissimilar things is considered in connection with it' (Gregory of Nyssa, 'On the Holy Spirit', 272, ¶3). Cf. Ayres, *Nicaea and Its Legacy*, 4–5, 141, 146–48, 186, 236, 278–88; and Holmes, *Holy Trinity*, 97–120.

and Aquinas in the next chapter, but here I want to show why it is not desirable to conceive of the divine persons as parts. If the persons are parts of God then several difficult problems emerge.[61] First, it is difficult to see how one would avoid a quaternity in God, comprised of Father, Son, Spirit, and their resulting divine essence.[62] One might attempt to avoid the conclusion of a quaternity by denying that the divine essence is in any way separable from the three persons taken together. However, if the three persons together *compose* a divine essence that is genuinely 'one', then the essence is not reducible to the three but is somehow additional to what the three are individually. Consequently, even if the essence is not 'separable' from the three persons who compose it, it is a genuine fourth in addition to the three, though of a different ontological order.[63]

A second danger is subordinationism, which makes Son and Spirit subordinate to the Father, rendering suspect the Son's and Spirit's full divinity. If the persons are parts but the essence is not a 'fourth thing', one might attempt to make one person of the Trinity the principal locus of the divinity that is then shared with the others. If, for instance, the Father is the fount of deity, and the persons are parts of God, then, as parts of God, the second and third persons cannot have received the full divinity but only part of it. The Father would still be the locus of full divinity, which is somehow now also composed of the Son and Spirit with whom the Father shares it. Consequently, the Son and Spirit would be subordinate to the Father, lesser deities by virtue of having only a partial share in the divinity proper to the Father.[64]

Finally, understanding the persons as parts of God inevitably entails that the persons themselves are not properly God. If 'God' is the name for what the three persons are together, then as constitutive parts the three persons cannot each be 'God'. And yet the *Quicunque Vult* (also known as the Athanasian Creed) and the Nicene Creed both insist on the full divinity of each person; stating, respectively: 'the Father is God, the Son is God, and the Holy Spirit is God; and yet they are not three Gods, but one God', and the Son is 'God of God, Light of Light, very God of very God' and the Spirit too is 'the Lord and Giver of life ... who with the Father and the Son together is worshipped and glorified'. Any view, then, that cannot affirm that each divine person is *fully God* is not an adequate interpretation of

---

[61] See also White, 'Trinitarian Simplicity', 727–35.
[62] Hinlicky, confusingly, makes the reverse claim, that viewing God as triune and simple results in a quaternity (*Divine Simplicity*, 105, 155).
[63] Which, as Balthasar argues, is obviated when simplicity is deployed to express the Trinity (*Theo-Drama*, 5:66).
[64] This is not to criticize the view of the Father as the fount of deity. I am only criticizing this as a tactic to defend a view of the persons as parts of God.

the trinitarian faith. To claim that the persons are *parts* of God which together compose God is to fail to affirm the full divinity of each and, therefore, to fail to express the content of the trinitarian faith. These three points together do not on their own entail the coherence of the doctrines of divine simplicity and the Trinity, but merely reject any construal of the relation between persons and essence of God in terms of part to whole.[65]

In the controversies through which pro-Nicene trinitarian theology was developed, opposing parties generally held to some form of divine simplicity, often appealing to it as justification for their divergent positions.[66] For Arius, the Son was disqualified from full identification with God because he is neither simple nor unoriginate; whereas for Athanasius simplicity and immutability together are what make intelligible the eternal generation and divinity of the Son.[67] Divine simplicity is the basis for two arguments in Athanasius' *Orationes contra Arianos* for the divinity of the Son, rather than understand him as an extrinsic production of the Father. First, if God is Creator and creates through the Son (following Jn. 1), then to deny the Son full divinity is to claim that the Father must 'accrue from without' the 'Framing Word ... by which He frames'. But this would further entail that God grows and becomes composite through the accretion of the Word and, consequently, that the Trinity is 'unlike itself, consisting of strange and alien natures and essences'.[68] The implication for Athanasius is clear: because scripture attests to the Son's involvement in creating, the Son must be fully divine, and not a part or addition to the divine essence.

Second, Athanasius argues that purging paternal analogies of materialist connotations displays that the Son fully possesses the simple divine essence and is generated from the Father without change or division. For God is not like human fathers who are 'passible and partitive', i.e., God does not generate according to change or by granting part of the divine being to another. As simple, God's being does not permit such partition. Hence, when scripture names Christ as God's Word and Wisdom, it does not name a part or external offspring but the

---

65 Barth agrees: 'The triunity of God does not name threefold divinity, either in the sense of a multitude of divinities or in the sense of the existence of a multitude of individuals or of parts within the one Godhead'. And: 'the "personality" of God belongs to the one and only essence of God, which through the doctrine of the Trinity is not tripled but rather recognized in its simplicity [*Einfachheit*]'; KD, I/1:369, 370 [CD, I/1:350] (my translation).
66 Cf. Anatolios, *Retrieving Nicaea*, 31, 36–41, 79–98. Cf. also Ayres, *Nicaea and Its Legacy*, 54–59, 112–13; and Holmes, *Holy Trinity*, 95–96, 97–120.
67 Athanasius, *c. Ar.*, I.17, I.28. See Anatolios, *Retrieving Nicaea*, 112–18; Ayres, *Nicaea and Its Legacy*, 112.
68 *c. Ar.*, I.17.

eternal Son who shares the divine essence: 'For, whereas men are capable of wisdom, God partakes in nothing, but is Himself the Father of His own Wisdom, of which whoso partake are given the name of wise. And this Wisdom too is not a passion, nor a part, but an Offspring proper to the Father'.[69] For Athanasius, then, it is *because* God is simple by nature that the identification of Father and Son in scripture refers not to parts of God or to greater and lesser divine emanations but to fully divine persons who without change or composition share the one divine essence.

How, then, does one avoid concluding either that the persons are identical to one another or that God's essence is internally differentiated, thereby compromising triunity or simplicity? The scholastic penchant for fine distinctions contributed fruitfully to answering this question. One option, associated with Aquinas, is to conceive of the persons in God as 'subsistent relations'. In the case of God, real relations do not terminate in distinct terms or essences, which would inevitably involve using part-language for God or result in tri-theism. For if each person of the Trinity is a substantial or essential term of a relation, and the Trinity taken together is God, then God is constituted of three distinct entities or parts. Consequently, Thomas argues that intra-divine relations function differently because they do not take distinct terms as creaturely relations do. Trinitarian relations are somehow relations *of the divine essence to itself*, taking no real distinct terms, and the persons are identical to these relations. Because the relations of paternity and filiation are *opposed* to one another, they distinguish Father and Son respectively (so the persons are distinguished by 'relations of opposition').[70] I discuss this more fully in the following chapters.

Another significant approach is put forward by John Duns Scotus. Scotus' trinitarian theology is constituted both by commitment to divine simplicity and his rejection of Aquinas' method for distinguishing the three persons as relations of opposition.[71] Scotus, however, rejected this manner of distinguishing the persons because, so Scotus argues, relations are posterior to the related terms and therefore cannot be constitutive of that which is related. The Father, then, could not perform the act of generating the Son if he did not possess existence logically prior to the act of generating.[72]

Scotus considers an objection to the doctrine of the Trinity that anticipates the modern critiques using the transitivity of identity, namely that if the Father is

---

69 *c. Ar.*, I.28, see also I.27 and I.29.
70 *STh*, I.28.3, *responsio*; I.29.4, *responsio*.
71 For Scotus' defence of simplicity, *Ordinatio*, I.8.1.1. Cross, *Scotus on God*, 99–114.
72 Cf. Friedman, 'Medieval Trinitarian Theology', 202–4.

identical to the divine essence, and the Son is identical to the essence, then the Father is identical to the Son.[73] He argues that this 'sophistical' objection requires that the identity claims denote both essential and formal identity. While he agrees that there is an essential identity between the Father and the divine essence, he rejects that there is a formal identity. There is a formal distinction (*distinctio formalis*) between each divine person and the common divine essence, a distinction that the mind apprehends and that has some basis in reality but does not entail a compositional difference. Consequently, the conclusion 'the Father is the Son' cannot follow for it falsely assumes a formal identity, which according to Scotus is not the case.[74] Each person is formally distinct from the divine essence, though essentially identical to it, and they are therefore formally distinct from one another. Their formal distinction obtains by virtue of having a personal property, *haecceity*, that is unique to each; in this trinitarian context, the *haecceities* are the relations of origin. Whereas for Aquinas, the persons are *identical* to their relations of origin, for Scotus each person's relation of origin constitutes a personal property by virtue of which the persons are formally distinct.[75]

Scotus is clearly addressing the problem of making identity claims within God while at the same time distinguishing between persons. While Scotus' own account is offered in conjunction with a doctrine of divine simplicity, many philosophers of religion today see this trinitarian problem as necessitating the rejection of simplicity altogether, or at least its modification, a position shared with many systematic theologians.[76]

---

73 For discussion of the transitivity of identity in recent discussion of the Tinity in philosophy of religion, cf. McCall, 'Trinity Doctrine', 57; and Hasker, *Metaphysics and Tri-Personal God*, 59.
74 *Ordinatio*, I.2.2.4.417. For this reason, Richard Cross argues that Scotus uses 'God' equivocally in regard to the Trinity on the one hand and each divine person on the other; Cross, 'Scotus on Substance and Trinity', 192–94.
75 *Ordinatio*, I.2.2.1–4.355–6; cf. Cross, *Scotus on God*, 153, 163, 183–85.
76 For recent witness to the importance of this question for philosophers of religion, see the partially overlapping collections: McCall and Rea, *Philosophical and Theological Essays on the Trinity*; and Rea, *Philosophical Theology 1*. See also Hughes, *Complex Theory of a Simple God*, 153–86; Moreland and Craig, *Philosophical Foundations for a Christian Worldview*, 524. For discussion, cf. McCall, *Which Trinity?*; and Hasker, *Metaphysics and Tri-Personal God*, 81–163. Amongst systematic theologians, see Gunton, *One, Three and Many*, 152; Gunton, *Act and Being*, 31–32, 51–52, 122–23, where he offers a more nuanced criticism and revision of simplicity; Hinlicky, *Divine Simplicity*; Moltmann, *Trinity and the Kingdom*, 174–78, preferring to talk of unity in terms of perichoresis; Nash, *Concept of God*, 85. For helpful discussion of the various theological challenges, see Ortlund, 'Simplicity in Historical Perspective'.

Colin Gunton is a particularly clear and influential theological critic of the classical account of divine simplicity.[77] For Gunton, simplicity itself is not a problem, except insofar as it smuggles Hellenistic assumptions about unity and knowledge of God into the Christian exposition of revelation, too often occluding the latter. Gunton considers the case of Plotinus, in whose thought he finds an unwarranted restriction on language about God. '[His] chief aim is as fully as possible to deprive the concept of God of any definite characteristics', Gunton explains, finding particular fault in the fact that Plotinus cannot 'attribute even goodness and love to God as an inhering, inner quality'.[78] Unfortunately, this negative approach very early influenced Christian thought, so that in Origen God is specified apart from any attention to scriptural witness to the economy or 'anything trinitarian'.[79] By the time we get to Aquinas, on Gunton's reading, impersonal attributes like simplicity dominate, pushing the personal, action-based attributes like the Trinity to the margins.[80] Consequently, theologians received an overly apophatic approach to God from Greek philosophers like Plotinus, which never sits easily with the positive, revelation-based approach of trinitarian theology.[81] For Gunton, a better, more biblical and Christian approach is exemplified by Karl Barth, whose characterization of the divine essence gives priority to the 'relational life of the Trinity', alongside which simplicity might still have a place, though revised.[82]

While Gunton revises simplicity in order to make it more amenable to Barthian trinitarian theology, others adopt a more polemical critique of divine simplicity, or any trinitarian theology that places primacy on 'unity'. Many of these critical responses to classical trinitarianism can be grouped under the heading of 'social trinitarianism'.[83] William Hasker offers a social trinitarianism that attempts to uphold a minimalist doctrine of simplicity. Hasker is concerned that

---

[77] Especially *Act and Being*, which influences Hinlicky's *Divine Simplicity*.
[78] Gunton, *Act and Being*, 43, 44.
[79] *Act and Being*, 45.
[80] *Act and Being*, 51–52; this reading leads him to the contentious conclusion that 'there is but a hair's breadth between Aquinas and Kant' (53). Compare this with the very different assessment of Aquinas and Kant in Gilson, *God and Philosophy*, 110–15: 'From Thomas Aquinas to … Kant … the line has been broken' (110). Consider Schwöbel's more charitable rendering of Aquinas, 'Where Do We Stand?', 33–35.
[81] Also Hinlicky, *Divine Complexity*, 160–61, 184, 193–99.
[82] Gunton, *Act and Being*, 32, 122–23.
[83] Representative examples of 'social trinitarianism' are: Hodgson, *Doctrine of the Trinity*; Moltmann, *Trinity and the Kingdom*; Brown, *Divine Trinity*; Boff, *Trinity and Society*; Plantinga, 'Social Trinity and Tritheism'; and Moreland and Craig, *Philosophical Foundations for a Christian Worldview*, ch. 29.

the strong version of simplicity necessitates the absolute identity of all persons in the Trinity, so that the three finally collapse into an undifferentiated one (similarly to Scotus, though for Scotus formal distinctions do not require revision of simplicity).[84] Jettisoning the entire tradition of 'strong' simplicity along with its 'Platonic doctrine of participation', Hasker concludes, 'The strong doctrine of divine simplicity, which threatens to become a cognitive black hole that swallows up everything positive we might want to say about God, needs to be excised'.[85]

Even in contemporary theology and philosophy of religion, then, we can see that several distinct approaches to the Trinity are on offer to respond to the concerns of the doctrine of divine simplicity. For trinitarian theology, simplicity captures the conviction that between the three divine persons, there is no gradation, division, or accumulated divinity. Somehow, all three are equally God without that rendering a straightforward part–whole relationship between the one and the three.

1.5 Conclusion

In this chapter I have introduced the main lines of debate regarding the doctrine of divine simplicity. Several factors have come to the fore, each of which complicates interpretation of the doctrine and also contributes to its proper formulation. First, I distinguished regulative and metaphysical functions of divine simplicity, noting that they can operate together though some theologians privilege one over the other. In this respect, there are varieties of metaphysical postures: agnostic, classical, revisionary, and explicitly non-metaphysical. In addition, divine simplicity pushes the boundaries of language, requiring careful attention to how our categories ought to be modulated in respect of God.

---

84 Hasker, *Metaphysics and Tri-Personal God*, 55–61.
85 *Metaphysics and Tri-Personal God*, 60, 61. Drawing on Michael Rea's constitution model for the Trinity ('Trinity', 403–23), Hasker suggests that the one 'simple' being of God is like a material that can constitute several objects simultaneous. For Hasker, this does not violate a minimal sense of divine simplicity for two combined reasons: first, a stipulated rule of constitution asserts of x and y, both of which are constituted by one trope, that 'x and y have all their parts in common at t'. Second, insofar as God is 'metaphysically simple, then neither x nor y will have "proper parts"; what they share, then, will be only their single "improper part"'. Taken together, these two points render the conclusion that the three divine persons ('life-streams', in Hasker's model) do not divide the divine nature but are entirely coincident with it, even if not strictly identical to it, being distinguished from it by the 'constitution relation' (*Metaphysics and Tri-Personal God*, 243).

I then presented three major theological deployments of the doctrine – the Creator–creature distinction, multiple divine perfections, and the doctrine of the Trinity – and I traced a variety of motivating factors, arguments, criticisms, and modern proposals particular to each. I have not attempted resolutions in this chapter but rather sought to illuminate the genuinely theological context of the doctrine of simplicity, the complex set of factors involved in the debates, and a sense of the diversity of proposals on offer. Given the degree to which the appreciation of divine simplicity is contingent on the assessment of its historical proponents and their arguments, in the next chapter I will offer more sustained readings of Gregory of Nyssa, Augustine, and Thomas Aquinas.

2 Simplicity in Christian doctrine: Gregory of Nyssa, Augustine, and Thomas Aquinas

> The search for the unity of being itself is at bottom a search for God and, at the same time, the recognition that no creature is God.
>
> –Hans Urs von Balthasar[1]

2.1 Introduction

Though Greco-Roman philosophers were motivated by different assumptions than early Christian thinkers, their discussions of the nature of God or ultimate reality often overlap in interesting ways with those of their Christian counterparts. They often shared, for instance, concern for the questions of how persons are united with God and how God is the unified source of reality. In Greek philosophy, this is a search for the *archē* (ἀρχή), a term that was stretched from its original political and causal uses to be deployed in pursuit of a metaphysical principle – the fundamental principle of unity and source of all being. Lloyd Gerson clarifies the *sui generis* character of the *arche*: 'genetic explanations which seek an original material for a complex phenomenon are unsatisfactory insofar as this material is subject to the same processes or changes as those observed in the phenomenon.'[2]

This philosophical pursuit of the simple *arche* finds resonance in the way in which the biblical tradition depicts God in the context of the doctrine of creation. For as the book of Genesis describes, the world was spoken into existence by the one God of Abraham, Isaac, and Jacob – the very same God who in the book of Exodus delivered Israel from Egypt. There is, then, a union of political authority/ power and initiating cause-like power in this one God. God is both politically sovereign – even beyond the local nation of Israel (revealed in God's power to liberate Israel from slavery to Egypt) – and is the initiator and source of the cosmos. Consequently, Israel's understanding of God exhibits parallels with the Greeks' search for the cosmic *arche*. It should therefore come as no surprise that some of the most robust meditations on the origin or ground of the phenom-

---

[1] *Theo-Logic*, 1:253.
[2] Gerson, *God and Greek Philosophy*, 6, cf. 5–14.

enal world happen in parallel and often through dialogue across these traditions.³

Before attending to how Gregory of Nyssa, Augustine, and Aquinas deploy the doctrine of divine simplicity, I look briefly at Plotinus (c. 204–270 CE), who is an exemplar on the Greek side and who presents one of the most coherent and systematic elaborations of the simplicity of the *arche* among Plato's ancient interpreters. Plotinus realized that the *arche* was not on the same ontological plane as the sensible multitude, and for this reason he approximates, even if he does not fully develop, the kind of distinction Christians would draw between Creator and creation. 'One', 'good', and 'simple' thus become markers of the ontological distinctiveness of the *arche*. The doctrine of divine simplicity finds its initial Greek-philosophical home here.

Plotinus' use of the concept of simplicity is more explicit than his predecessors', although it has roots in Plato and Aristotle. Plotinus adopts Plato's judgment on the utter uniqueness of each form and applies it to the *arche*, with modification.⁴ However, Aristotle expresses simplicity with greater precision than Plato when he says, 'the primary essence does not have matter, since it is an entelechy. So the unmovable first mover must be both formally and numerically single.'⁵ As Plotinus develops his concept of simplicity, he receives, synthesizes, and transforms the judgments of Plato and Aristotle on the unique singleness of the *arche*. From both thinkers he receives the contrastive use of simplicity – that the One, in contrast to sensible beings, is not composed of form and matter. From Plato he receives an affirmation of the *arche* as intelligible (in contrast to sensible) and, consequently, unique in a manner analogous to the forms. And from Aristotle he receives an affirmation of the actuality and singularity of the *arche*.⁶

---

3 Cf. Pannenberg, *Metaphysics*, 14–21, and 'Appropriation of the Philosophical Concept', 119–83.

4 Cf. Gerson, *Plotinus*, 6. The major modification that Plotinus makes is the elevation of the Good beyond all forms, so that the Good (the One) is not simply the highest form but is in fact ontologically prior to and distinct from the realm of forms. Consequently, the 'uniqueness' of each form for Plato is extended by analogy to the Good in Plotinus. Cf. *Enn.*, VI.9 [9].3.44–45: the One is '"itself in itself, uniform"; … it is formless, being prior to all Form'. All translations are from Gerson's edition. The Greek text is taken from Armstrong's edition in the Loeb Classical Library.

5 Aristotle, *Metaphysics*, Λ.8.1074a.

6 By suggesting that Plotinus uses simplicity to make 'affirmations', I am not suggesting that Plotinus is in this way not a radically apophatic thinker. On this, cf. Halfwassen, *Aufstieg zum Einen*, 9–17, 173–82. To say that these uses of simplicity are 'affirmations' rather than pure contrasts, I am drawing attention to the way that 'simple' is not simply the contrast of 'composed' as

During this time and following, Christians were also developing an understanding of God that required increasing reflection on the concept of divine simplicity in light of the emerging doctrine of the Trinity. Gregory of Nyssa (c. 335– 394 CE) represents a critical moment in Christian theology as controversies around the doctrine of the Trinity heightened the need to clarify the being and unity of God. In his polemics with Eunomius of Cyzicus, who challenged the divinity of the Son by appeal to his own construal of divine simplicity, Gregory deploys similar judgments to Plotinus, though to different effect and with greater concern for positive names for the simple divine nature. A defining figure for the medieval Latin theological tradition, Augustine (354–430 CE) takes up similar arguments from a new perspective concerning divine simplicity, and his approach is further refined and elaborated by Thomas Aquinas (1225–1274 CE). Tracing significant themes in Gregory, Augustine, and Aquinas will serve to highlight development within Christian construals of simplicity. Beginning with Gregory, I will argue that he and Plotinus each deploy distinct regulative principles toward the goal of identifying the object of genuine contemplation or worship, so that, even amidst many positive points of contact, they still have relatively distinct notions of divine simplicity.[7]

In Plotinus the regulative principle is *the principle of prior unity*, which can only be satisfied by a metaphysically simple source of reality. In Plotinus, prior unity and 'simplicity' first have a negative function, distinguishing the 'One' from other metaphysical first causes like Aristotle's *Noûs* and the Stoics *Psychē*. Because of this negative difference, speaking of and knowing the One involves a circumambulating motion *around* the One by means of an apophatic, contemplative return to the One.[8] Simplicity is, then, also about moral and intellectual honesty at the heights of intellectual activity, a purifying of the self in contemplation of the perfectly self-emanating and unified *arche*.[9] In Plotinus, one can detect the seeds for what became dominant aspects of simplicity in later developments. The One's simplicity, as is seen in the distinction of the One from *Noûs* and Soul, consists in a rejection of various forms of composition. Whereas *Noûs*, Soul, and all material beings are composite each in their own

---

if the two expressed a difference of quantity or degree. Rather, the distinction is qualitative, which emerges in part by virtue of the affirmations associated with simplicity as received from Plato and Aristotle. The qualitative distinction is closely connected with the deep apophaticism of Plotinus' thought concerning the One.

7 For a theological interpretation of Plotinus on divine simplicity, see Gavrilyuk, 'Plotinus on Simplicity'.
8 *Enn.*, VI.9 [9].3.51–54.
9 Pierre Hadot develops this relationship in *Plotinus or the Simplicity of Vision*.

ways, the One is absolutely simple and immaterial. Plotinus also uses several identity statements to express the One's simplicity, which are corollaries of the negative meaning of simplicity: whereas in all other beings a real distinction obtains between essence and existence (*ousia/hypostasis*), activity and existence (*energeia/hypostasis*), and will and essence (*thelema/ousia*), in the One they are identical. So Plotinus can say: 'We should not be afraid to posit the primary activity [ἐνέργειαν] as without substantiality or essence [οὐσίας]; this itself is to be posited as, in a way, its real existence [ὑπόστασιν]'.[10] 'Essence' (*ousia*) typically refers to forms or to a being according to its participation in a form. The One, which transcends the forms, is therefore beyond *ousia* and yet is in another sense identical to its *ousia*.[11]

For Gregory the regulative principle is *the strict distinction between uncreated and created*, crystalized by the development of the Christian doctrine of *creatio ex nihilo*. To avoid idolatry, only one being can satisfy the role of uncreated creator, and all perfections inhere in this one creator maximally and simply. Though Gregory's writings are not as systematic or philosophically exhaustive as Plotinus' *Enneads*, he makes some similar judgments concerning the divine essence. Consequently, they both have a strong commitment to a doctrine of divine simplicity, although coupled with *ex nihilo* Gregory's has greater openness to and explicit connection with divine infinity, which proves useful in his pro-Nicene trinitarian theology.[12] In Augustine and Aquinas we see an increasing philosophical sophistication in formulating the doctrine of divine simplicity from the perspective of the Trinity and *creatio ex nihilo* and a more thorough incorporation of a *principle of prior unity* in service to the *strict Creator–creature distinction*.

2.2 Gregory of Nyssa on the *adiastēmic* plenitude of the simple God

2.2.1 *Creatio ex nihilo* as a regulative principle in discerning the divine

A distinguishing feature of Gregory of Nyssa's theology and his context in fourth-century Trinitarian and Christological controversies is the growing Christian con-

---

[10] VI.8 [39].20.10–11 (translation altered).
[11] Gerson argues from this and other statements that Plotinus holds to an identity between essence and existence in the One; *Plotinus*, 11–13.
[12] Cf. Hart, 'Mirror of the Infinite', 545–46.

sensus on *creatio ex nihilo*. As Khaled Anatolios argues, at the threshold of Nicaea almost all parties to the debates held to a doctrine of creation out of nothing, in contrast to an emanationism in which divine being naturally overflows through intermediaries into the realm of corporeal, sensible beings.[13] The debate of Gregory and his brother Basil of Caesarea with Eunomius of Cyzicus is not over the sharp distinction between God and creation and the concomitant belief in *ex nihilo* but over how to identify the God who creates out of nothing – i.e., what names are appropriate for this God and whether or not the Son and Spirit share in the fullness of what the divine names signify.

The determinate belief in creation *out of nothing* is a regulative principle in Gregory's theology that distinguishes him from Plotinus. At most, Plotinus' view of the causal relation of the One to all other beings has 'creationist' tendencies without being completely distinguished from emanationism.[14] For even while the One is the sole *arche* of existence (and, as such, is not to be identified with anything that comes into being), the One's activity is mediated through *Noûs* and Soul. At times Plotinus speaks of the One's direct act of giving existence to sensible beings, while at others *Noûs* and/or Soul mediate the granting of existence by virtue of their roles as *archai* within the domains proper to them. For example, as any existent (other than the One and in a qualified sense *Noûs* itself) exists only by virtue of participating in the forms, all such existents receive existence *with form* through the intermediary activity of *Noûs*.[15] For Plotinus, the One is the uncontested *arche* of existence, but the granting of existence is co-administered by *Noûs* and Soul, who as lesser 'deities' can more directly act on finite beings. Consequently, there is some sense of a 'line' between uncreated and created – the One on the former side and everything else on the latter – yet the function of *Noûs* and Soul suggests that the line between creator and creation is

---

13 Anatolios, *Retrieving Nicaea*, 36, 38–39.
14 Contrary to Gerson, *Plotinus*, 26–36. Gerson argues that Plotinus is creationist and not emanationist, though the primary tactic he adopts is to show that several of Plotinus' claims often taken in a strictly emanationist sense can be squared with Thomas Aquinas's own claims on creation. However, this only clearly demonstrates that Plotinus is not merely or unqualifiedly emanationist. Any stronger claim on the basis of this argument has an air of anachronism. Yet on the other hand, contrary to Harry Wolfson, Plotinus's account of the activity of the One is more nuanced than a purely emanationist reading acknowledges ('Identification of *Ex Nihilo* in Gregory', 53–54).
15 *Enn.*, VI.7 [38].13.27–29: 'If then all the different Beings are prior to it, it would have already undergone motion under their influence. If they are not, then this Intellect generated all things … It is not possible, therefore, for Beings to be if Intellect does not activate them'.

graded and not fully disentangled from an emanationist articulation of the overflow of existence through intermediaries.[16]

Gregory of Nyssa, by contrast, has a clearly defined commitment to *ex nihilo* and a creationist conception of the production of finite being.[17] As Lucas Mateo-Seco puts it: 'There is nothing in the Greek philosophical tradition that corresponds to the Nyssen's distinction between created and uncreated ... This is an irreducible antithesis, one already manifest in his first works'.[18] The decisive motivating concern for Gregory is not the uncreated/created distinction *per se* – for this matter is settled in his theology – but how to identify the God who creates. Putting it this way highlights that both the epistemology of theology *and* the metaphysics of divine being are at play in Gregory's articulation of divine simplicity.[19] Whereas for Plotinus there are several candidates in philosophy for the position of principal *arche*, which then require adjudication and division of labor, for Gregory the matter is not as open – for him there is no possibility of division of labor in the production of the universe. By deploying a strict distinction between uncreated and created Gregory can focus on how to name and specify the uncreated Creator.

At one point, Gregory does consider multiple 'gods' or contenders for the role of creator. However, rather than making space for them in a graded scale of divinity, he demythologizes them. In the prologue of his *Catechetical Orations*, Gregory argues against a hypothetical polytheist, asking whether deities are characterized by 'perfection' – which he assumes would be answered affirmatively. From here, he maps perfection onto his strict distinction between uncreated and created, using this distinction as a rule for judgments about God:

> For if he should not discover a difference with respect to the greater and the deficient (since the principle of perfection does not admit deficiency), ... but rather the principle itself of divinity is one, not one particularity being found in a single thing, as is reasonable, it is altogether necessary for the erring fantasy about a multitude of gods to be pressed to the admission of one divinity. For if the good and the just, and the wise and the powerful should be admitted in the same manner, every difference being taken away in every respect, the multitude of gods is by necessity taken away from the teaching, the sameness throughout all things bringing him round to faith in the One.[20]

---

[16] For instance, in V.1 [10].6.29–40 Plotinus points to the necessary external emanation among all finite beings as an analogy for the radiating generation of *Noûs* from the One.
[17] See, for instance, *Cat.*, 39.2. Cf. Mateo-Seco, 'Creation'.
[18] 'Creation', 185–86.
[19] On the importance of the epistemology of theology for Gregory of Nyssa's doctrine of divine simplicity see Radde-Gallwitz, *Basil, Gregory, and Divine Simplicity*.
[20] *Cat.*, prologue 7–8.

This argument introduces several important themes for Gregory's doctrine of divine simplicity. First, perfections in divinity do not admit of degrees. Second, simplicity is a function of perfections in the Godhead. Third, diverse perfections do not entail multiple divinities or multiplicity in the Godhead but one divine being characterized by the plenitude of perfection. This last conclusion is simply the deployment of the prior judgment that God stands on one side of the absolute distinction between creator and creature.

2.2.2 Propria and perfections

Gregory's development of the doctrine of divine simplicity is in part constituted by his defence of his brother Basil against Eunomius. Eunomius developed a doctrine of divine simplicity in which God is identical to any divine attribute, and any such attribute would thereby serve as a definition of the divine essence. He argued that the essential definition of God is 'ingenerate' – all other attributes being identical (i.e., reducible) to it.[21] Basil and Gregory take issue with this because it disqualifies the Son from sharing in the divine essence; for insofar as the Son is generated from the Father, the Son does not share in the definitional predicate of 'ingenerate' and consequently is not identical to the divine essence. A biblical riposte is available to Gregory: 'if anyone thinks wisdom is to be honoured, "Christ is the power of God and the wisdom of God" [1 Cor. 1:24]. Since our mind will probably be disposed to admire to the greatest possible extent such and so many wonderful aspects of Christ, what superiority of honour will it be possible to conceive as especially rendered to the Father alone, in which the

---

21 Radde-Gallwitz, *Basil, Gregory, and Divine Simplicity*, 97–108. Radde-Gallwitz argues that Basil and Gregory can be read as arguing against the identity thesis – the view that all God's attributes are identical to the divine essences and hence actually identical to one another in the divine essence – because he associates the identity thesis with Eunomius. However, this conflates later, especially scholastic, understandings of simplicity and predication with Eunomius, who would more properly be labelled 'reductionist' or 'eliminationist' concerning the divine attributes. Rather than seeing the diverse attributes as identical in the divine essence, Eunomius makes the *meaning* of all attributes convertible with – and thereby reducible to – ingeneracy. Unlike Thomas, then, who can uphold alongside divine simplicity (and the identity thesis) a diversity of names each with distinct semantic content because he distinguishes the *modus significandi* and the *res significata*, Eunomius cannot maintain a diversity of senses for attributes predicated of God and instead eliminates any attributes' senses that are not strictly convertible with 'ingenerate'. Radde-Gallwitz use of the label 'identity thesis' is consequently misleading.

Son will properly have no part?'[22] Whatever the divine essence is, it cannot exclude the Son, for the Son is identified in scripture as the power and wisdom of God, and, as Gregory argued in the prologue to the *Catechetical Orations* cited above, such genuine perfections belong only to God. So, if a divine perfection is attributed to the Son then the Son is in fact revealed as divine by virtue of possessing genuine perfection.[23]

Committing to the witness of scripture, Gregory distinguishes modes of knowing to allow for genuine knowledge of God without thereby claiming definitional knowledge of the divine essence.[24] Essences are known according to the definition of a being, and no definition is attainable for the divine essence. Definitional knowledge, however, obtains only in cases where we can define a being by contradistinction from other beings. But God is the fullness of goodness with no admixture of opposition and contrast – God's being is not determined by distinction from others. Consequently, Gregory argues that to suppose the divine essence can be defined claims greater knowledge of the divine essence than is possible and renders divine immanence impossible. On the contrary, Gregory sees a positive connection between the simple, ineffable perfection of God and divine immanence, as Andrew Radde-Gallwitz explains:

> only the opposites of goods actually oppose those goods: the vicissitudes of human life are not evils, and consequently do not by themselves block our participation in God's life – or God's sharing in ours. ... [For Gregory] the world is no longer viewed as the opposite of God, such that God cannot enter into it and act within it. God and world are not opposites. This is no small part of the Cappadocian transformation of divine simplicity.[25]

Gregory is able to see simplicity as a positive judgment about God by associating the simple divine essence with a prior plenitude of perfection. This is due in part to his and Basil's shift in theological epistemology. A perfection can be recognized as a proper attribute or name of God in a non-definitional manner: although the perfection does not define the divine essence, it is a true *proprium* of God – where *propria* (e.g., power, incorruptibility, purity, justice) are 'proper-

---

[22] *Eun.*, 1:133 [*GNO*, 1:126–27; *NPNF²* 5:66]. As Basil had also noted before him (*Against Eunomius*, II.27, p. 172).
[23] Similar reasoning is used concerning the Holy Spirit in Gregory of Nyssa, 'On the Holy Spirit', 273, ¶5. Cf. Anatolios, *Retrieving Nicaea*, 215–20.
[24] Gregory explicitly charges Eunomius with abandoning the witness of scripture, privileging his own definition of God above the names God provides. Cf. *Eun.*, 1:109–10; 3:146 [*GNO*, 1:86; 2:175; *NPNF²*, 5:53, 196]. For Gregory, all names fail in respect of God, naming in various ways God's power (cf. *Life of Moses*, II.177).
[25] Radde-Gallwitz, *Basil, Gregory, and Divine Simplicity*, 187.

ties co-extensive with and intrinsic to the divine essence, but not individually definitive'.²⁶ The Latin term *propria* covers the set of Greek terms derived from ἴδιος, which can refer to essential or accidental properties. Whether essential or accidental, *propria* are features that are proper to a being because of the particular kind of being it is. So Aristotle says, 'A property [ἴδιον] is something which does not show the essence of a thing but belongs to it alone and is predicated convertibly of it'.²⁷ That is, *propria* (*idia*) are features by which God can be identified or recognized, though not comprehended essentially.²⁸

In Gregory, simplicity is a positive recognition that whatever *propria* can be attributed to God – each of which is derived from scripture and liturgy – these *propria* (or whatever is named thereby) inhere in God without diminishment or commingling with its contrary. If God is good, God is untarnished Goodness absent any trace of evil.²⁹ This is an outworking of Gregory's mapping of perfection onto the Creator–creature distinction, attributing genuine perfection to the Creator alone. He clarifies the logic of perfections so:

> the personal being [ὑπόστασις] of the Onlybegotten and that of the Holy Spirit are indefectibly perfect in goodness [τελείαν ἀγαθότητά] ... For all good things, as long as they do not admit their opposite, have no limit to their goodness, since they are naturally circumscribed only by what is opposite to them, ... and all in all individual good things cease where they meet their opposites. ... But if the divine and immutable nature is irreconcilable with what is worse – and that is something granted even by our enemies – then it is perceived as altogether unlimited in goodness, and unlimited is the same as infinite.³⁰

Something is limited by whatever bounds it, and according to Gregory only something's opposite can provide a bound. A good or perfection can only be bound by a corresponding *imperfection*, as weakness is to strength.³¹ Consequently, perfection inheres in the divine without circumscription and is therefore unlimited.

Later, Gregory explicitly connects unlimited, infinite perfection with simplicity. In one passage, Gregory interweaves these concepts and argues for their interconnectedness, warranting extended quotation:

---

26 *Basil, Gregory, and Divine Simplicity*, 107.
27 *Topica*, 102a19–21.
28 I am here following Radde-Gallwitz, *Basil, Gregory, and Divine Simplicity*, see xx.
29 *Eun.*, 1:104–5, 115, 122 [*GNO*, 1:77–78, 95–96, 107; *NPNF*², 5:51–2, 56, 60–61].
30 *Eun.*, 1:104 [*GNO*, 1:77; *NPNF*², 5:51].
31 As Radde-Gallwitz notes, the conflation of opposite and contradictory is a questionable equivocation in Gregory's thought, though it is not unique to him at that time (*Basil, Gregory, and Divine Simplicity*, 187–88).

> How could anyone take that to be pluriform [πολυειδῆ] and composite [σύνθετον] which has neither form nor shape, and to which no concepts of size and magnitude apply? … strictly speaking simplicity [ἁπλότης] does not allow concepts of more and less to apply to the Holy Trinity. In a case where it is not possible to conceive any mixture and combination of qualities, but the mind apprehends a power [δύναμιν] without parts and composition, how and by what logic might the difference of greater and lesser be understood? One who determines that such comparisons be made must inevitably envisage the incidence of some qualities in the subject. He either conceives the difference between them in terms of exceeding [and] falling short, and thus brings the concept of size into the debate, or he is arguing that it is superior or inferior in goodness, power, wisdom and whatever else is piously attributed to the divine; and thus he will not escape the imputation of composition [συνθέσεως]. There can be no lack of wisdom or power or any other good thing in one to whom goodness is not something acquired, but who is by nature constituted essentially such; so that whoever claims to apprehend lesser and greater beings in the divine nature has unwittingly argued that the divine is composed of dissimilar elements, so as to consider the subject to be one thing, and the attribute quite another, by participation in which what is not goodness comes to possess it. But if he truly envisaged the being as "simple [ἁπλῆν] and altogether singular," being itself what goodness actually is, and not becoming such by acquiring it, he would not think about it in terms of more and less. … In cases where the existent by its nature does not admit of the worse, no limit is applicable to goodness; the infinite is not such by its relation to something else, but itself by definition evades limitation. I do not know how anyone who has thought about it can agree to say that one infinite is more or less than another. So if he allows that the underlying being is simple [ἁπλῆν] and is properly related to itself, let him agree that it has attached to it the attributes of the simple and infinite [τό ἁπλοῦν καὶ ἄπειρον κοινωνίᾳ συναπτομένην]. But if he detaches and alienates the beings from each other, envisaging another being of the Onlybegotten alongside the Father, and yet another of the Spirit alongside the Onlybegotten, and applies to them concepts of greater and less, let it be noted that, while he appears to delight in what is simple [ἁπλοῦν], in reality he argues for the composite [σύνθετον].[32]

In this passage, Gregory is arguing that his opponent Eunomius is not following the logic of simplicity to its conclusions, insofar as he is admitting degrees of perfection or goodness in the Son and Spirit. Whether his argument is a convincing response to Eunomius is questionable, for Gregory seems to assume that the Son and Spirit do have proper claim to divine perfections – which is precisely what Eunomius denies. However, the argument clarifies some important aspects of simplicity for Gregory.

He notes, once again, that divine perfections – and simplicity itself – do not admit of degrees. He also clarifies why degrees of perfection compromise simplicity: attributing a partial perfection to God imagines the relation between being and perfection incorrectly by assuming a distinction between the subject and the quality. Because God is identical to the perfection (since simplicity al-

---

[32] *Eun.*, 1:115–16 [*GNO*, 1:95–96; *NPNF*[2], 5:57].

lows of no distinction between quality and subject), and the only perfections befitting God are unbounded, God is simple *and* infinite. Gregory does not claim that in God all perfections are identical to one another, rather he leaves the interrelations of perfections open.[33] However, he does positively identify the divine being with the divine perfection so that there is no subject–quality distinction.

In one elegant move, Gregory connects perfection, infinity, and simplicity. Starting with perfection, the argument is that God possesses every perfection. In God, however, these perfections should be understood as without any delimitations, for such would imply a comingling of the perfection with its contrary. Absent any contrary and limitation, the perfection is qualitatively infinite and unbounded. Moreover, as unbounded, the perfection is in fact not a quality separate from its subject to which it is predicated but is – in some unspecified way – to be thought of in identity with the subject.[34] The same judgment seems to identify God as simple, infinite, and plenitude of perfection. There is only one being on the 'Creator' side of the uncreated/created divide; consequently, whatever lies on that side (whether a perfection or a *hypostasis* like Father, Son, or Spirit) must in some manner be identical to the being of the Creator. Divine simplicity, in this sense, is a function of Gregory's use of the distinction between Creator and creature.

2.2.3 Infinity, simplicity, and *diastēma*

There is another concept that plays an important role in specifying divine simplicity as well as connecting infinity and simplicity for Gregory: *diastēma* and

---

33 Joseph O'Leary considers but rules out the possibility that Gregory sees 'the divine as pre-containing all perfections in a supreme degree, where they are entirely one … so that our language can attribute them to God in an analogical way' ('Simplicity and Plurality of Attributes', 325). This seems to overstate the case. Although Gregory himself does not say it, it is a possible inference from passages like the one I am presently considering that all perfections analogically co-inhere in God. If subject and perfection are identical, and God can be named by more than one perfection, then it is plausible that all perfections are entirely one and precontained eminently in God. However, I admit that such an inference moves beyond Gregory's own claims and prefer to maintain that Gregory remains undeveloped on the issue.
34 Contra Radde-Gallwitz's claim that Gregory explicitly rejects an 'identity thesis' according to which propria are identical to the divine essence (*Basil, Gregory, and Divine Simplicity*, 5–7 and *passim*). However, it is necessary to not overinterpret Gregory's rejection of a strict distinction between subject and perfection through the lens of later thinkers like Thomas. However, Radde-Gallwitz's more recent articulation of Gregory's position avoids his earlier, more 'ontological' reading of the *propria* ('Gregory of Nyssa and Divine Simplicity').

its opposite, *adiastēma*. This concept provides a point of comparison between Plotinus and Gregory, and perhaps has a role in explaining the greater degree of emphasis and clarity in Gregory's use of infinity.[35] *Diastēma* is a noun with several overlapping meanings: 'a) a standing apart, b) extended or distended existence, c) a gap or interval, d) the distance between two points or two astral bodies, or e) the temporal distance between two events'.[36] *Adiastēma* is the opposite, so that *diastēma* refers to a gap or interval and *adiastēma* denotes the closure or absence of any interval. Plotinus uses the language of *diastēma* and *adiastēma* in his discussion of time and eternity.[37] For Plotinus, time is a moveable (κινήτον) image of eternity, following Plato.[38] Time comes into being as Soul departs (*diastasis*) from *Noûs* and the One – for Soul 'wanted to keep on transferring what it saw [in eternity] to something else, it did not want the whole to be present to it all together', which leads to a different temporal mode of life for Soul, characterized by 'spreading out' (*diastasis*): 'So the spreading out [Διάστασις] of life involves time; life's continual progress involves continuity of time, and life which is past involves past time. ... time is the life of soul in a movement [κινήσει] of passage from one way of life to another'. By contrast, eternity is 'the unextended [ἀδιαστάτου] and unity'.[39] This leads directly to the conclusion that eternity is 'infinite [ἀπείρου] from the start and whole'.[40]

In Gregory's writing, all creaturely being is consistently characterized by *diastēma* – not just according to temporality. In fact, creation itself *is diastēma*, and so is a constant traversing of an interval.[41] In contrast, God is without any interval or extension – hence, *adiastēma* – both concerning the divine essence as distinct from creaturely being and in respect of the divine *hypostases*.[42] In *Contra Eunomium* book I, Gregory provides an argument against any interval between Father and Son that also demonstrates how God cannot be the term of any

---

35 John Rist compares Gregory's emphasis on infinity with that of Plotinus, arguing that both hold that the divine essence is infinite, yet divine infinity is clearer, more central, and less ambiguous for Gregory than in Plotinus ('Plotinus and Christian philosophy', 399–400).
36 Verghese, 'Διάστημα and Διάστασις', 245.
37 *Enn.*, III.7 [45]; cf. also I.5 [36].7.
38 Plato, *Timaeus*, 37D.
39 *Enn.*, III.7 [45].11.54.
40 *Enn.*, III.7 [45].11.55 (translation altered).
41 *Eun.*, 1:135, 184–85 [*GNO*, 1:129, 207–8; *NPNF*², 5:144, 215]. *In Eccl.*, or. 7, 125. This aspect of Gregory's thought was brought to prominence especially in the pioneering study of von Balthasar, *Presence and Thought*, 48, 156, 166; cf. also Verghese, 'Διάστημα and Διάστασις', 251; Mateo-Seco, 'Creation', 186.
42 *Eun.*, 1:134–37, 140–42, 184–85 [*GNO*, 1:128–33, 137–40, 207–8; *NPNF*², 5:67–68, 70–71, 215].

2.2 Gregory of Nyssa on the *adiastēmic* plenitude of the simple God

interval whatsoever.[43] If there exists an interval between Father and Son, as Gregory takes Eunomius to imply, then the interval is either infinite or finite. If infinite, then there would be no actual connection between Father and Son, which Gregory takes as impossible. However, if the interval is finite, then it is bounded on each side by a determinate term, in which case the Father would be a determinate entity in relation to another and would consequently be bounded and, hence, finite. As finite, the Father could no longer be considered God.[44]

This is a striking argument both for trinitarian theology and for a doctrine of divine simplicity. On the former, it completely rules out any construal of the three persons such that they become terms constituted by an interval or gap between them. On Gregory's logic, any such interval would render each person finite – bounded – and hence not identical to the divine essence, which is infinite.[45] For the nature of divine simplicity, it would seem to imply that a simple, infinite God cannot be a term in any relation, for by being a term in a relation, God would thereby be delimited and rendered finite. This fits with what Kathryn Tanner calls 'non-contrastive transcendence'.[46] As she puts it, 'a God who transcends the world must also … transcend the distinctions by contrast appropriate there. A God who genuinely transcends the world must not be characterized, therefore, by a direct contrast with it'.[47] This resonates with Gregory – God must transcend the discursive space within which identities are determined contrastively (or by 'intervals'). Divine simplicity and infinity function together to identify God non-contrastively, which further clarifies and strengthens Gregory's strict Creator–creature distinction while allowing the Creator genuine immanence.[48]

---

[43] *Eun.*, 1:134–37 [*GNO*, 1:128–33; *NPNF²*, 5:67–68].
[44] The argument bears striking resemblance to an argument in Plato's *Parmenides*, according to which any temporal relations presuppose a bounded term of the relation. Parmenides then rules out any temporal relations in the One by appeal to simplicity (*Parmenides*, 137D).
[45] In referring to an 'identity' between each divine person and the one essence, I mean simply that the persons are not 'additional' or 'incidental' to the divine essence, nor do they add up to *comprise* the essence but are entirely coextensive with it.
[46] Tanner, *God and Creation*, 42–46.
[47] *God and Creation*, 46.
[48] As Tanner analyses, 'God's transcendence and involvement with the world vary inversely … when God's transcendence is defined contrastively'; *God and Creation*, 45. Hence, the remedy is to conceive of God's transcendence non-contrastively to recognise genuine immanence. This point, however, remains undeveloped in Gregory, who does at times use διάστημα for the creator/creature distinction. This might be chalked up as analogical usage, but it is not clear. Cf. Verghese, 'Διάστημα and Διάστασις', 253–54.

In Homily 7 on Ecclesiastes, Gregory aptly expresses the issue of non-contrastive transcendence under the category of *diastēma:*

> In the contemplation of what is, one is compelled to go beyond *diastēmic* conception [διαστηματικὴν ἔννοιαν], yet one does not get beyond it. Together with every concept it thinks of, it surely envisages, comprehended at the same time as the being of what is conceived, its *diastēma*; but *diastēma* is nothing other than creation itself [δὲ διάστημα οὐδὲν ἄλλο ἢ κτίσις ἐστίν]. Yet that Good which we have learned to seek and to guard, and which we are advised to grasp and cling to, being above creation, is above comprehension. How could our understanding, which moves about within diastēmic space, comprehend the nature which is *adiastēmic*?[49]

This non-contrastive, *adiastēmic* conception of God confirms that the strict distinction between Creator and creature functions as a regulative rule for Gregory, forming part of the grammar of transcendence according to which God is properly identified.

In sum, Gregory of Nyssa develops a deeply integrated conception of the divine being according to which divine simplicity, infinity, and plenitude are mutually implicating, and are, in a sense, expressions of the same judgment concerning God's radical ontological otherness. God is that being who is all perfection without limitation, has perfection without distinction between quality and subject, and is *adiastēmic* – bears no interval or distance within or without. Although he has not developed a systematic theory or practice of analogical predication, Gregory is able to conceive of perfections inhering in God in a manner utterly distinct from their exemplification in finite beings. This is so because God bears perfections without limitation, beyond *diastēmic* apprehension, and without distinction or *diastēma* between subject and the perfection itself. When put into practice, Gregory's understanding of simplicity assists him in developing a Trinitarian theology. As the divine essence cannot be divided, multiply instantiated, composed, or conceived according to degrees, any identity that bears divine perfections is as such fully God. So, for instance, following the scriptural naming of Christ as the power and wisdom of God (1 Cor. 1:24), Gregory determines that Christ does in fact share the one divine essence.[50]

God's simplicity, for Gregory, includes God's ineffability (at least *qua* divine essence[51]) and ontological difference from creatures (*qua* infinitude and pleni-

---

49 *In Eccl.*, or. 7, 125 (translation altered) [*GNO*, 5:412].
50 *Eun.*, 1:133 [*GNO*, 1:126–27; *NPNF*² 5:66]. For elaboration, Hart, 'Mirror of the Infinite', 545–46.
51 *Eun.*, 3:96–97 [*GNO*, 2:63–64; *NPNF*², 5:146–7].

tude, and as the ground of finite participation⁵²), while permitting a positive similitude between God and creatures – for creatures actually enjoy participation in God's goodness – and allowing for genuine conceptualization and recognition of God through liturgical celebration of the divine names provided in scripture. For Gregory, this leads him to draw an analogy between the infinity of the divine nature and the ongoing growth of human knowledge of God, an eternal *epektasis:*

> Since the First Good is infinite by nature, the participation of the one which enjoys it must also perforce be infinite, ever apprehending more, and always discovering what exceeds the apprehended, and never able to draw level with it, since neither can what is shared be fathomed, nor can what grows by participation desist.⁵³

Consequently, in union with God, the human becomes a mirror of God's simple infinity, enjoying the 'marvelous' coincidence of rest and motion that characterizes God's own trinitarian life.⁵⁴

2.3 Augustine on the self-same (*idipsum*) triune God

Writing in the Latin West within just a few years of Gregory of Nyssa, Augustine of Hippo (354–430 CE) articulates a new level of clarity and integration for the doctrine of divine simplicity. The thought of Gregory of Nyssa and Augustine (as well as Aquinas, who will be the focus of the next section) are each regulated by the affirmation of *creatio ex nihilo*, so that their common conception of divine simplicity can differ in language without radically differing in content.⁵⁵ As Lewis Ayres says, 'To understand that Christ is uncreated rather than created is, for Augustine, to understand that Christ's life is the source of our continuing to live and of our eternal life. The uncreated must be life itself (and divinity does not come in degrees)'.⁵⁶ This could equally be read as a gloss on Gregory's argu-

---

52 *Eun.*, 3:145–51 [*GNO*, 2:174–82; *NPNF*², 5:196–99].
53 *Eun.*, 1:125 [*GNO*, 1:112; *NPNF*², 62]. Rist argues that Gregory's more consistent understanding of infinity enables this eschatological '*epektasis*' – an option that Plotinus' understanding of essential knowledge could not entertain ('Plotinus and Christian philosophy', 399–400).
54 *Life of Moses*, II.243. On the unity of motion and rest in God, cf. von Balthasar, *Presence and Thought*, 153–57.
55 Richard Cross has recently argued that Gregory and Augustine have much in common on the doctrine of divine simplicity, contributing to the ongoing reconciliatory readings of 'Eastern' and 'Western' theologians ('Divine Simplicity and Trinity', 53–65). On Augustine's regulative commitment to *ex nihilo*, cf. Anatolios, *Retrieving Nicaea*, 242–44; Ayres, *Augustine and Trinity*, 189–97.
56 Ayres, *Augustine and Trinity*, 189.

mentation presented above and betokens their overlap in theological grammar. I will present Augustine's development of 'pro-Nicene' theology in three steps: (3.3.1) his exposition of divine simplicity with special emphasis on *idipsum* as a divine name, (3.3.2) his clarification of the act of predication in respect of God, and (3.3.3) the use of divine simplicity in his trinitarian theology.

2.3.1 Augustine's exposition of divine simplicity

Augustine relies on the grammar of divine simplicity from early on in his Christian writings, understanding it as concomitant with *creatio ex nihilo*. Two aspects of the connection between simplicity and *ex nihilo* can be seen from passages of *De vera Religione* (c. 390), one of his first post-baptismal writings.

First, Augustine argues from the ontological dependency of creatures, who, because they are mutable, manifestly do not possess being in the 'supreme degree'. That they do not possess being in the supreme degree further displays that they were created by 'the one who *is* in the supreme degree'. The relative difference in mode of existence is not a matter of quantitative variation in form or actuality, as if creaturely being is on a single continuum with God, for the whole scale of actuality and form is created by – and thus utterly distinct from – God.[57] Rather, the difference has to do with the relationship between a subject (e.g., God or a creature) and existence. To say that God '*is* in the supreme degree' is to say that God, distinctly from creatures, *has existence* (*esse*) in the supreme degree, which means by identity rather than by reception or participation. In this way, creatures are composite by virtue of their dependence on God for existence, whereas God is simple by virtue of perfect identity with existence.

Second, Augustine argues that there is a positive, though imperfect, similitude between the relative wholeness or harmony of created bodies and the perfect wholeness of God's simple being: 'the body too, then, was made by him who is the source of all harmony. The body gets a kind of peace from its shape, without which it would be nothing. He therefore is the fashioner of the body also, from whom all peace is derived and who is shape unforged, and of all shapes the most shapely'.[58] The concinnity of composite bodies is a received perfection, given with the body's form or shape, and it therefore witnesses to a source of peace and harmony in the one from whom it is received: God, who in the utterly perfect simplicity of divinity is not *without shape* but rather 'most shapely'.

---

57 Augustine, *De Rel.*, 18.35. Cf. also Augustine, *Conf.*, XII.8.
58 *De Rel.*, 11.21.

2.3 Augustine on the self-same (*idipsum*) triune God — 47

Later, in *De Trinitate* Book V, the same conviction about the source of all good in the unquantifiably good God is reformulated: 'we should understand God … to be good without quality, great without quantity, creative without need or necessity, … holding all things together without possession'.[59] In *De Trinitate*, Augustine is tightening his use of such terms as substance and essence, clearing conceptual ground for specifying how it is that the simple divine essence is shared among three persons.[60] He reiterates the lack of distinction between subject and quality in God, even concluding from this lack of distinction that God is not properly called substance at all on the grounds that *substantia* comes from *subsistere*, which connotes a subject in which distinct qualities subsist or inhere. God is better talked of as *essentia*, which has no such problematic connotations, and so is more compatible with simplicity.[61]

An important basis for the judgment that in God there is no subject–quality distinction, is the name *idipsum* (self-sameness), which Augustine derives from Psalm 121:3 (Vulgate): 'The Jerusalem that is being built as a city, it is a sharing [*participatio*] in *the selfsame, the identical* [*idipsum*]'.[62] In his commentary, Augustine reflects on the meaning of *idipsum*: 'What is *idipsum*? It is simply *idipsum*, Being-Itself. How can I say anything about it, except that it is Being-Itself? Grasp it if you can, brothers and sisters, for whatever else I may say, I shall not have defined Being-Itself'.[63] '*Idipsum*' is for Augustine a fitting name for God as simple because God is identical to God's existence. As simply 'Being-Itself', God is without the creaturely limitation of mutable and dependent existence.

For Augustine, then, the Creator–creature distinction, explicated in terms of the different manner in which God and creatures each possess perfections or existence (creatures by means of participation and God by means of identity), provides a crucial framework for understanding divine simplicity. Lewis Ayres comments on this: 'The language of simplicity is thus part of Augustine's attempt to articulate the intelligible structure of reality and the possibility of our progress towards contemplation of its source'.[64] In *De civitate Dei* XI.10 Augustine

---

59 Augustine, *Trin.*, V.1.1.
60 *Trin.*, esp. Books V–VII. See Ayres, *Augustine and Trinity*, 199–205.
61 *Trin.*, VII.5.10. For commentary see Ayres, *Augustine and Trinity*, 201, where he notes, 'For this reason perhaps God *alone* should be called *essentia*'. However, having made this clarification about the improper use of *substantia* for God, Augustine does continue to use the term somewhat synonymously with *essentia*, though it seems clear he intends that his criticism of *substantia* be borne in mind in its use.
62 Based on the numbering for the Masoretic text (and hence for modern English translations), it is Psalm 122:3. Translated from the Latin by Ayres, *Augustine and Trinity*, 202.
63 Augustine, *En. Ps.*, 121.5.
64 Ayres, *Augustine and Trinity*, 208–9.

makes explicit the connection between participation and divine simplicity. Creatures have qualities and perfections by participation, yet as the source of all God does not participate in anything, being simple.[65] This understanding of God's distinction from creation, based on the implications of an ontology of participation according to which God is understood as the sole source of creaturely being, allows Augustine to maintain that God is infinitely different from creation and at the same time discernible through the similitude of created effects to their creative source. This infinite difference entails that God is ineffable *qua* essence, yet because we seek to worship and praise God we must attempt 'to say things that cannot altogether be said as they are thought by a man'.[66] Our thinking itself is accommodated to use for creatures who are substances modified by qualities. However, God is 'most truly and supremely *to be*' and consequently is unchangeable and does not admit of modification.[67] In God, all perfections are identical to the self-same (*idipsum*) essence of God, for God simply *is* all that God *has*.[68]

2.3.2 Predication and divine simplicity

The simplicity of God as *idipsum* creates a special problem for thinking and speaking about God, for we typically use predicates like 'wise' to express an accidental quality of a being or substance. When we say, 'the child is wise', we are modifying the subject (the child) with a quality that is not included in its definition, for there is nothing in the definition of a child that necessarily entails being wise. So, 'wise' expresses an accident or modification of 'the child'. As Augustine has clearly claimed, however, God is not subject to such modification and so has no accidents – which is to say that God is whatever God is by virtue of the divine essence, and not by virtue of anything else or a modification thereof. Consequently, as Roland Teske argues, Augustine carefully distinguishes our speaking about God (*dicere*) from our thinking about God (*cogitare*), and both from the being of God (*esse*).[69] Our *speaking* about God necessarily involves multiplicity, in terms both of multiple predicates and of the distinction between the subject and quality or accident. In our *thinking*, we can strive to remove this multiplicity by recalling that in God there are no such distinctions. Although we can

---

[65] Augustine, *Civ.*, XI.10; Ayres, *Nicaea and Its Legacy*, 380–81.
[66] *Trin.*, V.1.1. He goes on to say: 'when we think about God the Trinity we are aware that our thoughts are quite inadequate to their object, and incapable of grasping him as he is'.
[67] *Trin.*, V.2.3.
[68] *Civ.*, XI.10.
[69] Teske, 'Predicaments in *Trin.* 5'; Augustine, *Trin.*, V.1.1.

neither discard the multiple meanings of the predicates nor reduce their meanings to one, we can approximate the perfect unity in the reality of God by thinking of how divine predicates might converge.

Augustine undertakes this process in *De Trinitate* XV.5.8 by taking twelve predicates of God and showing how they might be reduced to a smaller number.[70] Because, for example, 'just', 'good', and 'spirit' are all somehow present to mind with the predicate 'happy', one can see how different concepts with distinct meanings can be thought and said in a single predicate, because one cannot predicate 'happy' of something that is not also just, good, and spirit. Although Augustine only reduces the twelve predicates to three rather than one, his point is simply to suggest how it might be that despite the unavoidable use of multiple predicates and their multiple meanings, the one, simple essence of God is all that is expressed by this multiplicity.[71] Teske expresses this relationship well:

> Hence, at the level of speech about God (*dicere*), many statements about God may seem to signify or designate an accident in God, but at the level of thought about God (*cogitare*) they must not be so understood, because in the being of God (*esse*) there is no accident, that is, no reality in God that can be lost or gained or that can increase or decrease.[72]

We may be able to think about God better than we can speak, but both operations ought to be continually disciplined and regulated by attending to the simplicity of God's being.

2.3.3 Simplicity and Trinity

Augustine continues to refine the act of predication to God as he turns directly to matters of the Trinity. The goal of Augustine's theology of the Trinity is *not* to affirm two separate truths – i.e., that God is simple and that God is triple – except insofar as these are two aspects of one truth. Which is to say that the aim is to know, think, and speak (to the extent it is possible) of the three persons of God in their perfect simplicity. As Ayres says of Augustine:

> We do not find the unity by focusing on something different from the persons: it is focusing on the persons' possession of wisdom and existence 'in themselves' that draws us to rec-

---

70 Teske, 'Predicaments in *Trin.* 5', 97.
71 *Trin.*, XV.5.8.
72 Teske, 'Predicaments in *Trin.* 5', 101.

ognize their unity. The triune communion *is* a consubstantial and eternal unity – but there *is* nothing but the persons.[73]

Putting it this way circumvents Colin Gunton's and Paul Hinlicky's critique of Augustine's doctrine of the Trinity (viz., that there is in fact a 'quaternity' of Father, Son, Spirit, and simple substance), and at the same time it focuses in on the mystery expressed in trinitarian doctrine.[74] Augustine's theology of the Trinity attempts to think through the internal logic of confessing three divine persons of whom it can be said that they are each the full perfection of the divine life, which is itself perfectly simple insofar as it is self-same (*idipsum*).

In order to explicate this confession, Augustine argues in three basic steps.[75] First, in order for Father, Son, and Spirit to be spoken of as being God *and* as being in relation to one another, they must each in some manner be an essence, for only where there is an essence can there be relation. Taking 1 Corinthians 1:24 ('Christ the power of God and the wisdom of God') as his starting point, Augustine asks how the Father can be his own essence by which he is wise and powerful if he is only such by virtue of the Son.[76] If the Father is only wise and powerful by virtue of being related to the Son, then the Father's act of uttering the Son is also the act by which the Father *becomes* wise and powerful, and because the Father is only truly God insofar as he is wise and powerful, the Father's act of uttering the Son is also the act by virtue of which the Father becomes divine. But the Father cannot give divinity to the Son apart from being divine himself, so the Father must be wise and powerful according to his own essence and not by way of relationship.[77]

---

[73] Ayres, *Nicaea and Its Legacy*, 380.

[74] For their criticisms, see Gunton, *One, Three and Many*, 54–58, 83–84; Gunton, *Act and Being*, 134–35; Hinlicky, *Divine Complexity*, 160–61, 184, 193–99; and Hinlicky, *Divine Simplicity*, 104–34. For a response to Gunton's criticisms, which goes a decent way toward settling Hinlicky's recapitulations as well, see Green, *Gunton and Augustine*.

[75] *Trin.*, VII.1.1–2.3. I am following Ayres in presenting Augustine's argument in this manner; Ayres, *Nicaea and Its Legacy*, 378–79.

[76] *Trin.*, VII.1.1.

[77] William Hasker takes such points as evidence that the persons 'are' an essence and, therefore, *not* 'subsistent relations', implicitly claiming that Aquinas's later trinitarian thought diverges from rather than develops upon Augustine; Hasker, *Metaphysics and Tri-Personal God*, 58n8. However, in making such a strong claim, Hasker is removing this step of Augustine's argument from its broader context, the cumulative effect of which is to undermine the sense in which the three persons are 'each' an essence, insofar as that can be taken as entailing *three* essences. As will be clear from steps two and three, each person 'is' an essence – the self-same simple essence of God. Hence, according to essence the three are identical, distinguished only according

But, second, the Father genuinely generates the Son, giving to the Son all that the Father is in essence. The Son, then, is according to essence wisdom and power in himself, just as is the Father. Because the Father is God in essence, and because the divine essence that is simply God is not distinct from divine power, the Father's power/act of giving the divine essence to the Son is not distinct from the Father's own essence. Therefore, the Son is in himself fully identical with the divine essence, for he receives in perfect simplicity all that the Father is in essence.

Consequently, third (and in qualification of the first step), Augustine insists that by virtue of the eternal generation of the Son, the Father is both fully identical with the divine essence and has this essence by way of the Son's identity with the essence. 'It is only because [the Father] has begotten his own being or "is-ness" that he is what he is with reference to himself. Just as he is only great with the greatness he has begotten, so he only is with the "is-ness" or being he has begotten, because for him it is not one thing to be and another to be great.'[78] The Father's identity with the divine essence is not in competition with the generation of the Son who is also identical with the divine essence; and this further entails that the Son is not divine by partition of the Father's divinity, both because the divine essence is simple and therefore indivisible and because for God power-in-act (i.e., generation) is not distinct from the simple essence, as if it were an accident. The power of God, *qua* Father, simply is the Father's perfect power generating the Son. Augustine deploys this kind of reasoning – what Ayres calls the 'grammar of simplicity' – to deduce that the Father, Son, and Spirit, are each perfectly identical to the divine essence. Augustine can consequently say, 'Thus Father and Son are simultaneously one wisdom according to one essence, and singly wisdom from wisdom in the same way as essence from essence'.[79]

This third step, in which Augustine affirms that each person is identical to the divine essence, comes into direct conflict with the concern in present-day philosophical theology with the transitivity of identity, which would seem to require that if Father, Son, and Spirit are each identical to the divine essence then they are also identical with one another, subverting the intentions of such trinitarian speculation. William Hasker raises this issue directly for interpreting Augustine. Either Augustine was aware of the transitivity of identity and did not rec-

---

to relation. This certainly is not yet to articulate Aquinas's concept of subsistent relations, but it allows for the latter to be a genuine development of Augustine's own position.
78 *Trin.*, VII.1.1.
79 *Trin.*, VII.2.3 (my translation): '*Unde pater et filius simul una sapientia quia una essentia, et singillatim sapientia de sapientia sicut essentia de essentia*'.

ognize its implications in the case of the Trinity, or he did recognize its problem for the Trinity but held to his doctrine in spite of its 'incoherence'. Hasker finds both of these options unlikely, for they fail to treat Augustine as a serious thinker. Instead, Hasker prefers to think that Augustine simply did not identify the persons with the essence 'in the sense of identity that is recognized by modern logicians'. Unfortunately, Hasker does not believe an alternative account of identity is available in Augustine or in the rest of ancient philosophy and theology, and consequently the collusion of strong simplicity and the Trinity is a 'tangle of confusion' that cannot be disentangled but must simply be rejected.[80]

While Hasker is correct insofar as Augustine never names a principle analogous to the modern transitivity of identity, he is incorrect to think that Augustine is unaware of the problem identified thereby in trinitarian theology. Hasker's mistake may be due in part to an inattention to the polemical edge of *De Trinitate*, where Augustine emphasizes the perfect identity in essence of the three persons so heavily in order to correct Arian subordinationism. But Augustine does recognize that by speaking of Father, Son, and Spirit as each identical to the divine essence the conclusion is forthcoming that the three are in fact identical to one another. As I noted above, in one sense Augustine concedes as much in explaining that the Father only 'is' by virtue of the being he has in the Son, because together they are one essence and one wisdom.[81] But Hasker has missed the importance of the distinction Augustine draws to clarify in what mode the three are one and in what mode they are three. For this purpose, Augustine goes to great lengths to distinguish how we speak of God's substance/essence and how we speak of the three divine persons according to relations.

Each divine person is an essence. But each person's essence – as simple, unbounded, and unparticipating – is identical with the essence of the others. Which is to say they are all identically God. Augustine must find a unique manner of distinguishing the three persons, for anything said of the triune God according to substance or essence is said of all three (because they possess the one identical essence). In this context, Augustine returns to the unique difficulties of predication in respect of the simple God. Typically the only way of predicating of a being is according to accidents (*secundum accidens*).[82] Augustine rejects this option, proposing that the names 'Father', 'Son', and 'Spirit' apply to God neither by way of substance nor of accident, but according to relation (*se-*

---

[80] Hasker, *Metaphysics and Tri-Personal God*, 59–60, quotations from 60.
[81] *Trin.*, VII.1.1, VII.2.3.
[82] *Trin.*, V.4.6.

cundum relativum) – that is, by reference to another (*ad alterutrum*).[83] By essence the Father is simply God, but *qua* 'person' he is identified by relation to the Son. So, *contra* Hasker, the transitivity of identity applies and is followed by Augustine according to predication of the divine essence, but this is not the only manner of predicating of God, and even in this case the grammar regulating such predication is quite different from the normal entities about which we speak. Differentiating by relation or by reference to another does not modify the essence (for it is not an accident). Consequently, it neither leads to multiple deities (tritheism) nor reduces the three persons to identity *qua* person (modalism).

Finally, part of the warrant for such an approach to trinitarian confession is Augustine's axiom of inseparable operations, and it is this commitment that connects his 'psychological analogy' of the Trinity with the trinitarian grammar of simplicity discussed here.[84] Because all that the Father is essentially is fully shared by Son and Spirit, so also the external acts of the Trinity are inseparable. Commenting on John 5:19, Augustine says:

> with God … there is not one thing, substance, by which he is, and another, power, by which he can, but whatever he has is all consubstantial with his very self, and he is whatever he is, because God simply is. It is not the case that he is in one way, can in another, but he has 'is' and 'can' together … all simultaneously, identically.[85]

The three persons, then, do not act in isolation or separation *ad extra*, because they act by the same power, which is predicated according to essence not relation. So, while the three persons are distinct according to relation, they are inseparable in external acts because action follows on the capacity of the essence, which is one and simple. By analogy, the human mind structured by the present-

---

[83] *Trin.*, V.5.6; see also V.2.3: '*Deo autem aliquid eiusmodi accidere non potest*'. It might help to register once again the difference between 'essence' according to the majority of analytic philosophers and according to ancient and medieval metaphysicians like Augustine. For the former, an essence is the set of properties a being possesses in all possible words in which the being exists, whereas for the latter an essence is the definition of a being according to genus and differentia, i.e., the internal structure or nature by virtue of which the being comes to bear the properties it does (consequently essence is prior to properties). Hasker seems to presume the former, anachronistically judging Augustine by it, for if the Father is distinguishable from the Son by virtue of a relationship, this entails that the Father has a property (being the Father of the Son) that would obtain in every possible world in which the Father exists, and, therefore, that the Father has a different essence from the Son. Augustine would reject this line of reasoning altogether because neither essences nor relations work this way for him.
[84] On the connection between inseparable relations and the psychological analogy, see Barnes, 'Latin Trinitarian Theology', 79–81.
[85] Augustine, *In Ioh.*, XX.4.

ly fragmented triple of memory, understanding, and love/will also strives toward inseparable action, a kind of mental positive simplicity of unity and wholeness. It is because God's utterly inseparable action is the origin and goal of our human striving for inseparable action that the human self *becomes* an image of the Trinity – and of the simplicity of the triune life – through approaching nearer in intimacy to God.[86]

2.4 Thomas Aquinas and the pure actuality of the simple God

Thomas Aquinas (1225–1274) lived eight centuries later than Augustine and Gregory of Nyssa. In some ways Aquinas represents the pinnacle of Christian thinking on divine simplicity in his highly systematized articulation of the varieties of composition and in the exhaustiveness of his deployment of simplicity throughout his theology. A significant historical factor in Aquinas's theology is access to Aristotle's writings, which had for some time not been available to Latin Christendom. In particular, Aquinas retrieves Aristotle's logic, his preference for attention to concrete particulars, and his articulation of the priority of act over potency. Plotinus also integrated some of these Aristotelian insights into his metaphysics, but Aquinas's own use of Aristotle is inflected by mediation through Muslim thinkers, especially Avicenna.[87] However, this does not mean that Aquinas's metaphysics and theology do not display Platonic and Augustinian influence.[88] Also important, his 'Aristotelian' emphasis on the concrete and particular receives its theological force from his commitment to the goodness of creation. As Frederick Christian Bauerschmidt notes, the Albigensians' denial that the God of Jesus Christ was the creator of the physical world was part of

---

[86] For elaboration on Augustine's 'psychological analogy' and how it is oriented toward the fulfilment of the self in God, see Hanby, *Augustine and Modernity*; and Williams, *On Augustine*, 155–91. Alfred Schindler, by contrast, assumes the psychological analogy works by relatively pure introspection apart from the self's pursuit of the triune God who is its *telos*, and he consequently takes a more negative interpretation of the analogy's role in Augustine's trinitarian theology; Schindler, *Wort und Analogie in Augustins Trinitätslehre*, 212–17.
[87] Gilson, 'Quasi Definitio Substantiae', 125–26: 'Between the metaphysics of Aristotle and that of Thomas Aquinas, the metaphysics of Avicenna acts as a kind of filter. The ontology of Aristotle reaches Thomas Aquinas Avicenna polarized'.
[88] On the Platonic/Neoplatonic aspects of Aquinas's thought, see Clarke, 'Meaning of Participation'; Perl, *Thinking Being*, 151–89; and Wippel, *Metaphysical Thought of Aquinas*, 95–131. On Aquinas's 'Augustinianism', see the collection, Dauphinais, David, and Levering, *Aquinas the Augustinian*.

2.4 Thomas Aquinas and the pure actuality of the simple God

what the Dominican order had been founded to correct.[89] As a Dominican himself, Aquinas took the Creator–creature distinction as centrally regulative for Christian theology, so much so that G. K. Chesterton quips that we could call him 'St. Thomas of the Creator'.[90]

Several recent studies, notably by Victor Preller, David Burrell, Herbert McCabe, and Denys Turner, have emphasized the apophaticism inherent in Aquinas's treatment of the Creator–creature distinction.[91] Divine simplicity, in this reading, becomes a way of regulating speech about God in order to distinguish the incomparable and ineffable nature of God from the composite and definable natures of finite creatures. Simplicity is, according to Burrell's reading of Aquinas, a 'formal feature' of divinity, and in this role it clearly functions to maintain the Creator–creature distinction. In Aquinas this apophatic role is joined to a cataphatic treatment of simplicity, especially according to the relation between God and creation as cause to effects, where Aquinas views God as a radically unique 'cause'.[92] I will argue that in this way Aquinas unites something like Plotinus' *principle of prior unity* within the more primary *strict distinction between uncreated and created*. I will proceed by (3.4.1) discussing how the apophatic element of divine simplicity works together with the causal relation, (3.4.2) showing how Aquinas integrates a *principle of prior unity* in his unique handling of the one-and-many dialectics, and (3.4.3) presenting the deployment of simplicity in his trinitarian theology, especially as he develops the concept of subsistent relations to express the identities of the three persons.

2.4.1 Simplicity, apophasis, and creation as causal relation

How one interprets Aquinas's doctrine of divine simplicity depends on what kind of exercise one believes Aquinas is engaged in throughout questions 2–11 of the *Summa Theologiæ*'s first part. A straightforwardly metaphysical reading would suggest that Aquinas is engaged in a *descriptive* account of the nature of God – i.e., as supplying an answer, even if limited, to the question 'what is God?'

---

89 Bauerschmidt, *Thomas Aquinas*, 107.
90 Chesterton, *St. Thomas Aquinas*, 53. See also Pieper, *Silence of St. Thomas*, 47–67.
91 Preller, *Divine Science*; Burrell, *Aquinas*; McCabe, *God Matters*; Turner, *Faith, Reason and the Existence of God*.
92 Cf. Franks, 'Simplicity of Living God', 278–82.

(*quid est*).⁹³ An alternative, apophatic approach capitalizes on Aquinas's prologue to question 3, where he explains that he will treat 'first, of the ways in which God *does not* exist'.⁹⁴ Burrell develops this apophatic reading in his *Aquinas: God and Action*, describing the sections on simplicity as 'philosophical depth grammar' for God-talk. In this view, Aquinas is seen as articulating formal features of divinity or regulative rules for talk of God, theology's principal subject.⁹⁵ Burrell's apophatic reading has received critique and qualification, even by Burrell himself in his later work.⁹⁶ Rudi te Velde praises but modestly supplements Burrell's early position by pointing to the significance of the causal relation between God and creation and the role of negative theology within Aquinas's *triplex via*, which ultimately aims toward knowledge according to supereminence.⁹⁷ This means that the grammatical reading of simplicity is correct, but should not be taken as excluding any positive knowledge of God throughout the discussion of 'what God is not'.⁹⁸

If, as I will assume, Aquinas is engaged in a grammatical exercise which also cultivates positive knowledge of God, then Aquinas's articulation of simplicity will display interconnected apophatic and cataphatic aspects. The discussion

---

93 As Long seems to take it, treating questions 2–26 and 27–43 (typically referred to as *de Deo uno* and *de Deo trino*, respectively) as comprising a single treatise on God; Long, *Perfectly Simple Triune God*, chap. 1.
94 Aquinas, *STh*, I.3, prologue (emphasis added).
95 Burrell, *Aquinas*, 13–15.
96 For some criticism, focused more directly on McCabe and Turner, see White, *Wisdom in the Face of Modernity*, 260–68. Burrell's development seems due in part to his greater appreciation of the difference between Aquinas's analogy and Maimonides' equivocity. So he recently argues: 'revelation gives direction to reason itself, inviting reason to give expression to its internal orientation to its source and goal. ... "the distinction" flowing from a revealed free creation will demand that certain terms be able to outstrip their use among creatures to indicate their source in the creator' ('Analogy, Creation, and Theological Language', 79). See also Burrell's other recent essays with similar effect: 'Act of Creation'; 'Metaphysics of Creation'; and '*Ex Nihilo* Recovered'. For commentary, especially comparing W. Norris Clarke and Burrell on analogy, see Rolnick, *Analogical Possibilities*, 285–300.
97 te Velde, *Aquinas on God*, 73–77. Peter Weigel also seems to agree, granting the apophatic element while treating it as a remotive moment in the *triplex via* (*Aquinas on Simplicity*, 190–91, 248–49).
98 However, I am still skeptical of Long's judgment that questions 3–11 are *descriptive* and prefer to say that the questions cultivate genuine knowledge. It seems that the apophatic element in the discussion precisely excludes *description* of God *qua* simple, though the negations offered do aid in the overall process of *knowing* God.

is apophatic insofar as it focuses principally on the way in which the composite reality of created natures distinguishes them from God. In this context, Aquinas speaks of God indirectly, by negating something about creaturely reality. And yet, the categories according to which creatures can be analyzed into component parts do not entirely fail in respect of God, at least not in the sense that they must *merely* be denied of God. Rather, insofar as God is the Creator – the 'cause' by virtue of which created effects receive their conditions and natures, as argued in the five ways – God possesses in perfect unity the diverse qualities that compose creatures. Consequently, the distinct categories used to describe composite creatures can be deployed to express knowledge not of what is distinct in God but of what is perfectly one and identical.

The meaning of what is expressed of God in this way is radically transformed from its creaturely meaning by being negated in its mode of signifying (*modus significandi*).[99] Consequently, as William Placher says, simplicity is not a *property* that applies to God, like we might assume for finite beings, but rather 'offers a good way of introducing a range of things we *cannot* say about God'. He elaborates by connection with the five ways:

> The project of understanding the world in its own terms remains always frustratingly incomplete ... And it happens to be the case that various people, realizing this limitation of reason's project of understanding the world in its own terms, have given the name 'God' to that 'beginning and end of all things' toward which reason puzzledly and unsuccessfully reaches without ever grasping.[100]

There is a name for the incompleteness of our quest to know and understand, which is no more definable or graspable for being named. One way of dealing with the ineffability we name 'God' is by unthinking any complexity and composition in respect of God, without undoing the connection we have to God as the creative source and end of all things.

How this works for Aquinas can be seen by looking at his treatment of the question of whether in God there is composition of essence (*essentia*) and existence (*esse*) in *STh* I.3.4. The whole of question 3 is dedicated to divine simplicity, and by the time he gets to article 4, Aquinas has already denied that God is composed according to bodily parts (a. 1), form and matter (a. 2), and subject and

---

99 Aquinas believes that even though our mode of signifying (*modus significandi*) is inadequate to God, it still can help draw one to form proper judgments about God as the reality signified (*res significata*). On this, see Rocca, 'Res Significata and Modus Significandi'.
100 Placher, *Domestication of Transcendence*, 22, 26.

essence/nature (a. 3).¹⁰¹ Carrying on, he also denies composition of genus and differentia (a. 5), substance and accidents (a. 6), composition according to multiple effects and by virtue of being perfect (a. 7), and by entering into composition with other things (a. 8). In article 4 specifically, Aquinas considers two potential objections to the identity of essence and existence in God, and they represent two opposing misinterpretations of the identity claim. On the one hand, to identify God's essence (*essentia*) with existence (*esse*) would seem to evacuate 'God' of any specifiable content, for existence is common to everything that is at all (*esse commune*).¹⁰² Something must be added to (*additio*) 'existence' to specify *which* existent is being named as God. Otherwise, 'God' would simply name any existing being. On the other hand, if God is essentially (i.e., by definition) *esse*, then it would seem we have precise knowledge of 'what' God is (*quid sit*), which Aquinas has already argued is impossible in I.2.2. The objections claim that the identity of essence and existence in God would permit either too little or too much knowledge of God.

In reply, Aquinas clarifies what kind of claim is being made in identifying God's essence with existence by showing that it is neither a reduction of existence to essence nor vice-versa. First, if essence and existence are distinct, then existence is either derived from the essence or has an external cause. The first option, however, is incoherent for it assumes that an essence can generate the existence by which it exists.¹⁰³ The second option, to say that the existence of a being has a cause external to its essence, entails that the being *derives* existence from another and therefore is caused to exist. Clearly, neither option fits God. The first fails by incoherence and the second conflicts with God as 'first cause' (I.2.3). Beyond conflicting with a prior claim of God as first cause (*primum causam efficientem*), the distinction implies both that an essence is potential in respect of existence and that an actual existent essence participates in existence (*ens per participationem*). But there is no potency in God (I.3.1), and God does not participate in anything else, for God is the primary existent as Creator of all else.

This allows Thomas to directly address the objections. In response to the first, he notes that there are two senses in which one might say an essence is 'unspecified' (*non fit additio*). One might mean that the essence excludes some 'ad-

---

101 Aquinas also demonstrates that God is not composed of actuality and potentiality, which is presented by way of rejecting composition of extended bodily parts; *STh*, I.3.1, *responsio*. He dedicates a chapter on denying potency of God in *ScG*, I.16. For commentary on each negation of composition in *STh*, I.3, see White, 'Simplicity and Trinity', 71–82.
102 This objection overlaps with Christopher Hughes' criticism that existence is too 'thin' a concept (*Complex Theory of a Simple God*, 21).
103 Cf. also *De ente*, IV.7.

dition' or specification, and he offers the example: 'reason is excluded by definition from irrational animals'. Or, one might mean that the essence is capable of being specified but in itself is not: 'as reason is not included in the definition of animals in general, though neither is it excluded'.[104] In the case of God, identifying essence and existence does entail that the divine essence is unspecified in the first sense, for God's existence excludes all additions or specifications; but in the case of *esse commune* (and *not* in God's case), existence is unspecified in the second sense.[105] For creatures, then, there is a sense in which their essence is something additional to their existence, so their essence 'specifies' existence as a particular actuality. However, for God there is no further addition or specification of God's act of existing.[106] Yet Aquinas insists that this does not deliver one into the trap of the second objection (viz., that one has thereby attained the impossible: positive knowledge of 'what God is'), for to identify God's essence and existence does not mean that *'esse'* directly signifies the act of existence of God but signifies rather God's status as the cause of existence in creatures. Thus, 'when we say that God is [*Deus est*] we frame a proposition about God which we clearly know to be true. And this, as we have seen, we know from his effects'.[107] Consequently, the essence–existence *distinction* as it applies to creatures does not obtain for God, because God's essence simply is existence.

While Aquinas is clear that this conclusion is primarily grammatical insofar as it helps us make and understand true propositions about God, two further points will clarify how this is both grammatical *and* informative. First, throughout the article, especially in the reply, Aquinas draws on the causal creative relation between God and creation to clarify his judgment that essence and existence are identical in God.[108] God cannot be defined *qua* essence, but, as Aquinas says in preface to the five ways, the *meaning* of 'God' can be recognized through the effects, and consequently creation as effect 'will take the place of a

---

104 *STh*, I.3.4 ad. 1.
105 For Aquinas *esse commune* – that in which all actual finite beings participate – is not identical to God, who is *esse subsistens*. There can only be one *esse subsistens*, as a purely actual, infinite act of being has no potentiality for individuation; whereas *esse commune* participates in God and is specified by the finite beings that participate in it (*STh*, I.3.8; *In div. nom.*, II.3). Cf. Wippel, *Metaphysical Thought of Aquinas*, 110–24. Further, *esse commune* is distinguished from God, who is *ipsum esse subsistens*, to the extent that Aquinas defines the former as in itself non-subsistent – 'completum et simplex, sed non subsistens' (*Pot.*, I.1). Ferdinand Ulrich's magisterial work, *Homo Abyssus*, develops a speculative metaphysic on the basis of this fundamental insight into the giftedness of finite being.
106 See also *ScG*, I.24.
107 *STh*, I.3.4 ad. 2.
108 For further elaboration and defence, see te Velde, *Aquinas on God*, 74–75.

definition of the cause in the proof that the cause exists'.[109] The identity of essence and existence in God is a judgment based on the causality of God as creator, for the crux of the distinction within creatures is their *derived* or *participating* existence. As their cause and as the ultimate source of all existence, God does not have existence as distinct from the divine essence but *is* existence by identity. Only as identical to existence can God be the ultimate source and cause of the existence of creatures.[110]

Second, although Aquinas insists that we cannot directly signify God's act of existence with the word *esse* but can only use *esse* to form a true proposition about God, when he discusses the ways we *can* name God he defends 'He Who Is' precisely because of the identity of essence and existence.[111] The name's meaning is still derived from the existence we encounter in composite creatures, and therefore must take into account the negative and grammatical aspect of divine simplicity. However, the generality of existence and its aptness to designate the whole being of God make 'He Who Is' the most proper name for God. Consequently, for Aquinas, the apophatic and grammatical work together with the cataphatic. As he explains,

> the understanding of negation is always based on an affirmation. And this is clear because an affirmative proposition proves every negative proposition, and so, unless the human intellect were to know something affirmatively about God, it could not deny anything about God. But it would not know anything if nothing said about God were to be affirmatively verified about him.[112]

It follows that the articles on divine simplicity, while consisting (even primarily) of grammatical and apophatic reflections, also concern cataphatic knowledge of God as the perfectly simple Creator of all things.

---

109 *STh*, I.2.2 ad. 2.
110 Aquinas makes the significance of the Creator–creature causal relation explicit for divine simplicity in *Pot.*, VII.1: 'Therefore, the being that made all beings actually exist, and itself proceeds from nothing else, is necessarily the first actual thing without any admixture of potentiality, since, if it were in any way potential, another being that made it actual would have to be prior to it. ... And so no composite thing can be the first actuality'.
111 *STh*, I.13.11, *responsio*. In these questions, Aquinas is discussing '*quomodo nominetur*' as planned in I.3, prologue.
112 *Pot.*, VII.5. The whole of question VII is concerned with divine simplicity.

2.4.2 Prior unity, participation, and the one and the many

The emphasis on the causal relation of God to creation already evinces the *principle of prior unity*. Yet the significance of *prior unity* for Aquinas can also be seen in the ways he responds to the relationship of the one and the many.[113] As John Wippel points out, there are two levels at which Aquinas handles the one-and-many. First, there is the question of how our language can express general being (*esse commune*) as both one and diverse, which is treated according to the analogy of being. Second is the question, 'How can there be many such beings, given the unity of being as indicated by the fact that each of them shares in being?'[114] The first is concerned with an order of *language* that is flexible enough to speak of that which is in different senses one and diverse (i.e., 'one' according to *esse commune* and 'many' according to the categories of substance, accident, etc.[115]); the second is concerned with the reality of multiple instances of existence that all share in the same perfection of existing.

'Being' is used analogically, even apart from any consideration of God, for accidents have being only derivatively as modifications of a substance, which has being primarily – accidents and substances are 'beings' in different modes.[116] Aquinas connects the metaphysical and linguistic senses of analogy by understanding 'being' through the Aristotelian act–potency distinction. 'Act' is given priority, so that primary being (substance) relates to secondary being (accident) as act to potency.[117] There is then an analogy of action as well, as substance is act to accidents' potency, form to matter, and existence to essence. In this way, Aquinas understands existence itself, the most general and basic metaphysical category, to be 'the ultimate positive core of all real perfections – an act which is multiplied and diversified by reception into various

---

113 Wippel dedicates four chapters and 132 pages to Aquinas's responses to the one-and-many (*Metaphysical Thought of Aquinas*, 63–194).
114 *Metaphysical Thought of Aquinas*, 65. On the first 'level' Wippel speaks of the analogy being in terms of concepts, where I would put the emphasis on the faculty of *judgment* as the primary site of analogy. On the significance of judgment over concepts, see Rocca, *Speaking the Incomprehensible God*, 165–87.
115 *STh*, I.11.1 ad. 2.
116 Wippel, *Metaphysical Thought of Aquinas*, 78. While there is a certain 'proportion' of 'being' between substance and accident, the analogy of proportion is subsumed, in this example, within the analogy of attribution because accidents are said to 'be' only by relation to substance. For application in the case of God, see Montagnes, *Analogy of Being according to Aquinas*, 25–27. See also Mascall, *Existence and Analogy*, 109–21.
117 *Pot.*, VI.6.

limiting modes of essence'.[118] Existence, then, is the 'prior unity' as the most general and profuse metaphysical principle, and it is received into the diversity of finite beings by virtue of the limiting modes of essence that distinguish beings according to kind. Essence is spoken of as 'limiting' because essences 'focus' or 'reduce' the unlimited active power of existence into a finite and particular mode or structure.[119]

Aquinas explicitly develops this insight in conjunction with Platonic thought, incorporating the relationship of participation between creation and God:

> We can understand ... this from the opinions of the Platonists, that something unshared needs to exist before finite and shared existing ... And so, since existing [*esse*] and other forms and perfections are in material substances in a particular way, as it were, inasmuch as the forms and perfections have been received in matter, an immaterial substance, which has in itself perfect existing [*esse*] in complete fullness, not in a particular way, necessarily pre-exists.[120]

Here we see that Aquinas deploys participation and *prior unity* to conclude to an immaterial act of perfect existence, from which all other beings exist by participation.[121] Earlier in the same book, *De potentia Dei*, Aquinas connects this argument directly with divine simplicity:

> we trace what exists by another as to its cause to what exists intrinsically. And so, if one heat were to exist intrinsically, it would necessarily cause all hot things, which have heat by sharing in it. But this is to posit a being that is its very existing [*esse*], and this is so because there needs to be a first being that is pure actuality, in which there is no composition. And so all other things, the ones that are not their existing but have it by participation, are from that one being.[122]

In this way, Aquinas incorporates into the causal relation of God as the active source of all creaturely existing the *principle of prior unity*, according to which existence from itself (existing intrinsically), as the simple act of self-subsistence, is the principle of all else, both in terms of the unique actuality of all other be-

---

118 Clarke, *Philosophical Approach*, 48.
119 Wippel, *Metaphysical Thought of Aquinas*, 124–31; Clarke, 'Limitation of Act by Potency', 79–82.
120 *Pot.*, VI.6.
121 Clarke, 'Meaning of Participation', 93–94.
122 *Pot.*, III.5.

ings and in terms of their diverse perfections through their limiting essences. But even here, the use of *prior unity* reasoning does not entail for Aquinas that that which is 'prior' denotes something univocally shared between God and creatures.[123] Creatures exist by participation in the divine act of simple existence, therefore receiving in a mode proper to finite beings the existence that is God's by nature.[124] That which is partial, limited, and multiple in creatures, in God is perfectly one and simple. Because Aquinas thereby links divine simplicity to God's status as 'cause', he maintains the priority of the *strict Creator–creature distinction* as a framework within which to understand the Creator as simple.

2.4.3 Simplicity and Trinity

Although Thomas' discussion of the Trinity only appears well into the *prima pars* and after much talk of God and the grammar of God, it is the primary and culminating discussion of God. As Gilles Emery argues, all the previous questions *enable* Aquinas to unite speculative and scriptural reasoning in the task of articulating the eternal Trinity.[125] There are several themes that display the significance of divine simplicity for Aquinas's trinitarian theology, especially salvation by participation in the Word, subsistent relations, and appropriation.

While Aquinas's trinitarian argument drawn from salvation is not entirely novel, the form that the argument takes is unique. In his commentary on the Gospel of John, Aquinas argues from the revealed path of salvation by participation in Christ to participation in the divine essence. His argument assumes the nature of participation as receiving by predication or gift what the participated being is by identity. In assuming this participatory grammar, Aquinas further argues for the identity of the Son with the divine essence:

> a person participating in the Word of God becomes god by participation. But a thing does not become this or that by participation unless it participates in what is this or that by its essence ... Therefore, one does not become god by participation unless he participates in what is God by essence. Therefore, the Word of God, that is the Son, by participation in whom we become gods, is God by essence.[126]

---

123 Cf. Wippel, *Metaphysical Thought of Aquinas*, 547: 'One kind [of analogy] involves a sharing in some single factor which is prior to all the entities that share in it. This kind of analogy cannot apply to God and any creature, just as univocity cannot.'
124 Consider *Comp.*, 68; *ScG*, I.32.
125 Emery, *Trinitarian Theology of Aquinas*.
126 *In Ioann*, 10.35, 1460 (vol. 2:215). Quoted in Emery, *Trinitarian Theology of Aquinas*, 12.

Simplicity is significant for trinitarian theology for soteriological reasons, because only if in sharing in the Son we are truly sharing in the essence of God can the Son's saving activity be truly efficacious. The Son could not give us divine perfection through participation if the Son is not himself the divine perfection by identity.

As Aquinas turns to a direct discussion of the three persons in relation to the simple divine essence, he explicitly frames his own arguments in response to Augustine's distinction between predication according to substance and according to relation.[127] Because Augustine's distinction is primarily in terms of predication, and so in terms of speech rather than being, there are multiple ways Augustine's position could be developed in attempting to clarify the nature of the divine persons and relations. John Duns Scotus' approach, which I introduced in chapter one, could be seen as one way of developing on Augustine by taking 'predicated according to relation' to entail a property given to the person. In this way Scotus avoids identifying person with relation. Aquinas takes an alternative approach, though he is equally developing on Augustine.[128]

The logical core of Aquinas's treatment of simplicity and the Trinity occurs in *STh*, I.28, where he considers whether the relations are identical to the divine essence (a. 2) and if there are four or more relations (a. 4). In article 2, he apparently recognizes the different readings that could be made of Augustine and consequently quotes him in the objections. However, it is clear in his response that he is not contradicting but clarifying Augustine's claims. Accepting that we speak of the persons according to relation, Aquinas distinguishes two ways that relation-language works. On the one hand, relations are 'accompaniments, not bound up inside' natures or essences ('*esse assistentes, non intrinsecus affixae*'). In this sense, relations do not actually inhere in an essence or derive being from it but apply to one being by reference to another. On the other hand, relations also fit in the category of accidents, so that the relation can actually inhere in the subject as an accident, internal but not essential. Aquinas allows that in certain respects both should be affirmed about God, though whatever is said according to accidents in creatures is actually said substantially of God: 'in God a really existing relation has the existence of the divine nature and is completely identical with it. When we think of relation as a "being to something" we signify a bearing, not on the nature, but rather on an opposite term'.[129]

---

127 *STh*, I.28.2.
128 Contra Hasker, *Metaphysics and Tri-Personal God*, 58n8. Thomas Smith discusses Aquinas's relation to Augustine in this respect in detail; Smith, *Aquinas' Trinitarian Theology*, 117–37.
129 *STh*, I.28.2, responsio.

Because the relation itself applies to God in both these ways at once, the relation does not entail another thing along with the relation (as in the case of creatures), for 'there are not two realities but one and the same which is not expressed perfectly by the term, since the meaning cannot cover it. ... Therefore one cannot conclude that there is in God yet another reality besides relation'.[130] While creaturely relations assume terms whose existence is prior and (generally) independent of the relation, in God this cannot be because relation as an accidental term applied substantially to God is in fact identical to the divine essence. Consequently, in God the relation does not connect two independently subsisting relata, but simply names the divine essence by reference to another – another who is also a relation of the divine essence. As Emery explains, 'it is a distinction from relative to relative, and not of relative to essence'.[131] This is why they are called 'subsistent relations', for they name the divine essence – not something over-and-above or distinct – and in this way they *subsist as* the essence considered under a certain aspect.[132]

However, this leaves four relations (paternity, filiation, spiration, and procession) where we confess three persons (Father, Son, Spirit), and in resolving this discrepancy Aquinas further clarifies the concept of subsistent relations (a. 4). Here Aquinas notes that relations are either by quantity or by the production of change.[133] Because, according to divine simplicity, quantity does not apply to God, Aquinas considers the second option, production according to action internal to God. If the relations are viewed in this light, it is clear that there are no longer four but two relations of procession (filiation and spiration) and one relation as source of procession (paternity). The four relational categories are only three susbsistent relations because insofar as they are predicated by reference to another the relations are determined by opposition.[134] Only where there is a relation of opposition is there a *real* relation in God, and this is true only of paternity, filiation, and spiration (both filiation and spiration are processions, but they each specify the relation of opposition whereas 'procession' does not). The relations of opposition express the *persons as act*. By connecting relation within God to *action*, Aquinas elegantly connects the pure actuality of the

---

130 *STh*, I.28.2 ad. 2. Note here the deployment of Aquinas's distinction between *res significata* and *modus significandi*, touched on above. Cf. Rocca, 'Res Significata and Modus Significandi'.
131 Emery, *Trinitarian Theology of Aquinas*, 97.
132 Cf. Dolezal, 'Trinity, Simplicity', esp. 82–85, 88–91.
133 Drawing on Aristotle, *Metaphysics*, Δ.15.1020b–1021b.
134 *STh*, I.28.3. Emery argues that 'relations of opposition' is a faithful development of Cappadocian theology; Emery, *Trinitarian Theology of Aquinas*, 71. He points to Basil of Caesarea, *Against Eunomius*, III.1–2.

divine *esse* to the meaning of the divine persons. The persons are the relations (I.40.1), and as subsistent the relations simply are the internal activity of the purely actual simple essence.[135]

Finally, Aquinas comes full circle in uniting simplicity and Trinity through his unique development of appropriation – i.e., 'appropriating' to one divine person a term that applies to the divine essence.[136] Appropriation acknowledges a unique fittingness between a divine person and a name or attribute of God, drawing from the revelation of the persons and their actions in scripture.[137] Consequently, Aquinas's emphasis on appropriation suggests that he gives priority to our knowledge of God's intratrinitarian distinctions (processions) 'only in the terms of revealed relations' (missions).[138] The appropriated terms (i.e., created terms of the triune missions) are not used to distinguish the persons in their intratrinitarian relations (i.e., their processions), for the practice of appropriation already assumes the processions; instead, appropriation is a biblically grounded practice of contemplating the richness of God's being through the revelatory actions of the divine persons.[139] Because revelation displays the particular actions of the Trinity, appropriation enriches our understanding of the essential attributes by connecting them with one of the three persons and their actions. Emery explains that we can consequently speak of an 'essential attribute' and an 'appropriated essential attribute':

> the latter is a much thicker complex notion. Combining the attribute of power and the person of the Father, 'power as appropriated to the Father' says more than 'divine power'. The appropriated attribute is envisaged in the person: one finds unity 'in the Father', equality 'in the Son', and bonding 'in the Holy Spirit'. Otherwise put, the appropriated attribute is the attribute considered *within the person to whom it is appropriated*.[140]

Through the practice of appropriation, our knowledge of God as Trinity further discloses how replete the simple essence of God is. Further, in Aquinas' particular use of appropriation, it provides a way of naming the divine persons in their personal identity, and not merely by their distinctions according to opposi-

---

135 Cf. Dolezal, 'Trinity, Simplicity', 91–94.
136 See Emery's impressive and comprehensive discussion of appropriation in *Trinitarian Theology of Aquinas*, 312–37.
137 *STh*, I.39.7–8.
138 Smith, *Aquinas' Trinitarian Theology*, 132; see also pp. 132–37 for further discussion of appropriations in Aquinas's trinitarian method.
139 *Aquinas' Trinitarian Theology*, 132.
140 Emery, *Trinitarian Theology of Aquinas*, 326.

tion.¹⁴¹ Cumulatively, Aquinas's discussion of divine simplicity and the Holy Trinity depicts God as *active* – as finally most adequately spoken of in verbs: infinite *esse* subsisting in three relational acts.¹⁴²

2.5 Simplicity, prior unity, and the Creator–creature distinction

Gregory of Nyssa, Augustine, and Thomas Aquinas each arrive at a strong conception of divine simplicity, and for all of them it is a mark of the Creator, the absolute source of existence. I began with the claim that Plotinus and Gregory approach divine simplicity from distinct regulative rules, *the principle of prior unity* for Plotinus and *the strict distinction between uncreated and created* for Gregory. In Augustine and Aquinas it becomes increasingly explicit that Plotinus' *principle of prior unity* can be incorporated *within* the strict *Creator–creature distinction*. It is now possible to reflect on the material differences these regulative rules produce.

On the one hand, there are overlapping conclusions even between Plotinus and Gregory, despite their different argumentative paths. Taken simply as propositions, each might endorse the regulative rule of the other in some form. Gregory would most certainly accept the logical and metaphysical priority of unity.¹⁴³ Plotinus might accept a creator–creature distinction, although it is not as strict a line as we find in Gregory due to the kind of intermediating roles he apportions to *Noûs* and Soul. They agree about divine ineffability, eschewing any attempt to define the essence of God, and this carries over into Augustine and Aquinas. Further, for both, ineffability is not simply the sort of epistemological reserve appropriate to fallible beings but is rooted in their metaphysics – for Plotinus, it is rooted in the spiraling emanation-and-return scheme, for Gregory in the qualitative (*adiastemic*) infinity of divine perfection.¹⁴⁴

Nonetheless, Plotinus and Gregory do come to identify the meaning and function of divine simplicity differently, in part because they pursue divine

---

141 Cf. Smith, *Aquinas' Trinitarian Theology*, 134, who suggests that this distinguishes Aquinas from his predecessors.
142 *STh*, I.28.4, *responsio*: 'realis relatio in Deo esse non possit nisi super actionem fundata'. On using verbs to express the divine life in general, cf. Kerr, *After Aquinas*, 187–91.
143 On the importance of what is 'prior' – though for us it is also what we 'become' – cf. Gregory of Nyssa, 'On Perfection', 118: 'But what benefit do we derive from believing that He is the beginning? We become ourselves what we believe our beginning to be.'
144 On Plotinus' apophaticism, see Halfwassen, *Aufstieg zum Einen*, 12–17.

'unity' differently, and here the preference for different rules to guide their philosophical and theological metaphysics distinguishes them.[145] In Plotinus, the *principle of prior unity* becomes something of a negative eligibility criterion for the highest *arche*. His task consists of analyzing the potential deities put forward, especially by Aristotle and the Stoics, to discern whether they satisfy the *principle of prior unity*. In both cases, motion (*kinesis*) evinces potentiality, passivity, and dependence.[146] Even the definition of *Noûs* as self-thinking thought implies for Plotinus a movement from subject to object, and this motion – as for all motion – is oriented toward perfection in the Good. Because moved toward the Good, *Noûs* must not be identical to the perfect Good.[147] These factors give the sense that, perhaps contrary to Plotinus' better intentions, divine unity comes to be conceived on a univocal, contrastive continuum with ordinary instances of unity. *Noûs* and Soul, while approximating the simplicity of the One are just not quite simple *enough*.

For Gregory, on the other hand, the *Creator–creature distinction* permits more diverse means of specifying and naming the creator while radically distinguishing the kind of unity conceived for God. Because there is an absolute, nongradable distinction between the created and the uncreated, any name or identity that bears divine, uncreated perfection is discerned as in fact identical to the divine essence.[148] So, for instance, Gregory encounters a problem concerning the Son that is analogous to Plotinus' *Noûs* who precisely by virtue of a kind of motion might be deemed external to the Good or the One. Eunomius charges that the Son cannot be the one God because the Son is *generated*, and according to Eunomius God as uncreated is essentially 'ingeneracy'. Gregory challenges the value of 'ingeneracy' as a definition of divinity, and he argues that 'generation' must be purged of materialistic conceptualizations when used of the Son. For Gregory, once the material overtones are purged and the Son's bearing of divine perfections is recognized in accordance with scriptural witness, this 'gener-

---

145 Tanner, *God and Creation*, 42–44, concludes that Plotinus vacillates between univocal and contrastive speech, which raises the question of whether Plotinus' conception of the unity of the One could really accommodate the kind of Creator–creature distinction pro-Nicene Christian theologians like Gregory articulate. Cf. also Bussanich, 'Plotinus's metaphysics of the One', 60–61.
146 In the case of Soul (*Psyche*), Plotinus' issue appears to concern motion when one recognizes the analogy he draws between how the human mind moves the human soul in its activites and how the divine *Nous* moves divine *Psyche*; cf. *Enn.*, IV.1 [21].1.60–65; IV.3 [27].2–3; IV.3 [27].12.30–32.
147 *Enn.*, V.6 [24].5.10–19.
148 And this does not entail, for Gregory, any particular ontological picture of 'how' these properties or names inhere in God's being. Cf. Radde-Gallwitz, 'Gregory of Nyssa and Divine Simplicity', 452–66.

ation' is not a motion like anything we encounter in finite embodied beings. For all these motions are characterized by *diastema*, whereas between the Father and Son there is no *diastema*. By admitting multiple identities (*hypostases*) on the 'uncreated' side, Gregory must think of relation, motion (like 'generation'), and simplicity together.[149] While his approach does not end in a completed systematic 'position', he significantly advances Christian understandings of relation and divine simplicity by persistently thinking of God's unity non-contrastively and as *adiastemic*.

In Augustine this same set of problems is addressed through attention to modes of predication. We can predicate a relation of motion – generation – to God without predicating a substantial change (viz., motion/change according to essence), because in so predicating we are speaking according to *relations*, or with reference to another, and not according to the essence. So, despite predicating by reference to another, no separation of essences is being named. Aquinas develops Gregory's and Augustine's concern with how we name/predicate of God, primarily through his distinction between the mode of signifying and the reality signified, a codified articulation of what Gregory expresses when he distinguishes our *diastemic* mode of thinking from the *adiastemic* nature of God.[150] However, Aquinas also takes up Augustine's distinction concerning predication according to relation vs substance and develops it into an understanding of the persons *as* 'subsistent relations', which advances the understanding of simplicity's function in trinitarian theology.

Further, Gregory makes positive use of infinity to argue that the divine nature cannot be a term in a sequential or ontologically graded relation, as if generation entailed the begetting of one discrete divine entity (Son) from another discrete divine entity (Father). For such a relation would constitute a bound for each person, thereby rendering each finite. The persons – Father, Son, and Spirit – are *adiastemic*, there is no interval between them which an extrinsic relation would have to traverse. There cannot be multiple and diverse actual infinities. Rather, there is one uncreated, infinite, simple, *adiastemic* divine essence, identified triply and irreducibly as Father, Son, and Spirit. While Gregory does not articulate the later Latin view of the divine persons as *subsistent relations*, his conception of *adiastemic* relations among the divine persons seems patient of this technical concept.

---

149 Cf. von Balthasar, *Presence and Thought*, 153–57. The unity of motion and rest also appears in Gregory's interpretation of contemplative ascent (*Life of Moses*, II.243).
150 *In Eccl.*, or. 7, 125.

Plotinus neither conceives divine simplicity with such openness to multiple naming nor has reason to. However, it is difficult to conceive how a doctrine of divine simplicity regulated primarily or exclusively by the *principle of prior unity* could accommodate the rich biblical naming of God found in Gregory, Augustine, and Aquinas. For Plotinus, any apparent multiplicity – in perfections or identities – is indicative of an underlying and prior actualizing principle (*arche*) of unity. The apparent multiplicity must then be sublated – either by reduction or transcendence – to a distinct, undifferentiated unity. Gregory's emphasis on an uncreated/created distinction allows for more initial openness in the use of divine simplicity, which through positive description as infinite plenitude of perfection is amenable to the self-donation of being, *ad intra* and *ad extra*. Within God's *adiastemic* life, Father, Son, and Spirit share in the self-donation of infinite perfection, as the one, simple, uncreated being. This self-donation is extended in the act of creating, allowing an endless participation (*epektasis*) of finite being in the one infinite Triune life.

In Augustine, there are hints that the Plotinian concept of *prior unity* is being deployed to express the *strict Creator–creature distinction*, especially as he speaks of the harmony of bodies evincing the perfect harmony and 'shapeliness' of God.[151] But in Aquinas, the metaphysical integration of *prior unity* is maximized, though clearly regulated by the *strict Creator–creature distinction*. Several factors come together to keep Aquinas's use of *prior unity* from resulting in Plotinus' barer conception of divine simplicity. Metaphysically, Aquinas avoids concluding to Plotinus' conception due to his enriched notion of existence (*esse*). Because for Aquinas *esse* is the source of a being's perfections, it is not necessary for the diversity of forms in created beings to have a distinct and mediating principle like *Noûs*; instead, they can be elegantly grounded directly in the absolutely simple *esse* of God by participation. While form is a genuine principle for creatures, it is the limitation of the perfection of *esse*'s actuality and is consequently potential (and therefore posterior) in respect of *esse*. For Aquinas, this metaphysical position is developed in conjunction with the scriptural naming of God as 'He Who Is' (Gen. 3:14), which presents God simultaneously as Creator and as the perfect act of self-subsisting existence (*ipsum esse subsistens*). If creation occurs by the divine act of self-subsisting existence, then ontological priority lies in *esse* as the act by which creaturely finite forms stand forth from nonbeing. By rethinking the nature of existence, Aquinas can continue to give primacy to the *strict Creator–creature distinction* while deploying in its service the *principle of prior unity*, thereby contributing to a Christian articulation of non-con-

---

151 Augustine, *De Rel.*, 11.21.

trastive divine unity. And in so doing, Aquinas holds together – as Gregory does before him through the concept of divine *adiastema* – the simplicity and the plenitude of God, so that simplicity and plenitude are not distinct aspects but name the same reality: that God is unlimited and uncomposed perfection, Creator of all else, subsisting as the threefold act of paternity, generation, and spiration.

2.6 Conclusion

What is clear, then, is that amongst the thinkers explored here divine simplicity is a shared category for explicating God's transcendence as Creator, and that for all of them this included rethinking the kind of unity and wholeness humans receive through communion with God.[152] While they each distinguish the unity of the *arche*, or Creator of all, from other immanent causal powers and political forces (as *arche*-language originally denotes[153]), they nonetheless articulate a sense that God, as the perfectly simple source of all, also communicates the perfection of wholeness and unity to creatures toward the goal of their own perfection and union with God. For all of them, simplicity is a regulative feature of God's life, explicated with the aid of metaphysical categories, that benefits their various efforts at expressing the mystery of God's triunity. At the same time, there is no single shared list of commitments that characterizes divine simplicity for these Christian thinkers.[154] However, for the Christian thinkers surveyed here, the kind of transcendence conceptualized through divine simplicity required some new theological and philosophical interrogation and refinement, primarily due to the developing trinitarian dogma. Their pro-Nicene efforts, responding to the challenges of Eunomius, Arians, and Albigensians, pushed language to the limits, requiring reflection on how God the Father could be spoken of as eternally generating a Son and eternally breathing a Spirit, with all three being of the same substance (*homoousios*). Gregory, Augustine, and Aquinas each develop ways to articulate how the otherness of God disrupts the normal relation between our language and the reality of which it speaks. For if in God

---

152 Gregory of Nyssa, *Eun.*, 1:125 [*GNO*, 1:112; *NPNF*², 62], and *Life of Moses*, II.243. Augustine, *En. Ps.*, 121.5; (also cf. Williams, *On Augustine*, 155–91). Aquinas, *In Ioann*, 10.35, 1460 (vol. 2:215).
153 Cf. again Gerson's *God and Greek Philosophy*, 5–14.
154 Duby's list (*Divine Simplicity*, 80–89) represents something of a consensus for reformed scholastics, but it is questionable whether all ten items could be attributed to Gregory of Nyssa or even Augustine. As helpful as such lists can be, they risk overcommitting divine simplicity to a particular metaphysical system.

there is eternal procession, somehow God is not simply incapable of motion – as Plotinus' concept of simplicity would suggest – and yet whatever motion might be proper to God is not univocal to the motion of finite beings who move by virtue of act–potency composition and an orientation to a good not reducible to themselves. They must, then, render anew their concept of simplicity through the exigencies of pro-Nicene trinitarian theology. But it is because they are committed to divine simplicity that they go about the task of revising it.

In the twentieth century trinitarian revival, however, this prior commitment to divine simplicity is undercut. Consequently, much of the recent work to give centrality to the doctrine of the Trinity has been done either with less attention to divine simplicity or in explicit rejection of it. Developing a doctrine of divine simplicity today, then, is not simply a matter of developing a shared, received commitment to simplicity in comportment with the doctrine of the Trinity. In the following chapters, I consider how simplicity declined in recent trinitarian theology and engage in discussion with the revisionary metaphysics of the American Lutheran theologian Robert W. Jenson.

Part II **Divine simplicity in the revisionary metaphysics of Robert W. Jenson**

3 The contemporary crisis of divine simplicity

> For a time I shared the German supposition that the tradition culminating with Hegel was identical with metaphysics as such, and that we were past all that. This was an error on my part... The question 'What is it to be?' has not gone away, though it is now often discussed in egregiously jejune fashion. ... [I] attempt to continue Western theology's work of revising inherited pagan Greek metaphysics to fit the gospel.
>
> –Robert W. Jenson[1]

3.1 Introduction

As the last chapter demonstrates, ancient and medieval articulations of God used the doctrine of divine simplicity to elucidate the Creator–creation distinction, the multiple names of God, and the logic of the Trinity. In recent theology, however, divine simplicity has become contentious. One textbook introduction to theology boldly asserts, in stark contrast to much of the tradition, that simplicity 'has no real biblical basis and has in fact worked to defeat the resources of a full-fledged trinitarianism'.[2] What has led to this recent ambivalence – even animosity – toward divine simplicity? Is there hope for the doctrine in the wake of this shift? In this chapter, I will provide a brief response to the first question and then begin a more extensive response to the second, which will be the subject of the remaining chapters.

First, I argue that divine simplicity has become a problem in large part due to a growing distrust of metaphysics and extra-biblical concepts. In the eighteenth and nineteenth centuries, this distrust resulted in difficulties also for the doctrine of the Trinity.[3] Along the way, the increasing Protestant emphases on the primacy of scripture and on the practical, spiritual orientation of theology marginalized metaphysics and speculative theology. And with this rejection of speculative and metaphysical theology, divine simplicity tends to be either refor-

---

[1] 'Preface', vii. Consider also: 'Were the gospel fully spoken, it would be a word about every item of reality that already is: every person, every atomic particle, every galaxy, every animal. And it would be an evocation of futurity, a creation of new language, infinite in its openness. Were the gospel fully spoken it would therefore be a communication in which art and science were one' (S&P, 76–77).
[2] Plantinga, Thompson, and Lundberg, *Introduction to Christian Theology*, 104. By contrast, two recent studies have attempted to demonstrate the biblical basis of divine simplicity; see Barrett, *Divine Simplicity*, esp. 133–62; and Duby, *Divine Simplicity*.
[3] Cf. Powell, *Trinity in German Thought*, 60–103.

mulated in ethical terms or rejected altogether. The question of revitalizing divine simplicity, therefore, partly hangs on the function and viability of metaphysics in theology. Second, I will begin a dialogue with Robert Jenson's 'revisionary metaphysics' as a way of considering metaphysics' viability. Jenson writes from within the Protestant (and, more specifically, Lutheran) tradition that contributed to the marginalization of metaphysics and divine simplicity in the first place, and yet in Jenson one can see a self-conscious attempt to sympathetically engage the early and medieval church's use of metaphysics. Consequently, in this chapter I will introduce Jenson's metaphysical project, and in the next chapter I will explore the revised notion of divine simplicity this produces.

3.2 Scripture, metaphysics, and the problem(s) with divine simplicity

The story of divine simplicity's unsettling has no single determinative moment. There is no one isolated event on which to rest the blame for destabilizing simplicity and its former givenness. However, because the historical formulations of simplicity are deeply rooted in metaphysical language – especially in the theologians I have discussed so far – I take it that shifts in perspective on the value of metaphysics in theology is at least a significant factor in simplicity's eclipse.[4] It is tempting to reduce the shift to a single event – perhaps John Duns Scotus' turn to univocity, Cajetan's interpretation of Aquinas on analogy, Descartes' epistemological privileging of the ego, Hume's critiques of the classical 'proofs' and of causal models of the God–world relation, Kant's agnosticism toward the noumenal, or the logical positivists' decrying of all 'metaphysics'.

---

[4] The historical presentations available do not adequately cover simplicity's unsettling. For instance, Barrett's historical account (*Divine Simplicity*, 35–132), which is both elegant and more comprehensive than any other study, does not provide an account of simplicity's demise. Rather, he keeps distinct his broad account of simplicity's historical acceptance and the modern criticisms. What he and others do not address is the conditions for the possibility of these modern criticisms. Similarly, see also Dolezal, *God without Parts*, 1–30; and Duby, *Divine Simplicity*, 7–53. For one exception, see Peterson, 'Parting of God', 130–73. Peterson's account gives special attention to the way that process theologians developed the procrustean category of 'classical theism' that inevitably reduced the rich diversity of views on divine simplicity to a caricature that fit none in reality. His argument helps illuminate the role that the polemics of process theism have played but does not fully account for why theologians with little to no sympathies with process thought nonetheless concur in criticizing simplicity. To this extent, my argument provides a complementary angle on a similar set of historical shifts.

Caricatures that they are, each of these factors may share some of the blame for the recent critical attitude to simplicity.

However, I see the contemporary unease with simplicity as closely connected to a broader trend within Protestantism that finds radical expression in the early twentieth-century, namely a difficulty in connecting biblical revelation with the philosophically and metaphysically laden conceptualities of dogmatic tradition. This shift alone does not excise simplicity from modern theology – for, as I have noted, there are a variety of live options concerning simplicity today – but it does render simplicity optional in a new way, and therefore simplicity is no longer a 'given' as it once was. One source of this difficulty is Martin Luther's ambivalence toward metaphysics, which can be seen in theses 19 – 21 of his 1518 *Heidelberg Disputation:*

> 19. That person does not deserve to be called a theologian who looks upon the invisible things of God as though they were clearly perceptible in those things which have actually happened [Rom. 1:20]. 20. One deserves to be called a theologian, however, who comprehends the visible and manifest things of God seen through suffering and the cross. 21. A theologian of glory calls evil good and good evil. A theologian of the cross calls the thing what it actually is.[5]

In this quotation, one can sense two possible postures towards metaphysics. On the one hand, thesis 19 might be taken as rejecting all forms of metaphysics as so much 'theology of glory', which attempts to directly penetrate into the 'invisible things of God' by natural reason. This is the interpretation Martin Heidegger takes, with direct reference to this passage of Luther.[6] On the other hand, theses 20 – 21 might be taken as commending a procedure for *true* metaphysics – through the cross one comes to see what a thing '*actually is*'. As Timothy Stanley has argued, 'the difficulty here for future interpretations of Lutheran metaphysics, is on which thesis to put the emphasis'.[7]

For some followers of Luther, the emphasis fell on thesis 19 as a natural consequence of the preference for scriptural revelation over-against any philosophical or traditioned reasoning. So, in his first edition of the *Loci Communes*, Luther's colleague Philip Melanchthon took a strong stance against speculative reasoning in preference for the explicit revelation of scripture.[8] This preference worked to the detriment even of the doctrines of the Trinity and Christology,

---

5 Luther, *Heidelberg Disputation*, 15.
6 Heidegger, *Phenomenology of Religious Life*, 213. Cf. Stanley, *Protestant Metaphysics*, 72–73.
7 Stanley, *Protestant Metaphysics*, 28.
8 Melanchthon, *Loci Communes Theologici*, 18–22.

though later editions attempted to correct this deficiency.⁹ What is sown here in these early reformers is a nascent skepticism for extra-biblical categories.¹⁰ The result was not an immediate rejection of all metaphysics, even in a scholastic mode. Despite Luther's and Calvin's harsh words for scholasticism, Lutheran and Reformed theologians in the seventeenth and eighteenth centuries exhibited a heavy dose of scholastic metaphysics.¹¹ These early reformers expressed a distrust of speculation for its own sake, challenging contemporaries to root speculative and metaphysical thinking in the core commitments of the gospel and the life of faith.¹²

After this positive use of metaphysics (including robust reflection on divine simplicity) in Protestant thought during the early modern period, nineteenth- and twentieth-century theology evinced a preference for Luther's harsher judgments on metaphysics, radicalizing the more modest censure on speculation expressed by Luther and Melanchthon. Albrecht Ritschl and Rudolf Bultmann each contributed in different ways, as Samuel Powell explains:

> It was Ritschl's belief that Luther achieved a major revolution in the Christian understanding of Christ, whereby ... attention was shifted from belief in the predicates attributed to Christ to trust in Christ's lordship. Trust is the basis for our ascribing divinity to Christ, since, as Luther argued in his *Large Catechism*, God is that in which we put our trust. The effect of this alteration was, in Ritschl's estimation, dramatic. With the emphasis on trust in Christ, the medieval attempts at reconciling faith and reason lost their motive. ... Bultmann like Ritschl eagerly and frequently employed statements by Melanchthon in a sustained effort to restrict theology to God's saving activities toward us.¹³

During the same time that Ritschl was radicalizing the Protestant anti-metaphysical stance, Isaak Dorner, a German Lutheran theologian deeply influenced by Hegel, was revising the doctrine of divine simplicity. Dorner's revision consists

---

9 Cf. Powell, *Trinity in German Thought*, 16–18.
10 John Calvin's relationship to metaphysics and 'scholasticism' is also ambiguous, though Calvinist Reformed theologians seem to have returned to scholasticism more quickly than Lutherans. On Calvin's relation to metaphysics, see Billings, *Calvin, Participation, and Gift*, 26–38.
11 For example, Francis Turretin among the Reformed and Johannes Quenstedt for the Lutherans. For more on the complexity of Protestant metaphysics, especially in a way that problematizes the accusation of pure 'nominalism', see Aspray, 'Complex Legacy'. Duby, *Divine Simplicity*, draws heavily on Protestant scholastics in his own constructive defence and explication of divine simplicity, arguing that Protestant affirmations of simplicity are *both* metaphysically rigorous and exegetically based.
12 For one example of how this anti-speculative disposition generally serves to prevent excessive speculation rather than reject all philosophy or metaphysics *tout court*, see Harris, 'We Keep Our Eyes Fixed Upon Christ', 253–59.
13 Powell, *Trinity in German Thought*, 12–13.

primarily in inverting the relation between ethics and ontology. Rather than conceive the ethical constancy of God as an outflow of the ontological perfection of God's simple immutability, Dorner interprets immutability and simplicity first through the ethical lens of God's covenant faithfulness and historical self-identity.[14] In whatever sense we might speak of God's ontological simplicity, it is logically and not merely epistemologically posterior to the more fundamental ethical constancy of God revealed in scripture.[15] In this way, Dorner evinces a subordination of metaphysics – and with it divine simplicity in its metaphysical rendering – though not its outright rejection.

In the twentieth century, Karl Barth explicitly picks up Dorner's approach to immutability and simplicity after stringently criticizing the earlier Protestant scholasticism of Turretin, Quenstedt, and van Mastricht.[16] Of the latter group Barth says, 'Starting from the generalised notion of God, the idea of the divine simplicity was necessarily exalted to the all-controlling principle, the idol, ... devouring everything concrete'.[17] Barth especially approved of Dorner's appropriation of simplicity through the lens of *revelation*, so that the identity of all God's perfections is an aspect of positive, cataphatic revelation in scripture, rather than an apophatic interpretation of God's difference from creation.[18] Barth's polemic against the *analogia entis* accentuates the difference in his thought between metaphysical reflection and biblical theology. This differentiation gener-

---

14 Dorner, *System*, 235–37, 447–65. Dorner explicitly correlates immutability as an entailment of simplicity (236), but in his final analysis calls simplicity in question on the basis of his ethical inversion: 'No bulwark needs therefore be erected against what is anthropopathical by philosophy, – by ideas of Absoluteness, Simplicity, and Exaltation above space and time, peradventure asserted by philosophy. Theology combats what is necessary by its own means, by its ethical idea of God' (462). See also Dorner, *Divine Immutability*, article 2. For more on Dorner, especially in relation to P. T. Forsyth and later developments in trinitarian theology, see Holmes, *Holy Trinity*, 191–96.
15 Dorner, *Divine Immutability*, 171.
16 Barth is also influenced here by the judgment of his teacher, Wilhelm Hermann, who said, 'Our conceptions of the divine attributes express the way in which faith recognises God's working. We have no right to distinguish from this, as did the older dogmatics, a knowledge of God's nature. The conceptions whereby the older theology proposed to apprehend God's nature are un-Biblical and have no value for faith' (*Systematic Theology*, 97). On Hermann's influence on Barth, see McCormack, *Barth's Critically Realistic Dialectical Theology*, 49–68.
17 Barth, *CD*, II/1, 229 [*KD*, II/1, 370].
18 *CD*, II/1, 330 [*KD*, II/1, 371–72]. Dorner develops his biblical alternative through giving primacy to an ethical understanding of God as love, even offering 'love' as God's essential definition, so that love in freedom is the guiding and unifying attribute for all other divine attributes – an approach that might be seen as echoed in Barth's own theology of divine attributes; Dorner, *System*, 1:447–65.

ates a dichotomy whereby the more strictly one interprets simplicity as rooted exclusively in metaphysical reasoning (especially according to the *analogia entis*), the more likely one is to understand the doctrine as antithetical to positive biblical revelation.

Although I have thus far presented modern developments as evincing a *Protestant* problem with metaphysics, a similar dichotomy also appears in the Catholic theologian Karl Rahner. He detects in Aquinas's doctrine of God two separate treatises based in distinct sources of divine knowledge: first *de Deo uno*, based in general metaphysical speculation about the difference of God from creation, and second *de Deo trino*, based in the scriptural witness and economy of salvation.[19] Following this line of critique, many theologians in the trinitarian revival, influenced by Barth and Rahner, sought to reverse this sequence by developing their doctrines of God out of careful attention to the Bible's narrative identification of the three divine identities.[20] Often, this attention to the biblical depiction of God is presented in opposition to classical metaphysical conceptions of God. The lesson I draw from this historical sketch is *not* that the increasing hesitancy toward metaphysics entailed the loss of the doctrine of divine simplicity by any sort of logical necessity. Rather, there is a shift in posture toward metaphysics and the metaphysical language that had formerly been assumed in trinitarian and christological formulas, and this shift has rendered divine sim-

---

19 Rahner, *Trinity*, 16–21. Catherine Lacugna, though sympathetic to much of Rahner's reading of simplicity and Trinity, recognizes that Rahner's reading of Aquinas on God is not adequate to Aquinas' purpose or the *Summa Theologiæ*'s structure. However, she is still critical of Aquinas for *beginning his whole theology with the doctrine of God in God's immanent life*. In this respect, she also shows a preference for the salvific/economic as discrete from and over against the philosophical and speculative (*God For Us*, 146–57). However, Denys Turner clarifies further that Aquinas uses this particular approach in the *STh* for pedagogical reasons, using other structures in different contexts (*Aquinas*, 110–43).

20 Schwöbel concludes his summary of the influence of Barth and Rahner: 'Die Antwort auf die Frage nach der Identität Gottes ist darum für den christlichen Glauben eine dreifache und keine einfache' ('Trinitätslehre als Rahmentheorie', 33). The positive contributions of this development in late twentieth century theology should not be overlooked, considering the scriptural warrant of the doctrine was considered to be highly questionable after nineteenth-century scepticism, especially in Ritschl; on which cf. Powell, Trinity in German Thought, 142–72; and Holmes, Holy Trinity, 165–201. Exemplars of the first two of Coakley's 'three waves' of trinitarian revival ('"Relational Ontology", Trinity, and Science', 185–94) are: Barth, CD; Boff, *Trinity and Society*; Fiddes, *Participating in God*; Gunton, *Becoming and Being*; Gunton, *Act and Being*; Gunton, *One, Three and Many*; Jenson, TI; Lacugna, *God For Us*; Lossky, *Mystical Theology*; Moltmann, *Trinity and the Kingdom*; Pannenberg, *Systematic Theology*, 1:259–336; Rahner, *Trinity*; Schwöbel, *Trinitarian Theology Today*; Schwöbel, *Gott in Beziehung*; Torrance, *Doctrine of God*; Torrance, *Trinitarian Faith*; Zizioulas, *Being as Communion*.

3.2 Scripture, metaphysics, and the problem(s) with divine simplicity — 81

plicity *optional* (if not alien) rather than given. Once simplicity is considered optional, and there is no consensus concerning metaphysics in theology, the formerly standard arguments for simplicity become suspect, especially insofar as they rely on metaphysical categories and aims that are not obviously drawn directly from scripture.

A symptomatic assumption in many recent criticisms of simplicity is that metaphysics and scripture appear to be inversely related. That is, the more philosophically or metaphysically entrenched a doctrine like divine simplicity appears, the less biblical it is taken to be.[21] Theologians of several different commitments repeat this inverse-relation logic. A Wesleyan political theologian, Douglas Meeks, says, 'If we know God historically and history eschatologically, then God cannot be construed as simple substance or absolute subject. Rather, God is God as God uncovers Godself in the narratives of Israel and of the Son of Israel's God through the Holy Spirit'.[22] Reformed philosophical theologian Nicholas Wolterstorff also says, 'the doctrine of divine simplicity conflicts at many points with the picture of God that one picks up from reading Scripture and participating in the liturgy'.[23] Reformed dogmatic theologian Colin Gunton argues the same: 'the negative, metaphysical and impersonal attributes [viz., 'simplicity, unchangeableness and oneness'] so dominate the discussion that the personal and action-based attributes appear to have been marginalized'.[24] Similarly, German Lutheran Eberhard Jüngel says, 'it is only God's identification with this dead man that can serve as the basis for theological modes of thinking that corresponds to truth. Otherwise, theology drifts into speculation and props up the transcendent God of the philosophers, reducing theological discourse to abject apophaticism.'[25] Ted Peters, an American Lutheran systematic theologian, writes, 'the unity of the godhead is a unity of integrating love. It is not the primordial unity of some simple substance of which each of the three persons represents a different expression. It is rather a dynamic unity, a personal unity, an achieved wholeness.'[26] And Barth's great rival and contemporary, Emil Brunner, pronoun-

---

21 Viz., the textbook quoted above (Plantinga, Thompson, and Lundberg, *Introduction to Christian Theology*, 104).
22 'The Social Trinity and Property', 15.
23 'Is it Possible and Desirable?', 42. Consider also: Wierenga, *Nature of God*, 173.
24 *Act and Being*, 51.
25 *God as Mystery*, xxii. Though it should also be noted that Jüngel recognizes the false dichotomy such rhetoric often presumes, which he tries to overcome (see 110–11).
26 *God – The World's Future*, 210–11. See also his earlier critique of traditional impassibility and simplicity as 'substance metaphysics' that does not comport with biblical revelation in *God as Trinity*, 30–33.

ces, 'there is really no *usus practicus* [for divine simplicity] ... [we are] here dealing with a speculative *theologumenon* or *philosophumenon*, which has nothing at all to do with the God of the Christian Faith'.[27]

These verdicts on simplicity – diverse as they are in other respects – seem to share a conviction that the doctrine of divine simplicity is questionable in no small part because of its metaphysical and philosophical character, which purportedly does not sit well with the narrative depiction of God in scripture. This line of critique suggests that the viability of divine simplicity for systematic theology partially hinges on the relation between metaphysics and philosophical theology on the one hand and biblical theology on the other. Robert W. Jenson was a systematic theologian who, in the wake of Barth, privileged the biblical depiction of God and yet also came to see the need for metaphysics in the task of faithfully proclaiming this God. I intend, then, to call into question an *a priori* disjunction between philosophical/metaphysical theology and biblical theology. In the remainder of this chapter I will introduce Jenson's understanding of Christian theology as 'revisionary metaphysics'. After considering here how Jenson envisions the need for metaphysical thinking within the task of retelling the narrative of God's ways with God's people, I will be able in the next chapter to show how Jenson creatively develops a doctrine of divine simplicity. For the remainder of this chapter and the next, the task is primarily expositional and interpretive. Only after presenting Jenson's contribution on its own terms will I raise criticisms for the sake of my own constructive arguments.

3.3 Robert Jenson on the task of metaphysics

3.3.1 Situating Jenson

One benefit of the ambivalence towards metaphysics and divine simplicity is that space is created in which to re-evaluate their critical functions in Christian theology. Is 'metaphysics' a violent use of language that necessarily attempts to 'contain' objects within a predetermined concept?[28] Is divine simplicity a form of Aristotle's 'unmoved mover' (purportedly) hovering statically at a distance

---

[27] *Christian Doctrine of God*, 294. This is found in an appendix to his discussion of the 'Problem of the "Divine Attributes"', where he propounds the Hellenization thesis, laying the majority of blame on Augustine and Pseudo-Dionysius the Areopagite (241–47).

[28] On this particular critique of 'metaphysics', with attention to Heidegger, Jacques Derrida, John Caputo, and Jean-Luc Marion, see Hector, *Theology without Metaphysics*, 1–45. The remainder of Hector's book develops an alternative, pragmatic account of language.

from finite being? Or does it reify a 'fourth thing' alongside the three divine hypostases? If these are genuine possibilities within theological history, then the recent critical posture at least provides another occasion to excise them explicitly. Toward the goal of articulating the central mystery of God's triunity in our present theological context, Robert Jenson is an ideal dialogue partner because in his writing several major trends in contemporary theology converge. As Stephen Holmes put it, 'Barth's denial of a *Logos asarkos*, Rahner's insistence on the identity of the immanent Trinity with the economic Trinity, and Pannenberg's and Moltmann's desire to see God's life as open to the gospel history, all reach their most extreme, and most coherent, expression in Jenson's theology.'[29]

Jenson's expression of each of these themes is inflected by his own central concern with the relation of eternity to time. His Lutheran concern with the story of God's acts of salvation – God as *pro me* – drives his revisionary metaphysics. Consequently, when Jenson rejects the above-noted inverse-relation between metaphysics and biblical revelation, he at the same time adopts a particular understanding of their interrelation, namely that metaphysics is developed out of the exigencies of our engagement with the biblical narrative. In this section, I consider in more detail how Jenson relates scripture and metaphysics. In the following sections of this chapter, I discuss the core themes that drive Jenson's revisionary project, how these themes converge on the person of Christ, and how Jenson revises basic metaphysical categories. Throughout it will become clear that Jenson explicitly formulates and deploys analogues to the regulative principles I discerned in the thinkers discussed in chapter two: the *principle of prior unity* and the *strict Creator–creature distinction*. In Jenson, however, these are revised. I argue that he develops a *principle of dramatic unity*.

3.3.2 Scripture and revisionary metaphysics

In his early writing, Jenson associates theology's involvement with metaphysics as an evangelistic accident, now irrelevant. For instance, in *Alpha and Omega* Jenson explains the central concern of theology: 'The Church must always simply speak of Christ to man as it finds him'.[30] This justifies for Jenson a turn away from a timeless metaphysical deity, for 'so long as man lived in a world which thus reached from time into the timeless, it was indeed to this man that the Gospel had to be made understandable', but 'We no longer live in this framework …

---

29 Holmes, *Holy Trinity*, 24.
30 Jenson, *A&O*, 16.

The basic fact of our lives is that we do not live from day to day over against a timeless structure of reality, sustained and judged by unchanging certainties'.[31] Because pre-modern humanity was shaped by 'metaphysics' – which here seems to be identified with religious commitment to timelessness – the task of evangelism required the communication of the gospel in the medium of this antecedent conceptuality. Twentieth-century humanity evidently no longer has any stake in such metaphysics; therefore, neither need the church worry with it.[32] As Jenson later concedes, this stark distinction and simplistic understanding of metaphysics is a misrepresentation and grants too much to Heidegger's history of philosophy.[33] However, Jenson does not come to reject all elements of this story. He remains committed to an evangelical reading of theology's philosophical activity.[34] He also remains convinced of the fundamentally temporal character of human existence as the primary context within which the gospel must speak today.

But as he comes to question the identification of metaphysics with an obsession with *timeless* 'being' as such, he reconceives metaphysics as a task of critical reflection on the nature of 'being' from the perspective of God's self-revelation in scripture and in the person of Christ. This critical reflection happens in the interval between hearing and speaking the gospel: 'theology is reflection internal to the act of tradition, to the turn from hearing something to speaking it. Theology is an act of *interpretation:* it begins with a received word and issues in a new word essentially related to the old word'.[35] Consequently, for Jenson, there need be no conflict or competition between theology's speculative and practical modes, for 'gospel' is itself a discourse, a discourse that happens between human speakers and between God and humans. Insofar as God is recognized as the primary agent and object of the discourse, theology is speculative – i.e., 'a cognitive enterprise so captivated by a determinate object that it is its own reward'.[36] Insofar as the discourse of the gospel happens in the address

---

31 *A&O*, 15.
32 For a brief genealogy of the rejection of the metaphysics of timelessness, see Jenson, 'Triunity of Truth', 88–92.
33 Jenson, 'Preface', vii. He maintains his narration of humanity's relation to timelessness but equates the drive for the timeless with 'religiosity' rather than metaphysics. Greek theology's use of their privileged metaphysical predicates is simply a symptom of their religiosity rather than the core problem (*ST*, 1:94–95), see 15: 'It is the very purpose of normal religion to defend us from the threats and challenges of our temporality'. He initiates his updated critique against timelessness under the name of 'religion' through dialogue with Barth's *Römerbrief* – see especially *RAI*, 16–19; and *GaG*, 5–8.
34 *ST*, 1:6–7.
35 *ST*, 1:14.
36 *ST*, 1:11. See also *S&P*, 191.

of one human person to another, it is indeed a practical discipline, a critical reflection on what the church must *do*. Were theology purely practical – a posture the Protestant tradition has often been tempted to assume – then there would be no real value in metaphysics, but a theology that takes such a course risks losing any sense of having to do with a determine object.[37]

The key for Jenson's understanding of the role of metaphysics in theological interpretation is his conviction that God is not merely the object of the gospel's discourse but also the primary agent – which is both normative for theological activity and constitutive of the church's practice of reading scripture. He explains:

> The triune Creator, in this context the Source of being who is also the Word about being, is in person the metaphysical bond between determinate reality and discourse. If there is no such God, then, at least for all we can know, there is no such bond, and texts float free in a void of reference ... Believers in the triune God suppose that because the Creator and his Word are one God, reality and language can meet within this God's creation.[38]

The speculative and the practical, then, are in harmony in theology in no small part because in this respect theology reflects the union of being and speaking in God.

The church believes itself to be involved with God through reading scripture, discerning God's intention. If the church is to be oriented to God and God's intention as the goal of reading scripture, it must not only reflect carefully on the *activity* of reading but must also *discipline* this activity in pursuit of its end. The church must, then, reckon with the speculative character of its own theological activity.[39] Jenson's proposal is that the church treat the creed as the 'critical theory' for reading scripture – in other words, it is the church's creedal tradition that guides church members in critically penetrating beyond their own 'agendas' in order to discern the divine 'agenda'.[40] But this does not mean that for Jenson God somehow is reducible to the story narrated in scripture or to the intralinguistic realm of regulative discourse (contra Francesca Murphy), for this is precisely one point on which he distinguishes his 'postliberalism' from George Lindbeck's: in speaking the story of God narrated in scripture, we are in fact speaking *of who God is in God's own self*, and we strive to do so without reducing God to the act of our speaking. Indeed, the narrative telling and the regulative rules *work* because

---

37 Similarly Pannenberg, *Metaphysics*, 6.
38 *CC*, 81–82.
39 For similar reflections on the relation of theological speech to the reality of God, see Thiemann, *Revelation and Theology*, 81–82.
40 *CC*, 79–87.

of their relation to a stipulated 'extralinguistic fact'.⁴¹ The goal is not simply to understand the church's privileged narratives correctly, it is finally to understand the God to whom these narratives direct us.⁴² 'Intratextuality', while significant, does not exhaust the task of theology.

Jenson can thus affirm with classical metaphysics that the task of metaphysics is to discern the conditions of being's intelligibility.⁴³ That we experience life as a so-far unfinished story, and so our temporality as a positive condition of narratability, suggests that reality is fundamentally intelligible. However, because narratability is a basic feature of reality's intelligibility, metaphysics as a task cannot terminate in a comprehensive grasp of reality-as-such apart from the completion of history. If metaphysics terminated in creaturely reality *and* was supposed to be comprehensive, then the unfinished narrative of human existence either would be a threat to metaphysic's purported comprehensiveness or would require explaining away (i.e., by reducing the apparent openness of the future into an illusion, a by-product of our inability to calculate the determinations of the future by the past). Citing Wolfhart Pannenberg, Jenson says:

> This God, and only this God, can give us *history* as a *whole* – and so the meaning we seek for life. History is a contingency, which a knowledge of history as a whole would seem to cancel. Therefore, the wholeness of history 'can perhaps only so be thought, that the contingency of events and their connection' somehow 'have a common root'. The Power of the Future is this root: [God] is at once by his futurity the 'origin of the contingency of events' and by his personal oneness the 'origin of their connection'.⁴⁴

Drawing on Heidegger and Barth, Jenson takes it as fundamental that to exist is to be in motion from 'what is' to 'what is not yet'. As Jenson expresses it, *being* 'is the fact about any reality that it is not yet what it must be, insofar as this "not" upsets and moves the status quo away from itself'. The intelligibility and reality of this movement is not self-evocating: 'God, finally, is the miracle that this hap-

---

41 *ST*, 1:18–19, critiquing Lindbeck, *Nature of Doctrine*. Also *A&O*, 112–13. For Murphy's criticism, see Murphy, *God is Not a Story*, 16–18. For a similar defence of Jenson to my own, see Henry, *Freedom of God*, 94–97.
42 Hence it cannot be done apart from a communal commitment to the unity of truth and the concomitant discipline of worship and prayer; see Jenson, 'Triunity of Truth', 86–87.
43 Cf. 'Triunity of Truth', 84–86. On the centrality of intelligibility for classical metaphysics, see Perl, *Thinking Being*.
44 *GaG*, 178, quoting Pannenberg, *Grundfragen systematischer Theologie*, 73f.

pens'.⁴⁵ But narratability and the metaphysical instability this suggests is not, for Jenson, simply a postmodern proposition to which theology must bow. Rather, such insistence on historicity is internal to the gospel, because the 'gospel is itself an impeller and enabler of history'.⁴⁶

Consequently, according to Jenson one cannot avoid metaphysics by appeal to the priority of biblical narrative, for narrativity itself is inherently metaphysical and so the interpretation of scripture is already a metaphysical task. This is both because the unity of the biblical canon (and therefore its narrative) is itself internally related to a metaphysical affirmation of the unity of its divine author and because *interpretation* (hermeneutics) involves the conscious activity of understanding the narrative as a dramatic unity with universal claim.⁴⁷ Further, this construal of metaphysics and its relation to theology requires an acknowledgment of the performative nature of both. Metaphysics is an historical task, itself undertaken in the tension between 'what is' and 'what is not-yet', which means that the person who engages in the task does so from *within* this historical movement or tension. The doing of metaphysics affects the subject's own 'being' – i.e., the subject's movement from 'what is' to 'what is not-yet'. Theological metaphysics is therefore self-involving:

> Since we now live the story Scripture tells, Scripture does not merely inform us about the course of this story, for persons live historically by discourse, by address and response to one another. Thus Scripture is not merely a record of divine-human history but a proclaiming of it, not merely an account of God's life with us to date but a voice in that life. When we read Scripture in the church, someone addresses us.⁴⁸

As Jenson said earlier of theological utterances more broadly, 'The drama of Time, which we may come to regard as God's address to us, ... is the drama of our lives. ... Theological utterance is indeed not merely informative, but not because it is *un*informative. It is *formative*, creative'.⁴⁹ Within Christian theology,

---

45 *GaG*, 172, also 129, 159–60. On this understanding of temporality in Heidegger, see his *Introduction to Metaphysics*, 31–38, 226. On Jenson's reading of Barth in this light, see *A&O*, 74–75; citing Barth, *CD*, III/2, 158.
46 *ST*, 1:15.
47 *ST*, 1:20: 'if theology is hermeneutics, it is *universal* hermeneutics; the act of interpreting with which it is concerned can turn to anything at all. But when hermeneutics become universal they just so become metaphysics.'
48 Jenson, 'Scripture's Authority', 34.
49 *KTHF*, 123.

metaphysics is done in something of an ad hoc fashion, as scripture involves the theologian/interpreter in the dramatic world it presents.⁵⁰

Already, issues of 'unity' have emerged. First, Jenson understands metaphysics as involved in an interpretive act which attempts a unified conception of reality. From a Christian and biblical perspective, this is accomplished by taking particular revelatory events as hermeneutically normative for interpreting all reality. Therefore, there is a *hermeneutical* unity being sought in theological metaphysics. The hermeneutical unity takes its grammar from the *narrative* unity of scripture as a whole. This does not assume that the Bible is exclusively interpreted in the genre of narrative, but it does affirm that the Bible presents events that span time and that center on its principal character, God. In this sense, scripture does have a narrative unity which derives from the unity of its object. Because it is the triune God who is the agent of the hermeneutically normative revelatory events, the way one moves from particular events to the universal/metaphysical is shaped by the extratextual context and the intratextual relation of events.⁵¹ Consequently, metaphysics is concerned to foster a unified vision of reality in the metaphysician, is regulated by the narrative unity of scripture, and is directed toward the perfectly unified reality of its principal object, namely God. None of these forms of unity, for Jenson, can or should be thought in abstraction from our historicity – the particularity of our position in time, the temporal character of our living and thinking, and the temporal activity and incarnation of the triune God.⁵² In this sense, the task of metaphysics itself is for Jenson oriented to-

---

50 For reflections on how the Bible incorporates the reader, see Jenson, 'The Strange New World of the Bible'. As Josh Gaghan notes, this 'ad hoc' construal of metaphysics in relation to theology need not put Jenson at odds with Aquinas, for Aquinas also uses metaphysics in something of an ad hoc fashion, even if he allows a greater degree of autonomy to human reason ('Reason, Metaphysics, and their Relationship'). For a different exposition of Jenson's conception of the task of metaphysics, see Crocker, 'Jenson and Metaphysics'. Crocker restricts his reading of Jenson's method primarily to the prolegomena of *ST* 1, and he restricts the dialogue partners to contemporary analytic philosophers. While the prolegomena is definitely a necessary site of Jenson's metaphysical method, I have preferred to interpret it in light of and in continuity with Jenson's other writings. Consequently, I believe that for Jenson metaphysics is more complicated than a kind of Quinean task of populating one's ontology from the commitments of normative sentences. Nevertheless, I do not deny development in Jenson's thinking. I have already pointed to his own shift in appreciation of 'metaphysics'. I also acknowledge that his method in retrieval has shown development, on which see the excellent treatment of Williams, 'Parlement of Foules'. Nonetheless, my exposition shows that even where he shifts there are motivating factors that remain consistent and determinative for his approach to metaphysics.
51 For a sustained argument for this understanding of the unity of Christian scripture, see Gordon, *Divine Scripture*.
52 *GaG*, 178.

ward a *dramatic* unity, a unity which is sought within the vicissitudes of time and whose primary determinative object is revealed through temporal acts.[53]

3.4 Promise: developing a Christian revisionary metaphysics

So far, I have introduced Jenson's approach to revisionary metaphysics as a particular way of navigating the twentieth-century disjunction of philosophy and scripture in much western theology. For him theological metaphysics is the task of reflecting on what ultimately must be the case given the world revealed in Jesus. To see, then, how basic metaphysical categories function in Jenson's thought, one must observe how he fills in the content of these categories within his theological arguments. Jenson self-consciously engages in revision of basic metaphysical categories, especially 'being' and 'time'. Without neglecting the *theological* contours and convictions of Jenson's work, in what follows I home in on those issues that seem especially to display his *metaphysical* assumptions and proposals.[54] In this section, I discuss his use of the category of 'promise' toward a Christian interpretation of reality, in particular 'reality' under the aspect of time. In the following sections, I will look at how this framing of history through the lens of promise – and thus his construal of the category of time – leads him to proposals on the nature of 'being' and how these proposals usher in other metaphysical revisions.

In Jenson's view, time is the category in greatest need of metaphysical revision, both because of its complicity in theological errors and because of its centrality in human experience. In his words, time 'is our one ineluctable metaphysical experience'.[55] Time is also a fundamental catalyst for religion, and it is what distinguishes Israel's religion from its ancient near eastern neighbors'. Jenson explicates this difference in two ways, both of which are developed out of his reading of the Old Testament. First, Israel understands her relationship to God

---

53 The discussion at this point goes some way toward absolving Jenson of Scott Swain's criticism when the latter contends that Jenson distorts the task of identifying God by displacing the event of creation by 'midstream' events like exodus and resurrection (*God of the Gospel*, 83). In particular, Swain's critique insufficiently acknowledges that Jenson's privileging of 'midstream' events is hermeneutical and is analogous to Israel's own hermeneutical priority of exodus. See also Jenson, 'Aspects', 23.
54 For sympathetic expressions of Jenson's theology, cf. Henry, *Freedom of God*; Lee, *Trinitarian Ontology and Israel*; Nicol, *Exodus and Resurrection*; and Wright, *Dogmatic Aesthetics*.
55 Jenson, 'Some Riffs', 127; also 'What Kind of God?', 3.

by means of a narrative that has a beginning, or perhaps a few beginnings (exodus, Abraham, creation). By granting genuine origin, Israel conceived of reality as history and not circuit. Second, Israel's own temptation to the religious status quo received continual interruption by the prophets who pointed forward to a promised future as the measure for the present. By emphasizing the inadequacy of Israel's present to God's promised future, the prophets bore witness to an interval between now and then, between history and hope – an interval that only God could truly rhyme and within which creaturely reality occurs.[56]

The interval between present and promise sets two postures toward the future into stark contrast, a contrast that Jenson interprets through the lens of the classical Lutheran distinction between 'law' and 'gospel'. Law responds to the interval between present and future by a word 'that ties the future to the past' while demanding 'that I live for someone or something'. It consequently attempts to secure the future by means of the past, by mandate. Gospel, on the other hand, 'is the pledge to me of one for whom I may live … the word that allows us to own our past from the future'. Although he distinguishes them, Jenson does not completely set law and gospel against one another:

> That the Gospel speaks to the one addressed by the Law gives the unity of past and present, gives the possibility of history. … That God's word is both Law and Gospel means that it is a future-opening challenge posed by the past: that is, that it is tradition.[57]

'Law' and 'gospel' provide a theological hermeneutic for the rhyming of past and future, which as an act of God remains partially future – an eschatological promise.

By applying this law-gospel hermeneutic to historical reality as such, Jenson conceives several possible postures toward time, which is complex due to the multiple levels of our experience of it. Because our posture toward time is mediated linguistically and interpersonally, our relation to time is social and political. Our posture to time also introduces ultimacy – especially the ultimacy of *death* as the ultimate extent of our personal obligations and commitments. Consequently, our relation to time is also moral and religious. These factors coalesce onto the two interrelated themes of futurity and promise. The social and political experience of time is connected to the fact that human language is not merely

---

[56] *S&P*, 13–31. The language of 'rhyming history and hope' comes from Russell D. Rook's fine book on Jenson's theology of culture, *Rhyming Hope and History*, its title a riff on Jenson's own language in *VW*, 29–30, and in *S&P*, 105.
[57] *KTHF*, 188.

3.4 Promise: developing a Christian revisionary metaphysics — 91

declarative but also performative.[58] The performative utterances most basic to social reality are promises.[59] When a person makes a promise, that person offers a postulated future to another for which the first person takes whole or partial responsibility. As a result, the two persons become joined together for at least the time that spans promise and fulfilment.[60]

But promises come in various forms, and so while promises are basic to Jenson's conception of 'gospel', the two are not simply identical. Not all promises are properly gospel. In fact, some promises function as 'law' and *not* gospel. Gospel-promise is distinguished from law-promise by the conditions attached to the promise. Gospel offers a future with absolutely no conditions on the recipient, whereas the future offered by the law is only granted pending the fulfilment of certain conditions. While many human relationships attempt unconditional promises, none can actually attain them because all human actions have conditions that the individual cannot fully compensate for. If I promise my son he will go to college, and even if I mean to take all the responsibility for the fulfilment of the promise, I can only actually bring it about if several conditions obtain: if my funds have not been compromised, if such institutions continue to exist, if I live long enough to see to it that my promise is made good, etc. The last factor – death – is, according to Jenson, the final condition that limits all human promises. Further, because promises are basic to the human project of living meaningfully in the world, death finally limits the ability for humans to reasonably expect their lives to have meaning.

This brings us to a problem. For in order to persevere in our political projects, we have to continue making promises and assume that there is a genuine and meaningful future that we can come to coinhabit. Yet there seems to be no reasonable basis for such hope and mutual trust, if we are limited to what we can ensure for ourselves and what our actual histories testify to.[61] It is this prob-

---

58 Which he develops through dialogue with J. L. Austin and Donald D. Evans (*How to Do Things with Words*; and *Logic of Self-Involvement*, respectively). See *KTHF*, 121–23.
59 'Is it not true that the entire web of our communication, by which we would humanly coinhabit a meaningful world, is the attempt to erect a promise between us?' (*S&P*, 29).
60 Gregory Walter picks up this theme from Jenson and develops an account of promise as a gift that is 'doubled' and 'extended' (*Being Promised*, 1–36).
61 So Israel herself plays out dramatically the options we all face: 'At the end, Israel's history works out to three possibilities: (1) a despair so consistent as not even to be heroic, a mere dribbling end of all human home in the experience of its implausibility, or (2) death and a resurrection, or (3) the religion of the Law. And these are not merely Israel's options. They are our options, if indeed the God of Israel is truly God' (*S&P*, 29).

lematic that has historically given rise to religion.⁶² According to Jenson, religion is the attempt to secure in advance a future for ourselves by appeal to some eternity.⁶³ In most religions, an eternity is posited by turning something that is available to our experience into an atemporal eternity – by which Jenson means an eternity that is completely abstracted from the ebbs and flows and vulnerabilities of actual history. Consequently, such religion is an act of projection. It projects onto the uncertainty of the future whatever it is that we most feel would give meaning to our lives and does so as if the future's uncertainty was irrelevant to the meaning found in the eternalized reality.⁶⁴

The gospel irrupts into this religiosity, cutting against it in two ways. First, according to Jenson, it does not posit a *timeless* eternity, but an eternity that is somehow positively related to time. As he says, God's eternity *embraces* time rather than *negating* it.⁶⁵ Second, the gospel proclaims that someone available to us in our history will grant the final meaning of our lives, but not as a fixed and closed item of the past – i.e., something we can comprehend and therefore use for ourselves to make meaning – but as a person within history whose future is never closed off – i.e., as one who is raised from the dead. 'The gospel-message ... is that the final outcome of the human enterprise will be an act of Jesus'.⁶⁶ Jesus is the act of God by which the promised future has a particular location within creation's past, and thereby Jesus is the union of past and future, the rhyming of law and gospel, and the possibility of genuine history. Jesus is in this way the center of Jenson's revisionary metaphysics:

> Any doctrine which claims to open up to men the meaning and purpose of their lives is necessarily also a description of reality. The Christian Gospel is no exception. If it says to me that Jesus Christ is the center of everything it thereby says that everything has Jesus Christ at its center and so makes a decisive statement about the nature of what is real.⁶⁷

Here we can see the theological bases for Jenson's understanding of the task of metaphysics as self-involving, history-encompassing, and christologically centered. Now we can proceed to consider his conception of 'being'.

---

62 And so Kant's argument for God as a postulate of moral reasoning is at least accurate to the function of God-talk in the religiosity Jenson criticizes.
63 *ST*, 1:16.
64 *ST*, 1:52–57.
65 *ST*, 1:139–43, 169–71, 216–21; 2:35.
66 *S&P*, 33. See also *KTHF*, 155.
67 *A&O*, 112.

3.5 Jesus Christ and created being

3.5.1 Election and predestination: Barth and Jenson's revisionary metaphysics

To be, for Jenson, is to 'have a role in the story of Jesus'.[68] With this decisive statement, Jenson summarizes his entire metaphysical project. At this point Jenson's unique debt to Karl Barth is pronounced. His doctoral dissertation, written at Heidelberg under Peter Brunner and approved by Barth himself, was a study of Barth's doctrine of election, climaxing in a treatment of predestination.[69] In Barth, Jenson finds an unrelenting meditation on what must be the case concerning reality given that God has chosen the *man Jesus*, 'predestining' those who belong to him within that choice. Not only 'has' God so chosen, *God is this decision*. Working out the implications of this claim generates a whole new metaphysic, a radical reworking of the fundamental intelligibility of reality. The revision revolves around a re-construal of the relationship between time and eternity, for, according to Jenson, faithful gospel proclamation requires that we construe the time–eternity relationship through the lens of their union in the event of Jesus' life, death, and resurrection.

Jenson worries, however, that Barth's own explication of the event of election ends up collapsing history into one pretemporal decree, thereby turning creaturely temporality into a merely platonic 'moving image of eternity'. Despite Barth's efforts, Jesus' historical work of reconciliation tends in his theology to float above our history, having been turned into an 'essential history' established in pretemporal eternity.[70] Such a move, in Jenson's view, threatens to evacuate the historical event of reconciliation of specifiable content. This will be a recurring theme in Jenson's thought: the concept of 'atemporal eternity' is problematic because it is void of content and thereby is the perfect object of our religious projections.[71] The *particularity* of the event of Jesus' life, death, and resurrection – i.e., Jesus' spatio-temporal specifiability – ensures that God's action and identity have content over-against us, and consequently that God is present to us in a way that accomplishes what is promised (viz., union between God and humanity) without allowing God to be a blank screen on which we project our ideologies.

---

68 *A&O*, 116–17.
69 Jenson, 'Cur Deus Homo?'; published as *A&O*, see 141–45 for discussion of predestination.
70 *A&O*, 161–67; *GaG*, 151–56.
71 *GaG*, 84–85, 123–29; *RAI*, 17–22; *KTHF*, 157; 'Proclamation without Metaphysics', in *TRM*, 4–17.

We, therefore, see *who* this God is – we can come to *identify* the God of the gospel – because Jesus Christ is the elected and electing God. It is because this particular life has been chosen by God that our human lives have a genuine future, and thereby genuine being in the present:

> The transcendence of the God who justifies the ungodly is thus the futurity of Jesus' love-unto-death. ... God, though not a being, is the transcendence *of* the being Jesus. Now we can interpret this: God is the futurity *of* the past event Jesus. The mystery of Jesus' resurrection itself, of the event which must lie between his death and his coming in life, is the mystery of God. ... *That we have a narratable future*, that we live *for* this past and only therefore knowable person, *is itself an occurrence*. It is a temporal occurrence, for it came after Jesus' death and before his appearances. This event is the occurrence of God. And since the reality of the resurrection is the reality of a promise, we must say that God now is real as this promise.[72]

In Jesus the promise of God's future is present; it is performed and achieved as an historical event and is not timelessly enacted apart from this historical actuality. Because Jesus is the presence of God's own inexhaustible future, we can actually intend our own future in its form as gift without falling into the trap of projection. All reality, it can also be concluded, has an asymmetrical temporal structure (that is, time has an irreversible direction) *because* the God who creates also lives one historical life within it *as* the possibility of the future of all creation.[73] This is Jenson's opening move in the task of revising any metaphysical categories that are not readily amenable to the gospel's proclamation that all reality has Christ as its center and future. This approach gives metaphysical and theological primacy to the future, and in what follows, I will attempt to explicate what this means. I offer a Heideggerian rendering of Jenson's ontology, in order to make more explicit the specifically philosophical/metaphysical content of this shift. In the process, I will show the centrality of language or the word-event for Jenson.

3.5.2 Being and the horizon of the future: Heidegger and Jenson's revisionary metaphysics

Jenson's debt to Heidegger has been underappreciated, though to emphasize a connection with Heidegger does not displace the influence of Barth. Rather, their influences could be said to converge here in Jenson's thinking, for as Jenson

---

[72] *GaG*, 162.
[73] As expressed, for instance, in Jenson, 'Paul-According-to-Martyn', 156.

himself says, 'I was tempted to think of Barth's revealed divine "essence," *das Wesen Gottes*, as a *Wesen*, which like Heidegger's is simply *west an*, which *is* in that it sheerly *comes on* to us. I am still tempted'.[74] I propose taking this statement as a launching point for considering the connection of being and time in Jenson's thought, given his belief that the decisive metaphysical boundary for the human creature is its relation to the future (as is clear from Jenson's understanding of divine transcendence, introduced above).

According to Heidegger, the question of 'being' has perpetually evaded philosophical history because thinkers have attempted to determine its meaning by coordination with atemporal concepts like becoming, seeming, thinking, and the 'ought' or the good.[75] However, these only work to define being by restricting being – i.e., by positing some principle or reality somehow external to being that determines being as such. This is clearly absurd, for anything that actively determines something real is also being, so these approaches simply push the question further: if the 'ought' somehow determines being, what, then, is the being of the ought?[76] Heidegger argues that this gets the question of being all wrong, precisely because it does not attend to the *historicity* of being. Being is the event of the present proceeding into the future. There is no principle or other reality that conditions being. Rather, the future is the horizon into which *being determines itself*. Being is the movement of the present beyond itself, actively asserting into that which is not-yet.[77] So being is *event* – structured occurrence – performed against the horizon of the future.[78]

Jenson shares with Heidegger this identification of being as event, structured by the ontological priority of the future. Seeing the Heideggerian affinity will help to clarify in the next chapter how Jenson's use of temporal categories to interpret divine transcendence and triunity are in fact ways of expressing the metaphysical *unboundedness* of God, which precludes identifying God with creaturely temporal boundaries. This use of temporality to identify God is explicitly in contrast to Barth, of whom Jenson is critical on this point, which further justifies an appreciation of Heidegger's contribution. How this works can be seen by look-

---

74 Jenson, 'Barth on the Being of God', 45. Consider also *ST*, 1:207–8.
75 Heidegger, *Introduction to Metaphysics*, 102–222.
76 *Introduction to Metaphysics*, 226.
77 Heidegger, *Being and Time*, §83.
78 See especially the later Heidegger: 'Time-space now is the name for the openness which opens up in the mutual self-extending of futural approach, past and present. This openness exclusively and primarily provides the space in which space as we usually know it can unfold. The self-extending, the opening up, of future, past and present is itself prespatial; only thus can it make room, that is, provide space' (Heidegger, *On Time and Being*, 14).

ing at an early argument Jenson makes from creaturely temporality to God's being. In *God After God*, one of Jenson's most central categories is language or word.

Jenson defines being as the temporal movement of existence into the horizon of the future, a happening that occurs between now and not-yet. But how is the future opened to a person, to the historical being? Jenson answers: the future is opened by the address of another. When another person speaks to me, a horizon of freedom is offered as the condition of the possibility of my response. In this context, the exchange of words is the event of 'being' between present and future, and my response is the event of my being. Further, because the exchange happens through the use of signs and symbols available to both persons in the shared givenness of language, being happens as a particular unfolding of the *past*, understood as the givenness out of which the present and future happen.[79] Jenson is here drawing on Ernst Fuchs, whose view of language he believes only needs one central alteration: 'Instead of saying that time is the possibility of the true word, we must say that the word is the possibility of true time'.[80] This quotation expresses not only a difference between Jenson and Fuchs', but also a difference with Heidegger on the historicity of being.[81] For, because Jenson believes that *word* is the condition of the possibility of time, it is inescapable to ask *whose word* it is that finally makes possible the time within which all other words take place.[82] Speaking directly of Heidegger, Jenson raises the question of 'whether "authentic existence toward death" ... is itself a possibility within its own terms, that is, without an intervention of something ... like grace', and he rejects Heidegger's affirmative answer.[83] This theological turn signals the point at which theology proper comes into focus once again.[84] Consequently, this discussion will be picked up in the next chapter, where I consider

---

[79] *GaG*, 188–89.
[80] *GaG*, 188. Cf. also Dalferth, *Radical Theology*, 83–94, especially for his discussion of how 'hermeneutical theology' insists on the human person as first the *interpreted being*, which suggests an ontological priority of word over event, while also insisting that word and event are mutually implicated (esp. 90–91).
[81] Jenson also uses this argument against Sartre to acknowledge the decision-character of 'human nature' and yet to deny the simultaneous nihilism and deification of humanity that Sartre's perspective entails (*S&P*, 139–40).
[82] Jenson's theological point here also demonstrates how his use of Heidegger is *theologically motivated* as well, led by his Lutheran theology of freedom; on which cf. Jenson, *OTH*, 40–45.
[83] *OTH*, 7. Jenson is here referring to Heidegger's *Sein und Zeit*, 267–301.
[84] I am not implying that Jenson has been involved in an exercise external to theology. As should be clear, Jenson's metaphysical developments are themselves regulated by his theological judgments.

the understanding of divine simplicity that results from Jenson's historicized metaphysics.

3.5.3 Being human: Christ and the communal concept of 'nature'

It is worth noting at this point how Jenson's general conception of the category 'being' relates to his definition of 'nature'. He discusses the meaning of 'nature' through reflecting on the Chalcedonian definition and is primarily concerned with the theological issue of God's relation to creation. Although these theological issues, too, will be discussed further in the next chapter, here we might get a handle on the metaphysical work he is doing. He argues that 'nature' should be understood as a *communal concept:*

> That Christ has the divine nature means that he is one of the three whose mutuality is the divine life, who live the history that God is. That Christ has human nature means that he is one of the many whose mutuality is human life, who live the history that humanity is.[85]

This definition has been noted by commentators, but I think that his Heideggerian perspective on being, which is less frequently noted, helps to clarify what Jenson might mean.[86]

According to Jenson, one's being – which can refer either to the fact of being (existence) or to the mode of being (essence/nature) – happens in the movement from the present into the future, and this movement, in turn, happens in the giving of a word. Because Jenson rejects the concept of a nature as a set of properties a subject 'timelessly' bears, he has to revise the language if it is going to have any continuing value for him. He does so by taking account of both the temporal character of being and the priority of verbal address.[87] Because he believes that the language of 'nature' is necessary for clarifying the meaning of the ecumenical definition of Chalcedon, Jenson is committed to using it. His revision can be seen as adding a step onto the conviction that a word of address is what opens a future in which one's being takes place as response.[88] For Jenson, I am a human (rather than some other kind of being) because my lived existence happens in response to the words addressed to me by the community of human speakers, *and* (this is the additional step) because I in turn speak words that open the fu-

---

[85] *ST*, 1:138.
[86] For instance, Holmes, *Holy Trinity*, 23–24.
[87] *S&P*, 139; *ST*, 1:138.
[88] *ST*, 2:16.

ture for other human persons as well.[89] 'Temporal self-transcendence is a mutual undertaking; the ground of our being occurs as the communication between us'.[90] Humans are thus strictly distinguished from God in two ways. First, the mutual address among human persons makes many beings, whereas the mutual address among the three persons of the Godhead makes only one being.[91] Second (and following from this), the content of my human being is given to me as possibility from beings other than myself (both proximately by other humans and ultimately by way of the creative address of God), whereas God is the source of the possibility of all other beings and caused to be by none.[92]

Finally, human nature is for Jenson neither purely constructed nor an abstraction, because there is in fact a completeness to the 'whole course of human conversation' insofar as the death and resurrection of Jesus is the conclusion of the human story.[93] 'Christ as a participant in human history is definitive for all other participants'.[94] There is, in other words, such a thing as 'human nature' because God gives dramatic unity to the whole of humanity through the complete human life of Jesus being spoken to us as promise. And the stability of this nature is not entirely deferred into an unrealized future promised state because our present history itself participates in the promised future by taking place in response to Christ's actual resurrected life.[95] Therefore it is intelligible to speak now of a human nature, because the present community of humans genuinely shares in the dramatic unity promised to it in Christ's resurrection. And I, as an individual human being, have a 'nature' because I share in a conversation that has its own dramatic continuity through participation in God's faithfulness, first to God's own self and secondarily to God's creation in and through Jesus Christ.[96]

---

89 'To the question, "What am I?" the appropriate answer is a specification of to whom I hearken and how I respond. Or we may say: *love* is being, the event *between* us in which we share a future. To the question, "What am I," the answer is a statement of who loves me' (*S&P*, 140).
90 *S&P*, 139.
91 *ST*, 1:138.
92 *GaG*, 190.
93 *S&P*, 140.
94 *ST*, 1:138.
95 Which logically leads to the conclusion, acknowledged and developed by Jenson, that the church is the location of true humanity (*OTH*, 25–31, 43–45).
96 *S&P*, 140.

3.6 Dramatic unity

Before moving on to dialogue with Jenson on divine simplicity in the next chapter, it is time to take a summative look at his metaphysics, as presented so far. I noted that in contrast to the 'principle of *prior* unity', Jenson's metaphysics privileges what might rather be called the 'principle of *dramatic* unity'. Just as *prior unity* served as a heuristic for interpreting the multifaceted and sometimes divergent metaphysics of Plotinus, Gregory of Nyssa, Augustine, and Aquinas, *dramatic unity* is a heuristic for capturing some distinctive elements of Jenson's metaphysics.

The discussion I have offered makes it clear that Jenson's criticism toward classical metaphysics is not primarily a rejection of the centrality of *unity*. Rather, Jenson conceives of unity within the context of an historicization of being itself. While this has resonances with Heidegger's integration of being and time, it should also be clear that Jenson's particular development of this integration is thoroughly theological. Central to his unique development is his eschatological orientation, which funds his emphasis on dramatic unity. The unity that is the object of Jenson's revisionary metaphysics is thus what he terms an 'achieved' unity – it is an event. In the case of human nature, as we saw above, this unity supervenes on the whole human story; it is therefore 'achieved' insofar as the ending of the human story renders the whole intelligible. The problem is that if death is the end of the human story, it would also entail the failure of the human promises by which human individuals and communities sustain themselves. Consequently, the end of the human story would finally signal its failure to achieve unity. Jenson finds this unacceptable because it is inadequate to the hermeneutical function of metaphysics as he understands it; that is, if our own share in the world is ultimately unintelligible, we cannot continue thinking of the world and our actions within it as if they were intelligible. But he also – and perhaps more importantly – views this conclusion as unacceptable because it is directly contradicted by the gospel. For in the face of the futility of our own human projects, the gospel proclaims that an event within humanity's history has achieved the possibility for humanity as such to have unity. In particular, the gospel offers the end of Jesus' individual story – death and resurrection – as the meaning of the whole human story. This person's resurrection is the word of promise that enables humanity itself – and *mutatis mutandis* all created being – to receive a genuine conclusion to its own story.

It is in this way that creaturely being can be said to have dramatic unity. Jenson explicitly connects this with Aristotle's definition of drama, stating that in drama 'events occur "unexpectedly but on account of each other"'.⁹⁷ Jesus' death and resurrection is, according to the gospel, the promised end of all humanity, and it therefore offers a hitherto unexpected conclusion that nonetheless renders all other events meaningful, so that they can be seen to happen 'on account of each other'. Jenson's dramatic unity is therefore a *christological* metaphysic, or a christological universal hermeneutic. According to Jenson, this understanding of unity is the most adequate one for scripture's depiction of the character of creation: 'To create, in Scripture, is not to make a *thing*, not even a big and beautiful and wonderful thing like a cosmos. It is rather to initiate, sustain and fulfill a *history*'.⁹⁸ The affirmation that history's unity is *dramatic* functions at least in part to affirm that its unity (and the unity of its participants) happens in the coherence of the contingent events that constitute it. The unity that Jenson's metaphysics seeks to articulate is not isolatable to one slice of temporal reality or to a quasi-geometrical figure related to time's line. Rather, the unity happens 'between' past and future insofar as these two poles rhyme or cohere.⁹⁹

Jenson's metaphysics, I have argued, take a particular narrative (i.e., the narrative of God and Christ within Israel) as the *hermeneutic* for all of reality. This opens up to the final sense in which Jenson's metaphysics is regulated by the notion of dramatic unity, here a unity of the activity of thinking itself. In particular, Jenson insists on the unity of what Hegel distinguished as *Vostellung* and *Begriff*.¹⁰⁰ *Vostellung* is typically translated as 'representation', which is potentially misleading if taken in too narrow a sense. Allowing for a broad meaning, we might say that in theology, for Jenson, the *Vorstellung* is scripture's narrative in its presentation of God, and the *Begriff* is the concept of God itself or God as the object of thought. In contrast to those who believe thought should culminate in the abandonment of the *Vorstellung* (which Jenson identifies with left-wing Hegelianism and believes that Bultmann and his followers exemplify¹⁰¹), Jenson believes that the *Vorstellung* is not left behind in the *Begriff*. Consequently, when theology and metaphysics attempt a descriptive account of God and reality, the narratives and representations for the reality are never superseded when thinking attains its object or forms a concept. On the contrary, the *Vortstellung* itself is

---

97 *ST*, 1:64; quoting Aristotle, *Peri Poietikes*, 1452a, 3.
98 Jenson, 'What if It Were True?', 26.
99 Jenson, 'What Kind of God?', 3–4.
100 *OTH*, 1n1; 'What Kind of God?', 4.
101 Jenson contrasts Plato and Bultmann, siding with Plato(!) against Bultmann: 'The difference is that Plato thought that in this life he could not escape myth whereas Bultmann thought he could see through it', continuing in footnote 12, 'Plato preserved the *Vorstellung* in the *Begriff*; Bultmann was on Hegel's left wing' ('Paul-According-to-Martyn', 160).

how the person and linguistic community are *able* to think, though this does not necessarily entail that the *Vorstellung* undergoes no change, clarification, or critical scrutiny through the act of thinking. Jenson simply holds that when our thinking comes to the *Begriff* it does so only by and with the *Vorstellung*.

When thinking holds *Vorstellung* and *Begriff* together, it also forms a 'dramatic unity' within the process of thinking itself. The unity happens *between* representation and concept, in a manner similar to the way in which the dramatic unity of reality itself happens between past and future. Rowan Williams captures well this understanding of the activity of thinking when he defines 'representation': 'the object that is my face in the mirror is a representation, but my perceiving of it is a making present to myself of what is there'.[102] This dramatic unity of representation is the proper context within which to interpret Jenson's otherwise contentious and perhaps mystifying claim that God is identified *by* and *with* historical events.[103] In this sense, if God were only identified *by* events, the events would be a representation only pointing us to God. We would, consequently, need to abstract from the events in order to attain a proper *Begriff* of God. By arguing that God is identified *by and with* historical events, Jenson is insisting that the events are themselves – to use Williams' phrase – 'a making present' of the God whom they identify – though in this case God is the primary active agent of the 'making present' rather than the person who contemplates the representation.[104] Understanding these identity theses is important for, as Jenson himself says, 'the whole argument of the [*Systematic Theology*] depends on this move'.[105]

I believe we can also sharpen the issue of the inverse-relation between scripture and philosophy by attending to Jenson's insistence on the unity of *Vorstellung* and *Begriff*. In this light, the concern of some critics of divine simplicity can

---

102 Williams, *Edge of Words*, 188. While explicitly discussing Hegel a few pages later, he says that thinking '"overcomes" the order of representation in the sense not that it supplants it but that it shows it is not exhausted by it and is the only thing that finally gives intelligibility to it' (192).
103 *ST*, 1:57–60. Barth expresses similar concerns throughout *CD*, II/1, §27.2–§28.
104 The issue of God's identity in relation to temporal events will receive more explicit attention in the next chapter, but for the moment my account of Jenson here can be contrasted with Thomas H. McCall's puzzlement in *Which Trinity?*, 128–38. McCall argues that Jenson's identity theses entail that God is *identical to* historical events. It seems obvious to me, in a perhaps superficial way, that the prepositions 'by', 'with', and 'to', link nouns in sufficiently different ways that identity 'by' and 'with' does not obviously entail 'identity to'. But more to the point, McCall neglects to consider Jenson's main point about mediation in revelation and our apprehension thereof – which is what his identity theses concern. Gunton takes better account of the theological context of Jenson's identity theses ('Creation and Mediation in Jenson', 80–93).
105 *ST*, 1:59.

be affirmed while leaving space for the development of a different solution, that is a solution that privileges the scriptural witness without rejecting outright contributions from metaphysics. With the critics of divine simplicity – including Jenson – we can be critical of any philosophical doctrine of God that claims to have achieved a *Begriff* of God that has left behind the *Vorstellung* of God in scripture.[106] If philosophical theology offers such a concept of God, then it imposes its own inverse relation between philosophical doctrine and biblical revelation, in which priority is given to the philosophical *Begriff* over the biblical *Vorstellung*. However, for Jenson the use of metaphysical categories does not require a departure from the *Vorstellung* of scripture but can rather be deployed for a deepening of our contemplation of scripture and may even be required in some form by the need to recognize the unity of the God that is being made present to us in the narrative of scripture. Consequently, in Jenson we can see an affirmation of the unsubstitutability of scripture in knowledge of God, while also finding a solution that *overcomes* the inverse relation between scripture and metaphysics.

Insofar as Jenson's theological metaphysics is regulated by what I have called the *principle of dramatic unity*, it evinces several analogically related unities: unity of history, which in turn constitutes the unity of reality itself, and the unity of thinking. These different unities are themselves normed by the unity of scripture, which trains the mind in perceiving dramatic unity in history as a whole. Through engaging scripture, the reader learns to discern the unity of its primary author and three *dramatis personae*, the triune God. God is the only condition of the possibility of the unity of scripture as a whole, for the multivocal witness of scripture can only avoid cacophony if these several voices do in fact share in the self-narration of God. Scripture narrates how the people of Israel came to see that the same God whose promise sustains their own existence in hopeful anticipation also creates and sustains all reality in the same manner – as the promiser whose word gives the future as an intelligible horizon, and thereby is the condition of the possibility of a coherent past and present. Scripture, reality, and thinking itself have unity by virtue of the same event: by sharing in God's rhyming of past and future.

---

106 Which seems to be one of Jenson's core complaints about Augustine (*TI*, 126).

3.7 Conclusion

In the first section of this chapter, I sketched an account of the shifts in contemporary thought that have rendered divine simplicity optional in a new way, ultimately by dislodging it from the philosophical-theological contexts in which it makes sense and assuming what I call an inverse relation between philosophy and scripture. In the wake of these shifts, the task of retrieving the doctrine of divine simplicity requires renewed attention to the compatibility of scripture and metaphysics. I introduced Jenson's thought here as a constructive way into this situation by presenting salient features of his project of revisionary metaphysics. The shape of his metaphysical practice forms a powerful antidote to the assumed inverse-relation by attending to the ways that reading the Bible *as scripture* requires certain metaphysical questions to be addressed. In particular, the Bible is only an authoritative holy voice for the church if the God to whom it witnesses and who it claims as its author is a coherent character throughout its pages.

Rendering the unity and coherence of scripture's God is a greater task than simple re-narration – it also requires speculative and analytical reflection on the 'grammar' of such narration. Jenson understands revisionary metaphysics to be this grammar, though it is a grammar that functions referentially and not merely regulatively. In other words, this grammar is involved in judgments and affirmations about the reality it is helping us narrate and so is not purely second-order discourse. In Jenson's view, scripture guides metaphysics to discern the unity of history, reality, and thinking itself *dramatically,* for the unities that happen 'between' – i.e., in the rhyming of – past and future, subject and object, or *Vorstellung* and *Begriff* are essentially dramatic in character. This raises the question: if God's own unity is also dramatically conceived, how might this dramatic unity relate to the classical conception of God as perfectly simple?

4 Simplicity and Trinity in Robert Jenson's theology

The triune God's personal being is constituted precisely in perfect contingency to – as one now says – the other. The wonder that God is, is the wonder that these contingencies are perfectly mutual, that Father, Son, and Spirit are but one God, so that with God contingency to the other is identical with *not* being an accident. God and only God can, if one likes to put it so, be substance precisely by virtue of infinite permeability.

–Robert W. Jenson[1]

4.1 Introduction

It has been consistently claimed that Jenson completely rejects the notion of divine simplicity.[2] But while Jenson has certainly named divine simplicity as a culprit in what he views as inadequately baptized Hellenistic assumptions about God, he also never fully rejects it. On the contrary, he explicitly affirms it – even if a bit bashfully. Even in a section often cited as evidence of Jenson's full rejection of divine simplicity, he begins by stating that he 'will find truth in the maxim by which Augustine states the divine simplicity, that "what (God) has, he is"'.[3] There have been some readers who recognize at least traces of the logic of divine simplicity in Jenson's doctrine of God. Fergus Kerr sees Jenson's theology of God-as-event as potentially convergent with Aquinas' use of the dynamic category of 'act' to explicate God's simplicity.[4] Stephen John Wright carefully traces shifts in Jenson's treatment of simplicity and shows how many critiques overread Jenson's own critical comments on simplicity as if they entailed a wholesale rejection.[5] And most recently, Peter Leithart has noted the clear affirmations of divine simplicity in Jenson's biblical commentaries.[6]

---

1 *OTH*, 70.
2 Hart, *Beauty of the Infinite*, 160 ff; Henry, *Freedom of God*, 199; Hunsinger, 'Review', 187–92; Isaac, 'Unity of the Triune God', 137–38; Peters, 'God Happens', 342; Schlesinger, 'Trinity, Incarnation and Time', 195; Sholl, 'Jenson's Trinitarian Thought', 28; Swain, *God of the Gospel*, 130; Wells, 'Aquinas and Jenson on Trinity', 348.
3 *ST*, 1:112. Schlesinger, for example, cites the encompassing discussion from *ST*, 1:104–13 as evidence of Jenson's rejection of simplicity entirely ('Trinity, Incarnation and Time', 195).
4 Kerr, *After Aquinas*, 203–6.
5 Wright, *Dogmatic Aesthetics*, 61–81.
6 Leithart, 'Jenson as Theological Interpreter', 50–52.

What accounts for the inconsistent perceptions of Jenson's relation to divine simplicity? First, Jenson does make several sharp criticisms of simplicity as well as other divine attributes generally associated with it, like atemporality and impassibility.[7] Second, I suggest confusion also arises due to the particular metaphysical idiom he develops.[8] With respect to this last point, the previous chapter sought to clarify the way Jenson engages in theological metaphysics and should consequently help clear away some hurdles in the way of a charitable engagement with his doctrine of God. His approach deploys different categories than are traditional in metaphysics, and this needs to be borne in mind as his specific critiques and proposals are evaluated. Because Wright has aptly traced Jenson's various positions and general development on the doctrine of divine simplicity, I will not dedicate space to that task.[9] Rather, in this chapter I attempt a reconstruction of what might be called Jenson's implicit doctrine of divine simplicity, taking account of the previous chapter's presentation of his metaphysics.

My account will unfold in three stages. First, I will turn directly to a reconstruction of divine simplicity in Jenson's theology. Naturally, this will include attention to his trinitarian proposals, but the aim will be to explore how those trinitarian proposals involve Jenson in judgments about the simplicity of the divine *ousia*. In the second section I will turn more directly to how these judgments about the divine *ousia* redound to judgments about the three *hypostases*, or, in Jenson's preferred translation, the three 'identities' of God.[10] In particular, this second section will reflect on how Jenson uses the category of subsistent relations, includes Jesus in the Trinity, and extends the logic of divine simplicity in articulating the economic action of the Spirit. In the third section, I will consider how Jenson's theology addresses the other theological deployment of divine simplicity I have identified, namely, the relation between the multiplicity of divine names on the one hand and the unity of the divine essence on the other. In this chapter, I will only raise criticisms of Jenson when they are relevant for interpreting his constructive aims or for showing how such criticisms might

---

7 Jenson, *TI*, 114–31, esp. 118–19; *ST*, 1:211–13.
8 For instance, Thomas Weinandy's criticisms ('God and Human Suffering', 99–116), illuminating as they are for his own constructive argumentative aims, seem to rely on a question-begging reconstruction of Jenson's own speculative system. Like David Bentley Hart's earlier eloquent critique in *Beauty of the Infinite*, 160–67, this approach seems to collapse what are arguably *entailments* of Jenson's position into the position itself, thereby failing to distinguish clearly the actual content of Jenson's program from its perceived problematic entailments. Jenson responded to Weindandy's charges in a similar manner to my observations here, in an essay that originally appeared in the same collection: '*Ipse pater*', 93–95.
9 Wright, *Dogmatic Aesthetics*, 61–81.
10 Which he develops and justifies in *TI*, 108–11.

be answered within my interpretation of his thought. In the next chapter I will argue that there are several benefits to making explicit the possibilities within Jenson's thought for a doctrine of divine simplicity.

4.2 Divine simplicity as lively event

In the previous chapter, I argued for a specific construal of Jenson's interpretation of being and temporality. Like Heidegger, Jenson construes being as constituted not by any external reality like 'thought' or 'goodness' but by its eventful movement into the horizon of the future. Being is thus structured occurrence, made intelligible by its orientation to what is not-yet. Jenson's major revision to this Heideggerian account is to make 'word' more fundamental than time, in that word itself is the condition of the possibility of temporal being. If *word* is that by which individual beings are opened to the horizon of the future as the possibility for their own self-determination as being, then we might naturally ask after that word which transcends all particular words. By what word are all finite words created? To follow this line of questioning shows that Jenson's revision of Heidegger is theological, filtering elements of a Heideggerian ontology through the narrative world of scripture. All reality is, in scripture, generated and sustained by God's creative address. So, from within a Christian metaphysic, Heidegger's ontological revision is only plausible if it can be fruitfully deployed to imagine how God's creative address constitutes our existence as creatures in time.

Creatures have, for Jenson, 'natures' to the extent that the particular word that they *are* is spoken within a network of relations that are mutually constitutive. The sphere that these unsubstitutable and irreducible relations constitute is the community of creatures who share a nature. For humans, it is because one's very being as word happens in the mutual exchange of human persons with a recognizable unity over time that one can be said to share 'human nature'. This holds analogously but not identically for God's nature, a difference that Jenson negotiates christologically:

> That Christ has the divine nature means that he is one of the three whose mutuality is the divine life, who live the history that God is. That Christ has human nature means that he is one of the many whose mutuality is human life, who live the history that humanity is. There is a difference between these propositions in that the three who live God's life make only one God, whereas the many who live humanity make many human beings.[11]

---

11 *ST*, 1:138.

What kind of ontology can make this difference intelligible? And how does Jenson develop a trinitarian ontology that avoids devolving into three antecedent subjects who collectively 'make' one God? His particular resolution can only be understood within the construal of being and time that he develops from Heidegger. And here, too, I will attend to how his use of these categories navigates the difference between the mutual discourse that happens among human beings and that which happens in God. Importantly, for Jenson this difference between God and creatures is only finally interpretable within the discourse of faith, for what Jenson said of Jonathan Edwards and his contemporary Puritan context is no doubt a key conviction also of Jenson himself: 'faith in God *is* a mystery, only to be approximated by discourse'.[12]

4.2.1 Divine persons and divine temporal infinity

For humans past and future are real boundaries, horizons that constitute our finite nature. This radically distinguishes us from God – not because time as such is undesirable, but because our being-as-event happens in the address we receive from beyond ourselves: both in the already-givenness of language and in the future-opening utterance of another. For God the situation is quite different:

> God is the communication that creates our communication – as the possibility of history. ... God is the word whose future-opening utterance does not depend on a prior word, on a language which would subsist even were this word not spoken. The word which God is does not depend on some other word already having been spoken to create the language now used. The language in which God is uttered and which he presupposes is always and only the new language which that utterance seeks as its future. We may put it so: the futurity of God is that the distinction of language and utterance does not apply to him. An utterance which utters its own language is a word whose futurity cannot be overtaken.[13]

Jenson insists that this is not an interpretation that begins from human conditions of linguistic finitude and then reasons up to a corresponding conception of God (that is, it is not a piece of natural theology). Rather, understanding God as future-opening utterance is precisely the conclusion required from the biblical view of God creating by speech – all things existing through the Word who is Jesus Christ (John 1:1–4).

In this light one can see that Jenson does not identify God with creaturely temporality, nor does he claim that God actualizes Godself through the vicissi-

---

12 Jenson, *AT*, vii.
13 *GaG*, 190.

tudes of creaturely becoming.[14] Such an interpretation of Jenson misses the logic of being and temporality in his revisionary metaphysics, and therefore misconstrues the analogies he wants to draw between the trinitarian *taxis* and temporality. God can be said to 'have time' because God is the inexhaustible act of personal address by which all creation receives its being, and mutual address is the locus of temporal being.[15] Address is futurity – the offering of a not-yet the response to which constitutes the being of the respondent.[16] God is the event or act of this address, and therefore all interhuman acts of address have their power as future-opening utterance by participating in God's creative address.[17]

There is, consequently, a definite difference between time in respect of God and of creatures, and it is a difference which parallels divine simplicity and its concomitant denial of the real relation between God and the world. 'God is infinite. That is, God can be limited by no temporal conditions.'[18] God's 'time' is not constituted by the distinction between the prior givenness of language and the act of address, a distinction that is fundamental to human existence. Jenson is not, strictly speaking, making a claim about the specific act of address by which God creates *ad extra* (though in a perhaps under-clarified way, this is somehow included in the eternal address that God is). On the contrary, Jenson's argument is that to predicate of God the temporality of mutual address is first a trinitarian claim. Consequently, Jenson is also not collapsing the eternal being of God into a creation-directed act, nor the event of God's being into a purely immanent event. If anything, it is the other way round: Jenson is drawing the triune God's creation-directed action into God's eternal intratrinitarian life. He is denying that the distinction between prior givenness and particular utterance obtains in the eternal mutual address that the Trinity *is*. This denial immediately resonates with divine simplicity, which denies that the most basic constitutive dis-

---

14 Contra Weinandy, 'God and Human Suffering'.
15 Jenson, 'Aspects', 27–28.
16 And so, for God: 'Eternity would be apprehended as the dramatic mutuality of Father and Spirit, of God as God's origin and God as God's goal, and therefore not as immunity to change but as faithfulness in action. Being would accordingly be apprehended not as persistence in what is but as anticipation of what is not yet' (*UG*, 138).
17 *GaG*, 190. This would be the home of Jenson's version of the primary/secondary agency distinction. So also: 'the speech of God by which he creates us human and our morally obligating mutual speech are the same event. There must indeed have been a first address of God by which he initiated our discourse, but we need not necessarily think of a voice from heaven intruding at some point in the hominid descent. We may think rather of an unpredictable event of initial linguistic community' (*ST*, 2:63).
18 'Triune God', 185.

tinctions of creaturely existence hold for God (such as the distinction between essence and existence or, in Jenson's metaphysics, that between language and utterance). For finite beings, metaphysical distinctions serve as bounds for a being; in God no such bounds obtain – and Jenson's argument comes to analogous conclusions. For while 'past, present, and future' can be used of both God and creatures, Jenson deploys them analogically (and so *differently*) across the Creator–creature divide.[19]

In creatures, 'past, present, and future' name real bounding conditions of being – not in the sense that past and future as such have independent being in their creaturely reference, but that they express the edges of being in its determinateness. Being is definite, this-and-not-that, in the relation of actual being to that which it is no-longer and that which it is not-yet, neither of which have actuality apart from being poles of the movement of present being. In God, 'past, present, and future' name *ordered relations*, but not boundaries or distinct moments. The distinctions are *meaningful* in respect of God because they express how in God there is movement of address and response that extends to become creative address *ad extra*: 'the distinction between the triune story as it is about God and as it is about creatures is not a distinction between the simplicity of timelessness and the differentiations of temporality: eventful differentiation is real on both sides'.[20] However, it is also true that the eventful differentiations are not '*measurable*' in God (Jenson's wording), for 'nothing in God *recedes* into the past or *approaches* from the future.'[21] In this way, what for Oliver Crisp and George Hunsinger are obscure claims bordering on a 'fast-talking shell game', could also be taken as simply one in a long series of attempts throughout Christian history to hint suggestively at the mystery of God's reality with the help of creaturely language, in this case drawing on the language of temporality.[22] The difference in interpretation depends on whether Jenson is reducing the subsistent relations of the triune persons to temporal moments or, as I am arguing, is *interpreting and explicating* the triune subsistent relations from a Heideggerian-style identification of being with event. Jenson rec-

---

[19] And later he says as much in *ST*, 2:35. In the earlier *God After God*, Jenson also uses the language of 'appropriation' for his deployment of temporal categories for God (*GaG*, 193). Also 'Aspects', 25; and '*Ipse pater*', 99.
[20] *ST*, 1:113.
[21] *ST*, 2:35. As Sang Hoon Lee notes, Jenson's talk of God's futurity is not of an empty 'not-yet' but is the personal Spirit and the risen Son's eschatological reality (Lee, 'Preexistence and Transcendence', 409). This is yet another important sense in which 'futurity' has some undergone analogical stretching in its use of God.
[22] Crisp, 'Jenson on Pre-existence'; quotation from Hunsinger, 'Review', 172.

ognizes the possible difference at stake here and recommends that we 'call this structure in God God's "time", and so use the word analogously, with God as primary analogate and the created phenomenon as secondary analogate, as we do when we use such words as "good" and "being" theologically'.[23] The analogy is that God simply *is* event – simply *is* ordered relation – whereas creatures continually receive their being as advent – as the 'coming on' of the future.

In other words, I am arguing that Jenson's claim that God's eternity is a 'temporal infinity' should *not* interpreted as an affirmation of an endless series of divine moments, extending interminably into the past and future.[24] This wrongly takes Jenson's phrase as a cataphatic claim about the extent of a divine temporality that is univocal with our own temporality. When purely cataphatic, infinity tends toward a quantitative attribution, as if God is the maximal extension of temporal being. Rather, infinity has for Jenson the classical *apophatic* function that attributions of infinity ought to have in respect of God – namely the absolute rejection of all limiting conditions. In the apophatic form, infinity gestures toward the qualitative incomparability of God. For much of the tradition, unboundedness in respect of time is simply what it means to say that God is eternal and *not* temporal. However, Jenson believes that 'temporal infinity' specifies eternity more precisely than as the 'opposite of time' and hence avoids the risk of deploying the concepts of eternity and time contrastively, which would then inevitably identify eternity most closely with one pole of the temporal line (most likely the beginning).[25] God's being, we might paraphrase Jenson, has an internal structure

---

[23] 'Aspects', 25. And consider: 'Now, of course, a God who has a life, or more precisely is a life, and whose being has personal structure, is no proper God at all by the standards of that part of our metaphysical tradition most indebted to the Greek theologians. We observed that at the start. He is not "simple" in the usual—and in my judgment disastrous—Christian-theological sense: his relation to creation in its temporality cannot be modeled by the relation of a point to a line or of a center to a circle' (Jenson, 'What Kind of God?', 9).

[24] *TI*, 165; *ST*, 1:219. Note how this plays out in Jenson's critique of Wolfhart Pannenberg ('Parting Ways?', 60–62), with whom he otherwise has so much in common. Jenson notes that he and Pannenberg attempt much the same theological moves, but in Pannenberg this comes without any significant revision of the modern conception of time and eternity. For Jenson, *our concept of time has be to revised*. Jenson could only be speaking of 'temporal infinity' as an infinitely extended series if he operated with the taken for granted linear view of time. His 'revisionary metaphysics' is an attempt to upset this assumption in the light of the gospel's narration of history.

[25] Consider Barth's discussion of God's 'supratemporality' (*Überzeitlichkeit*), whereby God encompasses and accompanies creation in its temporality (*KD*, II/1, 698–713; *CD*, II/1, 620–30). For discussion, see Langdon, *God the Eternal Contemporary*, 70–82. Langdon notes that one difference between Jenson and Barth—despite much convergence—is Jenson's willingness to appropriate the poles of time to the persons of the Trinity (24). Schwöbel has recently proposed a way of understanding the eternity–time relation that overlaps with my rendering of Jenson here and

that can be meaningfully correlated to distinctions we experience in our temporally structured being. In us, this structure constitutes our *boundedness*; in God, the structure of whence, whither, and present are pure relations – subsistent relations – which do not express any external *relata* or realities and, consequently, cannot be *boundaries* in God. Because God's internal relational structure is of this nature, Jenson affirms that God can, 'if he so chooses, distinguish himself from others not by excluding them but including them ... and the room that he makes is our created time'.[26] God's (temporal) eternity non-contrastively includes creaturely time.

This can be further confirmed by noting that for Jenson, God's 'utterance' is completely unlike ours by virtue of the fact that there is no prior given language by which God speaks. Presumably, then, even God's historical acts – interpreted as words of creative address – do not have the character and reality they do by relying on prior givens, as if the historical commerce between God and creatures constituted a shared language from which God and creatures equally draw to form new utterances or enact new events. On the contrary, God's utterance is simply identical to its own language: 'God is this mystery and presupposition, as the Call that calls for all things, as the Utterance who presupposes no other utterance than himself'.[27] This is strikingly similar to one central tenet of divine simplicity: God is in no way constituted by dependence on a creaturely given. Jenson has here framed this point in terms of language and address, an interpretation all the more interesting for its ability to connect with something very traditional (divine simplicity and the denial of the real relation) while also being readily amenable to God's activity *ad extra* of relating by creative spoken address. The ordering of the mutual address within the Trinity helps express how the poles of creaturely time are received as creative gift, all under the biblical category of God's speech. God speaks a generating word as Father, sustained in the Son's filial response, and actively opens the horizon of freedom as Spirit. While there are important differences that ought to be upheld, this structuring of the trinitarian relations can ground an analogy between the eternity of God's intratrinitarian life and creation's temporally structured existence by participation, perhaps even as a gloss on Romans 11:36: 'from him and through him and to him are all things'.

---

attempts to think of eternity, along with Barth, otherwise than as time's opposite ('Eternity of the Triune God', 345–55).

26 *ST*, 1:226; also 'Aspects', 24–25.
27 *GaG*, 193.

4.2.2 Identity of essence and existence

In chapters one and two, I have argued that one of the central theological uses of the doctrine of divine simplicity is to clarify the Creator–creature distinction. And so far, Jenson's doctrine of God is formulated with a similar end in view, even though this can be misconstrued in light of his use of temporal categories. Perhaps my reconstruction of Jenson's implicit doctrine of divine simplicity can be made clearer by connecting it with the form of the doctrine developed by Aquinas, namely as the identity of essence and existence. According to Thomas, creatures are composed of two irreducible metaphysical principles, essence, which names the 'whatness' of a thing, and existence, which names its 'thatness'. In creatures these are distinguishable although inseparable because no creaturely essence accounts for its own existence, and creaturely existence never happens apart from the particular essences actualized by existing. In God, essence and existence are not distinct metaphysical principles that compound to produce the unique individual, 'God'; rather God simply 'is' God's essence and simply 'is' God's existence. By implication, then, in God essence and existence are identical.[28]

The proposal I have been offering for interpreting Jenson's use of temporal categories for God centers on my claim that what Jenson discerns as constitutive boundaries in creaturely being – i.e., the distinction of temporal poles – are not in fact boundaries in God's case. From one side, it is clear that Jenson does not want to argue to the strict *identity* of temporal poles in God, for he uses the poles of time to interpret the intratrinitarian relations. However, from another vantage point, Jenson does argue to their identity in God, specifically in claiming that the event of speech (which is in a sense more fundamental for Jenson than the distention of time) for God is the perfect identity of the 'givenness' of language and the act of utterance.[29] *Mutatis mutandis*, this perspective can be seen, like Aquinas, to envision God as the unity of essence and existence.

But the reconstruction of Jenson ventured here need not depend only on speculative comparison, for Jenson himself connects his own proposals with Aquinas's essence–existence distinction. In a late essay entitled 'Some Riffs on Thomas Aquinas' *De ente et essentia*', Jenson improvises on Aquinas' use of the essence–existence distinction specifically by glossing it in terms of temporality and personal address.[30] In his rendering, 'matter' is the 'whence' of a creature

---

[28] See Aquinas, *STh*, I.3.3–4.
[29] *GaG*, 193.
[30] 'Some Riffs', 125–30.

and the 'form' is the creature's 'whither'. An individual creature is a 'composite' because it is a created *essentia*, which is the 'form' *as* the form of this specific matter.³¹ Following Aquinas, his initial theological 'riff' consists in understanding the creature's possession of *esse* – the act of existence – as an external gift from God and not a purely immanent principle. But he builds on Aquinas to conceive of this gift particularly as God's *spoken address*. Consequently,

> the inner whence and whither of a composite creature will be that of the partner in a conversation with God, in and by which it is granted its being: the whence, the 'matter', will be the hearing of God's address, the whither, the 'form', the responding to it, and the unity of both, the *essentia*, will be faith.³²

The identification of 'faith' with the composite reality of at least human creaturely existence is certainly a specifically Jensonian development on Aquinas' metaphysics, but it also demonstrates a sympathy with Aquinas' theological use of metaphysical categories.

Jenson moves on to affirm Aquinas' shift in the use of these categories for God, explicitly affirming that in God existence and essence are identical, as well as the corollary that God is *esse tantum* or *actus purus*.³³ Naturally, he argues that a 'pure act' that is not simply a static state is quite close to what we now mean by 'event'. So he concludes:

> how can we name the *simplicitas* of an *esse* that is not the being of anything but itself? If not with the word that in modern jargon has acquired a distinct appropriate resonance, event? With God, to be is to happen, 'to' nothing but the happening itself; to happen as the act 'of ' nothing but the act itself.³⁴

Jenson admits that this could sound as if he is conflating the teachings of Barth and Aquinas, which he acknowledges would be to stretch the matter too far. But what he does find is similar to what I have been arguing for between Jenson himself and the classical doctrine of simplicity – not that they 'espouse the same teaching [o]nly ... that they both lead us into the same mystery'. And here we

---

31 'Some Riffs', 127.
32 'Some Riffs', 128.
33 'Some Riffs', 129–30. In a footnote he acknowledges his criticisms of simplicity, 'Any readers who have some acquaintance with my writing will know of my problem with the Western doctrine of divine simplicity. Here it will suffice to say that it does not extend to the precise use of this term in the specific present context' (129n17).
34 'Some Riffs', 130.

can see that despite Jenson's otherwise critical remarks about divine simplicity, he is willing to follow its logic as far as affirming the identity of essence and existence, glossing it as God's eventfulness.[35]

4.2.3 Impassibility and God's being as lively event

So far I have presented a reconstruction of divine simplicity in Jenson that emphasizes points of connection with long-standing aspects of the doctrine, especially in the form in which Aquinas articulates it. The central differences have concerned mode of expression. The reconstruction from this point on will begin to shift, as I trace aspects of Jenson's doctrine of God that are not as readily amenable to standard accounts of divine simplicity. Specifically, I consider how Jenson's critiques of atemporality, impassibility, and analogy set apart his doctrine of God.

Jenson rejects divine atemporality in particular by emphasizing the *liveliness* of God's being-as-event. God's triune life can be said to be structured occurrence, principally according to the relations of the three persons and, connected with this, according to God's identification *by* and *with* historical events. I have already attempted to offer an alternative interpretation to the extreme charges that have been levelled against him on the basis of these claims. But here Jenson's treatment of impassibility also requires further attention. Jenson is well known for denying impassibility – *ipse pater non est impassibilis* ('the Father himself is not impassible'), he says, quoting Origen.[36] While the question of God's impassibility has long exercised Jenson, a late essay offers clarification of his position. He argues that impassibility should only be denied in the negative (so that God is *not impassible*), while maintaining that it does not follow that God is 'passible'.[37] Since he suggests that it is neither the case that God is passible nor that God is impassible, there must be something amiss in how the question is framed.[38] How, then, does Jenson attempt to resolve this problem?

Jenson turns to an examination of how identifying descriptions function in narrative time by analogy with musical time. Drawing on Jeremy Begbie's analysis of musical time, Jenson argues that the success of a straightforward attribu-

---

[35] And he much earlier denies subject–essence composition (along with Aquinas, *STh* I.3.3): 'It is not that we have a deed without a doer, or an act without an actor—which would indeed be nonsense; it is that the distinction does not apply to God at all' (*S&P*, 119).
[36] Jenson, '*Ipse pater*', 93–101.
[37] '*Ipse pater*', 95–96.
[38] '*Ipse pater*', 96.

tion of properties depends on within which 'hyperbar-level' one is referring.[39] In musical perspective, a 'hyperbar' includes multiple bars (and/or other hyperbars) in it, reflecting a higher level of metrical structure within the overall musical composition. Consequently, hyperbars provide a tool to analyze how 'within a piece of music there is usually a multiplicity of temporal continua, operating concurrently' so that as downbeats in one bar or temporal continuum receive different accents, they 'become new beats in another metrical wave (a higher hyperbar)', and so on as the piece becomes more complex.[40] Jenson adopts this as a fruitful analogue for narrative time in general, especially because it allows one to see how predication can be true of one hyperbar and false of a higher, overlapping hyperbar. So, if one attends to one narrative hyperbar – for instance, when in Ezekiel 16 the LORD narrates Israel's adultery and judges with wrath – the narrative suggests that God is passible by having pity on early fledgling Israel and wrath on her later waywardness. But is God, 'considered as the subject of his total history with us, impassible? By the testimony of Scripture, he is indeed – in any plausible sense of the word'.[41] Jenson's trouble with 'impassibility', then, seems to be the risk of abstracting the concept entirely from the narrative, which would be to attempt to form a *Begriff* completely independently of scripture's narrative *Vorstellung(en)*.[42]

Jenson's proposals here raise immediate questions for a reconstruction of his implicit doctrine of divine simplicity. In particular, if God is identified with predicates differently according to the narrative hyperbar-level, does this not entail that God is in fact composed of multiple temporal moments and of the different hyperbar levels these moments themselves constitute? If so, this would completely undo the reconstruction I have attempted so far, which is only successful in constructing a Jensonian doctrine of divine simplicity to the extent that the 'time' Jenson predicates of God is not interpreted as a collected series of discrete moments. If God can in fact be said to be composed of moments that constitute hyperbars that in turn constitute higher-level hyperbars, then this reconstruction ultimately fails.[43]

---

39 'Ipse pater', 97; Begbie, *Theology, Music and Time*, 29–70.
40 Begbie, *Theology, Music and Time*, 35, 42.
41 Jenson, 'Ipse pater', 98.
42 'Is then God, abstracted from all such tales, passible or impassible? But that ... is a pseudo-question, since the abstraction cannot be performed on the biblical God' ('*Ipse pater*', 98).
43 We might express what is at stake here differently, by way of R. Kendall Soulen's critique of Jenson's early *Triune Identity* (Soulen, 'YHWH the Triune God', 41–44). Soulen notes the risk that Jenson's trinitarian theology might jettison 'the more fundamental insight ... that God's identity as YHWH the God of Israel is constitutive for trinitarian reflection' because Jenson treats the res-

I offer two observations that prevent directly concluding to this kind of 'hyperbar composition', one of which will clarify God's eventfulness and narrativity and the other concerning God's triunity (which will provide a segue into the next section). Whether Jenson's reflections on multiple narrative hyperbars entails composition in God depends on how God is related to the historical events that identify God, for the context of Jenson's discussion here is our identification of God within the narrative and not God's absolute being conceived independently of our narrative-normed thinking. Our reflections on particular biblical depictions of God's action or knowledge should not undo the dramatic location of the event.[44] And in this sense, it seems that Jenson is simply suggesting that there are multiple aspects under which a narrative event can be analyzed – i.e., according to multiple hyperbar-levels. Each hyperbar level should be allowed its appropriate narrative role. From this vantage, we might offer the following construal of his claims about God's passibility and impassibility, where the lower hyperbar of God's pity-turned-wrath is 'hyperbar^1' and the higher hyperbar of God's faithfulness to Israel is 'hyperbar^2'. *Qua* hyperbar^2, God is impassible as the unchangeable event of God's faithfulness to Israel and God's promises to her. *Qua* hyperbar^1, God is passible insofar as the hyperbar^2 event of God's faithfulness happens to the hyperbar^1 event of Israel's infancy and then infidelity *as* pity and wrath. God's dramatic unity, once again, is the 'rhyming' of past and future, of the multiple events within history's narrative, in such a way that even the unexpected events (say, of divine pity and divine wrath) can be seen to have happened 'on account of each other'. In this way, the multiple levels of hyperbars according to which God is identified in scripture do not have to be interpreted ontologically as referring to levels of composition in the divine being but can rather be seen as multiple narratival vantage points on the event that God is. If the multiple levels are narratival moments to which God *happens* as their dramatic unity, then God is not identical to those events in such a way that they are

---

urrection as '*a differentium that defines the subject of a new religion that logically stands on its own*' (41, 43). This would entail smuggling a form of supersessionism into the doctrine of God. In other words, if God is identified with the historical event of the resurrection in such a way that in God's life *it is a discrete moment in distinction from others*, then it changes God's identity radically enough that the unsubstitutability of the name of YHWH is displaced. Though it should be noted that Jenson later developed his theological interpretation of Israel more fully (see 'Christian Theology of Israel', 43–56). For consideration of how God's identification with Israel affects Jenson's ontology of God, see Lee, *Trinitarian Ontology and Israel*, 25–32, 146–72.

44 So reflecting on Genesis 22, where God responds to Abraham's obedience with 'Now I know', Jenson asks, 'Did God not know beforehand how Abraham would stand the test? If bound by a too-simple doctrine of divine omniscience, we say, "of course," we ruin the story' ('Bible and Trinity', 333).

compositional ingredients (or parts) of divinity. But God is identified *by and with* those events in such a way that the events are a real 'making present' of God to Israel.

If this rejection of hyperbar-level composition in the Godhead is to accord with Jenson's theology more broadly, two related caveats need to be offered. First, I have capitalized on the possibility that Jenson's different predications according to hyperbar-levels have to do with our *vantage point* from the side of the narrative, but, to follow Jenson's thought, this interpretation would also have to maintain that the multiple narratival vantage points are not simply a means one uses to come to understand the God hidden behind them – they are not *Vorstellungen* that one abandons in order to achieve the *Begriff*.[45] This requires that we allow Jenson to say that these multiple vantage points are in fact genuine 'representations' of God (in Rowan Williams' sense of that word), because they are a real 'making present' of God to us.[46] However, I do not see why this would *require* that the moments by which God is present to us are parts in a composite God, nor does it seem to me that Jenson has made such a claim.

Second, even if God is not 'identical to' the events that make up the various hyperbar levels by which we identify God, Jenson does still insist that God is 'identified *by* and *with*' such events – though decisively *not* 'actualized' by them.[47] This is another way of remembering the previous point that *Vorstellung* and *Begriff* are united in our identification of God. But it is also the opportunity to consider how Jenson understands God's eventful differentiation *in trinitarian terms*.[48] For while the claim, 'God is identified by and with', is a hermeneutical rule for preserving the unity of *Vorstellung* and *Begriff*, it is also for Jenson a way to hold together the Old and New Testaments in common witness to the Trinity. His paradigmatic expression of God's identity by and with events is his potent claim that 'God is whoever raised Jesus from the dead, having before raised Is-

---

45 As he expresses the issue in an early essay, God's identification with events has stronger import than the merely epistemological ('Three Identities', 2).
46 Williams, *Edge of Words*, 188.
47 As Timo Tavast misleadingly expresses it in 'Jenson on the Trinity', 362. Jenson explicitly rejects this characterization, though otherwise affirming Tavast's presentation of Jenson's doctrine of the Trinity ('Response to Tavast', 370).
48 A point Swain fails to recognize. He misinterprets Jenson's claim that the plurality of actors that make up God's story are not purely external to God as a claim about God's relation to creation, when it is in fact about the *triune relations* (*God of the Gospel*, 151). Jenson is arguing that because God has a story that involves 'a plurality of agents', God's identity is *either* determined extrinsically by creatures, immune to Gospel events, *or God's own identity is a plurality of dramatis dei personae*—and he clearly is opting for the third option (*ST*, 1:75).

rael from Egypt'.⁴⁹ Because Jenson identifies God's being *by and with the event of Jesus' resurrection*, it follows that he thinks of God's eventful differentiation by means of the trinitarian economy.⁵⁰ God can be identified by and with events – and so also with various hyperbar-levels in a narrative – because one of the triune persons is Jesus and therefore has a history. Consequently, whether Jenson avoids 'event composition' in God depends on whether he successfully articulates God's *trinitarian* incorporation of events.⁵¹ So I turn now to divine simplicity and the Trinity in Jenson, keeping this question in mind.

4.3 Simplicity and Trinity

4.3.1 Subsistent relations

God is a lively event. As simple, God is an event that happens to nothing other than God: in a riff on the classic doctrine of divine simplicity, there is no distinction in God between the event and that to which the event happens. Yet according to our encounter with God, God is identified by and with historical events. The tensions that emerge from these claims about God's being-as-event constitute for Jenson a trinitarian issue. God includes eventful differentiation by virtue

---

49 *ST*, 1:63. Cf. Stanley Hauerwas' discussion of this Jensonism in 'How to Write a Theological Sentence', 134–36. I agree with Hauerwas that this sentence 'is exemplary for what a theological sentence should be' precisely in the way it makes the word 'God' strange and unfamiliar for the reader (127).

50 Which is why Soulen's concerns about supersessionism (noted above, footnote 42) are relevant to how Jenson conceives the unity and eventful differentiation of God's being.

51 Considered *qua* God's 'oneness', if Jenson does escape event composition, we might be inclined to read him as what Francesca Aran Murphy has called a 'cinematic modalist'—and hers is a powerful argument in its aesthetic originality; Murphy, *God is Not a Story*, 264–66. Jenson is a cinematic modalist, according to Murphy, because his doctrine of God is analogous to the way a 'movie reel is a series of motionless pictures ... waiting to be run off their projector'; 'Jenson envisions God as "running himself off" an internal projector in just this way'. As I noted in the last chapter, however, this kind of 'essential history' that can be distinguished from the actual history is precisely what Jenson detects in Barth and is exercised to overcome (*A&O*, 161–67; *GaG*, 151–56). The most Murphy can claim to have established is that Jenson's theology *tends* in certain respects towards the problems she identifies, but she has by no means demonstrated, as her judgments seem to claim, that Jenson's theology is determinately a form of 'cinematic modalism'. In this respect, the reading fails to understand Jenson first on his own terms. For an exemplary treatment of Murphy's critique, see Henry, *Freedom of God*, 200–203. I return to Murphy's criticism in the next chapter.

of being triune, and God's eventful differentiation includes historical events by virtue of having Jesus as one member of the Trinity.

Jesus' role in the Trinity is one of the most hotly debated aspects of Jenson's thought. Many of the various threads of Jenson's writing come together in his christological orientation, because his christological convictions drive his theological and metaphysical proposals. Thus, christology is important in Jenson's thought for two related reasons. First, it is in Christ that God's self-knowledge and our knowledge of God come together, so that it is in Christ's own knowledge as God-man that we have human knowledge of God's reality.[52] For Jenson, knowledge of God is thus irreducibly christological. And second, the distinction between Creator and creature is established and sustained in the person of Jesus in Jenson's theology.[53] His explication of the two natures of Christ will prove to be the crucible of his understanding of the God–world relationship. The centrality of Jesus is both epistemological and ontological, and both interdependently. It is because God is identified by and with Jesus that our knowledge of God escapes fideistic nonfalsifiability, but this knowledge is also not reducible to mere information because the encounter with Jesus is both performative and transformative.[54]

In order to develop these points, I will begin with Trinity and move to Christ. First, I will show the way Jenson frames his trinitarian theology with the traditional trinitarian category of subsistent relations. Next, I will show how he uses this category to clarify his christology and its role in his critique of the *logos asarkos*, which will introduce the topic of Jesus in the Trinity. Because, according to Jenson, temporality is the most fundamental metaphysical fact of creaturely being, and because Jesus, one of the divine persons, is also a creature, temporality has a central function in his doctrine of the Trinity.

The interpretation of the temporality of God that I provided above is further clarified by Jenson's use of the category of 'subsistent relations' for the trinitarian persons. A subsistent relation is a relation that has no terms, no *relata* external to the relation by which it is constituted. Rather, the relation itself *subsists as* the substance of that of which it is a relation. Because it is a concept coined specifically in order to square trinitarian doctrine with divine simplicity, Jenson's adoption of it in his own speculative account of the Trinity is further evidence of his sympathy with some of the concerns of divine simplicity.[55] Furthermore,

---

[52] *ST*, 1:229.
[53] Jenson, 'Creator and Creature'.
[54] *KTHF*, 133–57.
[55] Jenson has consistently deployed the category: *S&P*, 127; *TI*, 107, 123–25; *ST*, 1:116–19; and 'Some Riffs', 130.

Jenson's use of subsistent relations is important both for his temporalizing of the Trinity and for his radical claims about the *logos asarkos*.

To the extent that Jenson is deploying *subsistent relations* in continuity with the tradition, this suggests that appropriating temporal poles to the divine persons need not culminate in reifying an absolute future in opposition to an absolute past. To conceive the divine persons as so starkly distinguished and extrinsic to one another would entail that Father and Spirit encounter one another as distinct terms, defined by their mutual incommensurability. The Father as 'Whence' could only encounter the Spirit as 'Whither' in utter external objectivity, and they would thus be related to one another only secondarily. However, for Jenson, the Spirit is 'Future' *as a relation*, a relation that opens up the ontological possibility of the Father's generation of the Son.[56] Whether the logic of subsistent relations is deepened or compromised by Jenson's insistence that such relations should be ordered toward a *goal* and not only *origin* is an important technical question that I will discuss in the next chapter.[57] But to understand what Jenson is up to on his own terms does not require a resolution of the matter. Jenson's appropriation of the poles of time to the inner-trinitarian *taxis* is usually offered to supplement and not supplant the definition of the persons by relations of origin. And it can be seen to relate closely to Jenson's emphasis on the horizon of the future as ontologically central. It is Jenson's contention that an act of generation defined only in terms of origin does not convey the dynamic *active* sense of divine being, for it obscures the sense that this being 'is' only as it *moves* actively into determinate actuality. It is also theologically freighted to the extent that it risks giving a privileged place to the Father as absolute origin, suggesting some sort of innertrinitarian subordination. To complete our understanding of the self-sufficient identity of God requires specification of God as both origin and goal, which Jenson believes the Trinity can provide.[58]

The movement into the future by which a finite being is constituted entails a distinction between that being's actuality and the horizon of the future that is its as-yet undetermined possibility. Because Jenson identifies the horizon of the future with the hypostasis of the Spirit, God can neither be said to stand in relation

---

56 'Or we can appropriate another of Karl Barth's maxims, which has been an axiom for me since I encountered it fifty years ago: it is not that there is not in eternity beginning, present, and goal; it is that in the eternity of the biblical God these are in no tension. Precisely God's goals are his eternal plenitude' ('What Kind of God?', 9).
57 James Henry defends Jenson's proposals on this front with less specific attention to the logic of *subsistent relations* but as a general biblical development of the doctrine of the Holy Spirit; cf. *Freedom of God*, 125–45, 168–77.
58 *ST*, 1:108, 119.

to an external range of possibilities from which God chooses one to actualize, nor to experience an interval between 'now' and 'not-yet'.⁵⁹ The horizon of possibility for God and for creatures is simply God's eternal being as the simultaneously perfecting and liberating Spirit. The Spirit, then, is the gift of the future in person both for God's innertrinitarian life and for humanity, albeit in different ways. In relation to humans, the Spirit is the future as a divine gift of freedom, giving what creatures do not in themselves possess. In relation to the Father and Son, the Spirit is 'future' as the *relation* of fulfillment, perfection, and freedom – and precisely as such the Spirit *gives* what the Father and Son always already *are* by being the divine identities they are only in their relation to the Spirit's perfecting identity.⁶⁰

What is less clear in Jenson's use of 'subsistent relations' is how it relates to a major tenet of pro-Nicene and Latin theology: the indivisibility of God's actions *ad extra*. In fact, Jenson is quite critical of how this *theologoumenon* functions in Augustine, claiming that he effectively renders the economic account of God's triune activity useless for identifying the three persons in their intratrinitarian relations.⁶¹ Jenson's criticism might give the impression that distinct agencies (and therefore wills) should be attributed to each of the divine persons based on the Gospel accounts.⁶² If this were the case, the divine persons could hardly be considered subsistent relations in the sense that the term is usually used and as Jenson himself uses it. However, to conclude to distinct agencies and wills would be to go beyond Jenson's actual arguments. It needs to be asked *why* Jenson is critical of Augustine on the unity of the Trinity's actions *ad extra*, whether this criticism applies to all affirmations that *opera trinitatis ad extra sunt indivisa*, and how his judgments here relate to the intratrinitarian relations. In ad-

---

59 Consider how Jenson articulates the finality of eschatological love, which, it would seem, is analogously true of how God's own loving futurity is a lived event of openness: 'The End will not close the future—if the End is love. For to love is to be open to the other-than-me, to what I do not yet know or will. And yet love can be the End, for when love is achieved there is nothing left unaccomplished, no not-yet still to seek. The End is when the future is open as future, without an intervening time in which the future must be achieved or prepared for—so that life is an event of openness' (*GaG*, 162).
60 *ST*, 1:157–60. Consider: 'Within the mystery of the triune God's specific eternity, the Son's subsistence must therefore be as much from the Spirit as *telos* as from the Father as *arche*' (Jenson, 'Once More', 121). For a thorough and rich discussion of Jenson's pneumatology, see Henry, *Freedom of God*, Parts I & II.
61 *TI*, 126–29; *ST*, 1:112.
62 As Matthew Levering and George Kalantzis suggest, where they acknowledge that Jenson is otherwise desirous to uphold aspects of the doctrine of divine simplicity, 'Why Think about Simplicity?', 413–14.

dressing these questions, it is important to note first that Jenson's critique of Augustine seems to be principally *hermeneutical*. He is concerned to preserve the narrative identification of God's triunity and believes that Augustine's particular moves generate an internal inconsistency that disables Augustine's trinitarian hermeneutic. In this sense, the problem for Jenson is not that Augustine wants to affirm a unity in God's action *ad extra*; the problem is that the way Augustine affirms it obscures the differentiation of the persons in their economic action, which is how theology came to recognize God's triunity in the first place. It follows from this that Jenson's critique need not apply to all uses of *ad extra indivisa*, as long as the particular use does not obscure the narrative's distinctions between the persons. Even within Jenson's own theology *ad extra indivisa* could potentially be a helpful way of seeing the unity of the Trinity.[63] How then do Jenson's concerns fit with his own use of subsistent relations for the internal life of God? If it is correct to characterize his criticism of Augustine in hermeneutical terms, then the criticism does not appear to directly conflict with identifying the persons as subsistent relations, rather he seems simply to be insisting on the fact that we truly *can* identify the relations by means of God's revelation in the economy. If the concern is hermeneutical, then his alternative does not require interpreting the economic distinctions between the persons as entailing distinct agencies and wills. Rather, he is insisting that the biblical narrative's depiction of the persons' distinctions according to God's acts *ad extra* do in fact characterize the identities of the persons.

4.3.2 Jesus in the Trinity: the body of God

Jenson also comes to deploy the category of *subsistent relations* in the context of clarifying his rejection of the *logos asarkos* – i.e., the pre-existent Son subsisting apart from and prior to any union with human flesh – which brings in the topic of Jesus in the Trinity. In his *Systematic Theology*, Jenson attempted to affirm the Son's existence 'prior' to incarnation without appeal to the *logos asarkos* by identifying the Son's antecedence to the historical life of Jesus with a pattern within Israel leading to the incarnation.[64] Jenson later admitted that this strategy was at

---

63 Which is, after all, Cappadocian and not only Augustinian. Jenson's own preferred teachers for trinitarian doctrine are the Cappadocians, especially Gregory of Nyssa (*TI*, 113), whom cites approvingly on the indivisibility of God's works *ad extra* (citing *Ablabius*, 125), which is in fact necessary for Jenson's main interpretive strategy, namely to claim that in the Cappadocians 'God' refers to the *creative activity* of the three persons together.
64 *ST*, 1:141.

best vague.⁶⁵ This is partly so because it is not clear what it means for a divine person to preexist as a pattern of movement. And further, this intra-historical description pushes the question of 'preexistence' too literally into a temporal frame, as if *from the perspective of God's eternity* there is a 'before' and 'after' incarnation; and this would also imply some kind of event-composition in God. It should be noted that Jenson explicitly denies in this context that God's life can be so plotted – further evidence that for him 'temporal infinity' is not endless extension of discrete moments.⁶⁶ To clarify his own position, Jenson insists that Jesus is one of the Trinity, but 'not as an individual instance of humanity as such, not as one among many who have the same human nature'. Rather, the eternal Logos is a subsistent relation and therefore 'it is Jesus' relation to the Father – and not Jesus as a specimen of humanity – which is the second hypostasis of Trinity'.⁶⁷ His rejection of the *logos asarkos*, then, is the rejection of *one entity* called 'the Son' who exists separately from *another entity* who lived as Jesus on earth and to which the latter is somehow united.⁶⁸

This clarification of Jenson's is strikingly compatible with a position that affirms divine simplicity.⁶⁹ For this christology insists that *qua* divine identity the Son is constituted by nothing other than the relation of filiation, which according to Jenson originates in Father as *arche* and culminates in the Spirit as *telos*. The Son is not constituted in his divine identity by membership in humanity, and therefore is not as such constituted by the human career of Jesus – though, as the created temporal life of the divine hypostasis, neither does this career identify some other person than the eternal Son. Insofar as Jesus is one of the Trinity by virtue of the subsistent relation alone, the second person's relation to creation and to human nature need not be construed in such a way that implies the historical events of the incarnation are compositional ingredients in (or metaphysical parts of) the divine being-as-event.

This suggests once again that Jenson's identification of God by and with events does not entail that those events constitute God's being. For if God's own eventful differentiation is conceived through the distinction of the triune

---

65 Which Sang Hoon Lee has attempted to help clarify against critiques in 'Preexistence and Transcendence', 401–14.
66 Jenson, 'Once More', 120, 124, where in footnote 20 Jenson draws attention to the need to remember time's creaturely status.
67 'Once More', 124.
68 This is a consistent concern of Jenson's in his presentation of christology (cf. also Jenson, 'Jesus in the Trinity', 308–18).
69 For example, cf. McFarland, *Word Made Flesh*, 85–88, rejecting a descriptive role for the *logos asarkos* while preserving a regulative role.

persons and the eventful differentiation of the persons are subsistent relations that simply *are* the divine event with no external terms that constitute them, then identifying God by and with historical events seems to allow Jenson to hold together the revelatory *Vorstellung* and *Begriff* without reducing God to a series of events that accumulate to constitute the whole divine identity. The divine persons as subsistent relations are able to include or encompass particular historical events because no terms *can* be constitutive of the relations *qua* relation. Consequently, the divine persons can take on relations to historical events – they can be identified by and with historical events – without being constituted by them, for the relation as which each person subsists is at once constituted only by the relations of the persons subsisting as the divine *ousia* and open to identification by and with historical events as the real presence of God to creatures.

The greatest hindrance to this reconstructive interpretation of Jenson's views is his speculation about the necessary eternal embodiment of God the Son. According to Jenson, the propositions 'God is love' and 'God has self-knowledge' are both only finally intelligible through an affirmation of God's embodiment.[70] Knowledge and love each, so Jenson argues, require embodiment, yet God can be love and have knowledge because God is triune, with one of the divine identities having a body. What Jenson means by this is unclear. For, on the one hand, Jenson insists that the Son is divine by virtue of being a subsistent relation and, therefore, '*not as an individual instance of humanity as such*'.[71] But, on the other hand, from the perspective of God's *ousia* as love and self-knowledge, it seems (though Jenson does not say it this way) that the Son's human embodiment *is in fact constitutive* of divinity, which would suggest that the Son's divine identity does not only obtain by virtue of being a subsistent relation but is also somehow constituted by having a human body. But this inference is, in turn, complicated by the fact that it is not clear exactly to what 'body' Jenson is referring in these arguments. He mentions the incarnate body – that which Jesus *does* have 'as an individual instance of humanity' – but then backs off from fully identifying the Son's 'bodiliness' with the incarnate human body when he says, 'the Son is available to the Father as the embodied human, Jesus. But also if there were a different creation, or none at all, the Son would somehow be available to the Father – though about that "somehow" we may not further speculate.'[72] The ambiguity here is due in part to an idiosyncratic and perhaps too minimal

---

70 Cf. Jenson, 'Body of God's Presence'; *ST*, 1:228–30; and *OTH*, 56.
71 'Once More', 124 (emphasis added).
72 *OTH*, 56.

definition of 'body': 'someone's "body" is simply the person him or herself insofar as this person is available to other persons and to him or herself, insofar as the person is an object for other persons and him or herself.'[73] If a 'body' is simply personal availability, then it is no wonder Jenson is so quick to insist on embodiment in God's intratrinitarian relations, for no doubt the persons of the Trinity are 'available' to one another.[74] But this definition does not account for the way that the concept of 'body' generally denotes a material object – i.e. something spatially extended – which leaves it unclear whether Jenson is claiming the necessity of *materiality* in God.[75] However, by not accounting for this aspect of the meaning of 'body', Jenson leaves it somewhat ambiguous exactly what he intends by insisting on God's embodiment.[76] I return to these questions in the next chapter.

4.3.3 The Holy Spirit in the Trinity: the simple event of futurity

Jenson deploys the logic of simplicity in two further ways, with the aim of reflecting on both the narrative of the incarnation and God's eventful being. These are perhaps the most explicit instances of how 'dramatic unity' is worked out in the

---

[73] *ST*, 1:205. Cf. also his *VW*, 20–25. Pannenberg also notes the weakness of Jenson's definition; 'Trinitarian Synthesis', 52.
[74] But if their mutual availability is articulated in terms of 'embodiment', how would the inference that the persons are thereby understood to be discrete entities be blocked? For there is at least a long tradition of understanding a 'body' to be form *individuated by matter*. If, however, the mutual availability of the persons requires such individuation, then it seems that they can only be 'three' at the cost of no longer being truly 'one'. Now, it might be claimed that Jenson does mean something different by 'body' than the traditional notion of 'individuation by matter' and so should not be charged with these objections. It is true that he does not deploy body in explicit continuity with this tradition, but his arguments for speaking of a 'body' of God seem to imply that it is *by virtue of embodiment that the persons of God have sufficient objectivity to be available to one another*, and it is hard to see how this does not assume some principle of individuation.
[75] So Jenson's project diverges from Stephen Webb's 'heavenly flesh' christology for different reasons than Webb seems to acknowledge; Webb, *Jesus Christ, Eternal God*, 97–108.
[76] Jenson provides his most comprehensive explanation of what God's bodiliness consists of in 'Body of God's Presence', 88: '(1) God is Word eternally in himself. "If he chooses to have himself as an object that is also our object, that is how it is." (2) To say God has a body is to say God transcends himself. God has himself as what he is free from, and just so free for.' But even here, what it means for God to transcend God is unclear, leaving it just as ambiguous what God's embodiment means in relation to human embodiment. I develop this question and what I believe is at stake further in Platter, 'Jesus, Trinity, and Creation'.

doctrine of God, and in both instances the activity of the Holy Spirit is central. First, there is a unity within the event of incarnation, which holds together the multiple moments of Christ's life through the action of the Spirit. Second, there is a unity of the word that Jesus *is* and the words *by which* Jesus is proclaimed. These two forms of dramatic unity concern Jenson's identification of the Son as God's Word – and they provide further clarity about how Jenson intends to identify God by and with historical events without making God identical to historical events.

Taking up recent interest in Spirit-christology, Jenson reflects on how the Spirit's involvement in several events in the incarnation reveals something of the incarnation's character. The culmination of his argument is a call for revising our conception of time in light of the unity different moments of Christ's incarnation display with one another:

> we must say that although in the account of [Jesus'] baptism the Father's word to an adult man is the Father's union with this man, Jesus does not first become the Word or the Son thirty years or so after his birth. But then it seems that Jesus' conception and what happened at his baptism must somehow happen at the same time – and indeed at the same time as his being begotten of the Father.[77]

What surfaces in Jenson's argument seems to be a twofold conviction. On the one hand, he will not interpret away the dramatic effect of Jesus' baptism, which suggests that the baptism is in some way itself the event of Jesus' union with God the Father. On the other hand, Jesus' divine identity is not an addition to an already existing human life, for divinity is not something that can be accrued piecemeal.[78] If Jesus is divine by virtue of the Father's word at his baptism, then he is just so also divine at his birth and death. Jenson's argument here is a particularly clear example of what 'dramatic simplicity' might entail, even though there is certainly some dialectical strain. On the one hand, Jesus is God the Son by virtue of the Father's word of address, 'You are my son' (Mark 1:11), but without thereby being 'adopted' as a divine Son, as if he were not divine beforehand. On the other hand, Jesus is God the Son by virtue of being conceived by the word that came to Mary from the angel Gabriel (Luke 1:30–35). Both these 'words' are the Father's address to the Son and occur in the presence of the Spirit who also shares in their enactment; and both events somehow 'make' Jesus to be God the Son.[79] These two events, according to Jenson, are the events that identify

---

77 Jenson, '*Conceptus*', 106.
78 In this context, Jenson explicitly rejects an adoptionist reading of Jesus' baptism; '*Conceptus*', 106.
79 '*Conceptus*', 104–6.

Jesus as God the Son, which means they are in some sense one event *both* happening eternally *and* happening at two moments in time some thirty years apart.

Jenson does not fully work out a 'solution' to this eternity–time dialectic; his aim is rather to illustrate how the Spirit is active in the incarnation in ways that disrupt our normal sense of the flow of time. The offense his rendering of the narrative causes to our sense of time is one of his explicit conclusions.[80] One way to interpret what Jenson is working towards would be to understand the generation of the Son as happening eternally as the Father addresses the Son in the Spirit, and the two historical events that constitute incarnation (conception and baptism) participate in that one eternal event. Another way to interpret Jenson is to shift focus from the unity of the eternal event onto the unity of the historical events. In this case, it would not be that the two historical events have the same transcendent point of reference, but that some part of the actual historical happening of each is identical to the other; the identity between the events is 'immanent' to their temporal occurrence. Perhaps he intends to suggest something that includes elements of both these construals in order to understand the eternal unity of God as somehow compatible with an immanent historical identity between events. This could then be seen as an extension of the logic of simplicity, in that the historical events that identify God might somehow bear an internal dramatic unity that itself displays God's eternal simplicity. Jenson does not make it clear which of these three possibilities he intends, though his claim that the problem requires a 'reconstrual of the succession of time' suggests he leans toward a resolution in terms that are immanent to the events, for only if the unity of the Spirit's agency in the incarnation is conceived most directly in immanent terms does the unity require a reconstrual of immanent categories (rather than, for instance, a clarification of how spatio-temporal events participate in God's eternal being-as-event).[81]

In another context, Jenson develops the unity of God's being and act by considering the role of the Spirit in gospel proclamation, and here he returns to the subject that first animated his study of Barth: predestination. 'The speaking of the gospel is the event of predestination in that the gospel gives what it speaks about, but this eschatological efficacy of the gospel is the Spirit.'[82] In this context, Jenson uses 'predestination' to mean the power of gospel proclamation to speak into reality the ultimate rhyming of one's past and future. From this per-

---

80 '*Conceptus*', 106.
81 Though, again, it is not clear that Jenson actually *opposes* the participatory option, it is simply notable that he does not explicitly pursue it.
82 'Holy Spirit', 138.

spective, the doctrine of predestination is properly conceived as a third-person critical hermeneutic for what is primarily a first- and second-person encounter – an encounter in which a word is spoken as genuine gospel promise.[83] Gospel promise is a distinct mode of promise because of its absolute unconditionality: its efficacy is not contingent on any prior action of the recipient or any unspoken limitations in the speaker; on the contrary, justification is by faith alone. For Jenson, recognition of the Spirit's role in justification provides some resolution to the well-rehearsed difficulties of predestination: i.e., that it threatens both to evacuate any genuine significance to the human will in responding to the gospel and that it threatens to render God's absolute sovereignty of will responsible for all evil along with the good of salvation:

> As seen in the gospel, God's will is absolute because it is immutably determined, as love; as seen in the total course of events, God's will is absolute in that it is absolutely undetermined – whatever happens, God has willed. Precisely the synthesis of these two determinations is the notion of spirit: a determinate reality that just by the actual character of its particular determination is utterly free.[84]

The Spirit's eschatological activity is evoked in gospel proclamation, rhyming in anticipation the absoluteness of God's love with the tumultuous experience of the present. But the Spirit's activity is neither a deluge of the perpetually new nor a simple repetition of what has always been. Rather, the Holy Spirit 'is the freedom of Jesus' future to transform and renew all previous events whatsoever'.[85] This is to say, the Spirit 'predestines' (or, as Jenson also puts it, 'postdestines') by offering Jesus' being-toward-the-future as the horizon of the possibility of the hearer's own being. Because Jesus' being is accomplished in his transcendence of death (i.e., his resurrection), his being-toward-the-future is an *achieved* future and not merely an empty horizon.

Again, Jenson is reflecting here on what is the case given that justifying faith is actually received in first- and second-person proclamation of the gospel. He is not attempting a description of some technique or process by which faith is received but is reflecting on the hermeneutics of the language of proclamation. The Spirit as the freedom of God's future is both active in the giving of faith (grace) and in the hermeneutical reflection internal to speaking the gospel.[86] Conse-

---

83 'Holy Spirit', 129–30.
84 'Holy Spirit', 139.
85 'Holy Spirit', 139.
86 So: 'the Spirit is precisely the fact that the gospel makes changes in us' ('Holy Spirit', 125); and: 'pneumatology must become hermeneutical reflection, reflection about Christian discourse done in the course thereof, as part of that discourse's accomplishment, reflection about how to

quently there is a dramatic unity within the *language* by which the church speaks the gospel:

> The continuity of language is the event in which, as I seek understanding with him to whom I *now* hearken, the agreements that regulate the language I already have are questioned so as to lead to new agreements ... the new person in the search for understanding with whom new Christian language is spoken is always the same Jesus, presented in the proclamation of Him as the coming one who is always new. ... that Jesus is indeed now present in the proclamation as the one who is never passed by, is of course a version of the central affirmation of faith: 'He is risen and will come again.'[87]

The church persists as a tradition by continuing in its linguistic activity to hearken to and so speak of Jesus – and the 'hearkening to' and 'speaking of' are in this case the one event of proclamation.[88] In other words, God happens in the eschatological language of promise. God happens as the 'same Jesus' who is the same precisely by being, in the Spirit, 'the coming one who is always new'.

Jenson can speak of Jesus 'happening' in our language because he understands Jesus as an inexhaustible event for whom distinctions between givenness and newness and between doer and deed do not apply.[89] In other words, the event of Jesus – the story that Jesus is – has a dramatic simplicity and is thereby present when the Spirit invokes genuine proclamation. Christian preaching can effect what it proclaims because it is a word-event that participates in the event of Jesus' death and resurrection.[90] Jenson's dramatic christological analogy between God and creatures comes into view. Like Christ, we too have our future in the address of the Spirit – which means that our very being is made possible by the eschatological horizon that the Spirit gives. Christ has this future both divinely and humanly. *Qua* divine, Christ has this future as a subsisting relation

---

speak the gospel done internally to the speaking' (130). While Jenson's own pneumatological rendering of justification by faith alone is offered by way of criticism of Augustine, Susannah Ticciati's reading of Augustine is actually quite compatible with Jenson's own constructive proposals, and therefore contrasts sharply with him as an interpretation of Augustine (*New Apophaticism*, 55–134).

87 *KTHF*, 235–36. Between this 1969 publication and his 1984 'The Holy Spirit' (which has guided the rest of my present argument), we can see an increasing attention to the role of the Holy Spirit in proclamation, justification, and predestination. This may not be irrelevant for his increasingly sympathetic posture to metaphysics.

88 Thus the Holy Spirit is central to Jenson's understanding of the Church's unity with Christ and persistence as a tradition. Cf. *UG*, 136 ff; Jenson, 'You Wonder Where the Spirit Went'.

89 *GaG*, 193; *S&P*, 119.

90 'God is real for us only as the word-event in which we then and there, as speakers and hearers, are condemned and rescued' (*KTHF*, 239).

from the Father *to* the Spirit and so shares in the mutuality by which the Spirit is also a subsisting relation to Father and Son. *Qua* human, Christ has this future by the same Spirit but by initiating *dependent and receptive speech*, or prayer.[91] Jesus has a creaturely beginning by birth from David's seed but is God the Son by the future-oriented action of the Spirit (exegeting Romans 1:3–4).[92] So Christ *enacts* the difference between God and creature through the invitation of the Spirit, being at once *homoousion* with the Spirit in divinity and dependent on the Spirit in humanity. And because Christ divinely *is* this relation to the Spirit as the Father's Word, our own words can share his human response to the Spirit and so become word-events of gospel as well. In other words, Christ can *be spoken* in our words because Christ simply *is* the Word, always breathed by the one Spirit. In this way, Jenson's retrieval of the Reformation's emphasis on proclamation and justification by faith alone itself constitutes an original extension of the grammar of divine simplicity.

4.4 Divine simplicity and divine names

There remain several open questions about Jenson's doctrine of God that I have not addressed here. I will be occupied with some questions in the next chapter, but for now I want to consider a potential lacuna in Jenson's doctrine of God that is especially pertinent to the doctrine of divine simplicity. As I have argued, simplicity has three main theological deployments: the Creator–creature relation, the Trinity, and the multiplicity of divine names or attributes. And although Jenson does not seem to have a full theology of the divine names in his *Systematic Theology*, his theology does not neglect the theme altogether.[93] In his contributions to the multi-authored *Christian Dogmatics*, for example, Jenson does provide dedicated discussion of divine attributes.[94] And in a later essay, Jenson offers some clues to how he conceives of the predication of attributes that the three divine persons share.[95] Still further, in his biblical commentaries, Jenson makes

---

91 'Creator and Creature', 159–61.
92 *ST*, 1:142, where he takes ὁρισθέντος (v. 4) as 'determined' to be Son of God 'according to the Spirit of holiness by resurrection from the dead'.
93 As he concedes, *ST*, 1:223.
94 'Triune God', 181–92. This work is often treated as a reproduction of his *Triune Identity*, but the discussion of divine attributes only appears in the *Christian Dogmatics* edition. Consider also 'Holy Spirit', 173–78.
95 Jenson, '*Deus est ipsa pulchritudo*'. Stephen Wright offers an excellent discussion of how Jenson's predication 'across the three' persons might be developed in *Dogmatic Aesthetics*, 79–92.

recourse to the identity of divine perfections in order to develop theological judgments on exegetical issues.[96]

Strikingly, Jenson urges that, 'Whatever we want to assert of the form "God is …" – that he is good, or great, or whatever – we must say three times for it to be true of the gospel's God.'[97] He concedes that this may only need be done explicitly to avoid ambiguity:

> But the *predicates* we use *of* the one identified in any of the three ways, can be made unambiguous – should ambiguity threaten – only by running them across all three identities. E.g., 'God is good in the way that a giver is good; and he is good in the way that a gift is good; and he is good in the way that the outcome of a gift is good.'[98]

Jenson's proposal here has a two-edged purpose. It is first a rule to preserve the fact that the divine *ousia* is not a proper subject in distinction from the persons, as unqualified predication to the *ousia* might be taken to imply. Second, the rule provides a way to avoid the possibility of analogical predication being reduced to agnosticism.[99] Jenson can affirm a kind of analogy – affirming the basic form of analogy that he finds in Aquinas – but he believes his own rule ensures that analogical predication retains content, for the mutual activity of the three persons specifies the manner in which God exemplifies a given attribute. And further, one of the three persons has a history and is therefore specifiable by means of ordinary identifying descriptions (i.e., Jesus, the one who was born of Mary, son of Joseph the carpenter, … was obedient to God unto death, etc.); thereby

---

96 *Song of Songs; Ezekiel.*
97 *S&P*, 126.
98 'Three Identities', 7; cf. also *TI*, 109.
99 In 'Triune God', 184–91, Jenson articulates each divine attribute as ways of explicating (or 'slogans' for) the central gospel claim 'Jesus is risen', distinguishing two types of attributes thereby: those which are made of the predicate (Jesus *is risen*) and thereby are slogans for the gospel fact of resurrection, and others that are attributes of the subject (*Jesus* is risen) and thereby specify the character of God as what happens between this man Jesus and his Father and their Spirit. In light of these reflections on how the *content* of divine attributes is determined, I find it hard to understand Timo Tavast's claim that Jenson deploys a 'negative natural theology', which he substantiates by appeal to Jenson's connection of the concept of 'God' to the concept of 'eternity' (Tavast, 'Identification of the Triune God', 157). However, Jenson's claim here is simply that 'God' and 'eternity' are interchangeable concepts in their religious function—not that we deduce God from natural knowledge of 'eternity'. By contrast, Jenson's doctrine of the Trinity is 'antireligious' (as Tavast rightly attends to) in the way it *challenges* any antecedent conception of 'eternity', thereby blocking any deductive or inductive move from experiences of temporality to the meaning or reality of the triune God's eternality.

the character of the attribute is knowable much like we come to know the character of other human persons and their properties.

For instance, God *is* freedom, according to Jenson. What this sentence means is ultimately conveyable only in trinitarian terms: in God, personal mutuality can be the complete gift of love one to the other precisely because the Spirit is the mutual love between Father and Son, opening each to the future as love.[100] And this reflection enables him to affirm a participatory analogy of freedom:

> enabling freedom is not a matter of causing but of sharing, and in yourself you no more have freedom to share than I do. Only the true God has freedom in himself, for only he is triune, only he is community with himself so as to be free in himself.'[101]

It is because God *is* freedom, rather than receiving it, that we can *become* free by participation.[102]

And Jenson makes a similar case for 'love' as a divine perfection, with interesting continuity as well as (potential) discontinuity with divine simplicity:

> God's love is intersubjective without needing to be the love of what is other than God, and indeed is consequent to its own intersubjectivity: the Father is the Father who begets the Son and breathes the Spirit, ontologically prior to there being simply God, of whom we may theistically say that 'he loves us' – or knows us or whatever else God does. Further, it is an ancient and ecumenical maxim of Christian theology: what God is and what God does or has are distinguishable only notionally. The God who loves us *is* love. And so the Godhead that is love is itself *founded* in intersubjectivity, for there is no Godhead antecedent to the Father's begetting the Son and breathing the Spirit.[103]

Several points are worthy of note here. Jenson yet again specifies the meaning of the attribution by explicating it in trinitarian terms. The application of the word (here, 'love') to God is even said to apply first to God *qua* the three persons before it refers to something the three are in common.[104] And, yet, for Jenson this still

---

100 *OTH*, 43.
101 *OTH*, 42–43; also 'Ontology of Freedom'.
102 Freedom has consistently been a key divine attribute for Jenson (cf. *S&P*, 23–24).
103 *OTH*, 53–54.
104 To the claim that the triune relations in God are 'ontologically prior to there being simply God', Jenson offers a qualification, saying that 'This is the great and in its own context true and indispensable contention of much modern Orthodox theology' (53n14). So, the ontological priority of the three to the one is true *in its own context*; such a qualification seems to imply that he would not endorse the statement in *every context*. And although he does not explicitly state what the proper context for the truth of the statement is, in the essay in which he uses the claim, it simply suggests that the *meaning* of terms predicated of God is derived first from how the predicate functions in respect of the three persons.

entails that the relation of God to a divine attribute or perfection is one of *identity*. In fact, for Jenson the identity of divine attributes to God and to one another is deployed to reinforce his own central trinitarian claims. In his commentary on Ezekiel, Jenson wonders what it was like when the prophet both 'saw visions of God' and 'the word of the LORD came expressly to Ezekiel' (Ez. 1:1–3) – entering into an excursus on the development of trinitarian doctrine and culminating in an affirmation of God as eternal triune conversation, in whom seeing and hearing are identical. For, God is 'identical to his attributes'.[105] The prophet Ezekiel experiences God's reality simultaneously by vision and sound, which elicits for Jenson an awareness of the triune conversation, known synesthetically by participating in the unity of God's own attributes. Other similar discussions of particular divine attributes could be isolated in Jenson's writing, which would populate a reasonable – if not somewhat unusual – list of divine attributes: e. g., eternal, faithful, omnipresent, unconditional love, almighty (and, in Christ, 'mortal'), and good, with the notable additions of jealousy and roominess.[106]

But perhaps most important to Jenson's theology would be 'infinite', which comes to Jenson through his reading of Gregory of Nyssa:

> For the great Greek thinkers, infinity meant the absence of being; for them, to be is precisely to have eidos, outline, so as to be knowable. For Gregory, on the precise contrary, infinity is fullness of being and the very essence of God, who therefore is known in discovering that we do not catch up with him.[107]

Divine infinity is not a new theme in this chapter's discussion of Jenson; and by saying that God's infinity is the obverse of our inability to 'catch up with him', Jenson takes up a long-standing name of God and explicates it in specifically temporal terms: 'God's infinity, in our view, is basically his temporal infinity, the unhinderedness of his transcendence through time.'[108] It is a driving conviction of Jenson's theology that the finite is capable of the infinite – *finitum capax infiniti*[109] – which is certainly part of his motivation for embarking on a temporal rendering of divine infinity:

---

105 Jenson, *Ezekiel*, 34–35.
106 This list, excepting the last two, is derived from Jenson, 'Triune God', 184–91. 'Indeed, if we were to list divine attributes, roominess would have to come next after jealousy' (*ST*, 1:226).
107 Jenson, 'Nyssa: *Moses*', 537; cf. also *TI*, esp. 162–66, 168–75.
108 'Triune God', 186.
109 As Gabriel Fackre notes in 'The Lutheran *Capax* Lives'; as well as, differently, Buckley, 'Intimacy'.

Participation in our finitude, alienation, and consequent disaster thus belongs to the event that in fact God is. Exegeting 'belongs'; it essentially characterizes the true God that, if there are creatures and fallen creatures, he is able and apt so to participate in their life. It is appropriate to what it means to be this God that in his second identity he died with and for us.[110]

The compatibility of the finite with the infinite, however, is first a claim about God's triune infinity. It is because of the character of the life God lives as Father, Son, and Spirit that God *makes room* for others. The 'roominess' of God is God's fugal musicality – the textured interweaving of three voices in perfect circumincession – which by already consisting of a harmonious diversity can become 'distended' to make space for creaturely time.[111] Which is to say that God's 'roominess' is not an emptiness into which creatures can be inserted but is instead a *fullness* that by taking a particular *action* the triune God can share with creatures. Jenson's musical rendering of divine roominess therefore contrasts his account of God's 'place' with that of Jürgen Moltmann. For Moltmann, God is the place of creation, withdrawing into God's own self in 'zimzum' to form the nothingness where the universe is created.[112] Because for Moltmann God's 'roominess' is in fact a kind of 'emptiness' for creation, God's inhabitation of particular places within creation undergoes strain and requires some kind of 'contraction' or self-humiliation of God.[113] However, Jenson is under less strain in depicting God's particular presence to creation because for him God's 'roominess' is not a quasi-spatialized withdrawal or emptiness but a fullness that God shares with creatures.

4.5 Conclusion

This chapter has demonstrated the uniqueness of Jenson's doctrine of God in relation to the other theologians I have discussed. His emphasis on the temporality of being and the temporal conditions of knowledge push him to think of creation

---

110 'Triune God', 189–90. Note that Jenson's 'exegesis' of what it means for something 'to belong to the event that in fact God is' resembles Aquinas' suppositional necessity, so that God's 'constitution' by undergoing death and resurrection is under the rubric of the supposition that there are in fact fallen creatures. Cf. *STh*, 1.19.3, *sed contra*.
111 *ST*, 1:234–36; 2:33–35, 367–69.
112 Moltmann, *God in Creation*, 86–93. Balthasar's theology is also vulnerable to strained spatialized readings; Jacob Lett has recently used Jenson's musical rendering to fruitfully 'repair' this potential weakness in Balthasar (see 'Divine Roominess', 267–77).
113 Moltmann, *Coming of God*, 302–8.

and God in a dramatic register. Yet it should also be clear that many of the judgments Gregory of Nyssa, Augustine, and Aquinas articulate are shared in Jenson's theology. In particular, Jenson has developed a theological metaphysics that affirms the radical dependency of all creatures on their Creator, thereby instantiating the regulative rule of the strict distinction of Creator and creature.[114] In this way, Jenson engages self-consciously in theological metaphysics in order to affirm God's triune, non-contrastive transcendence. He deploys the grammar of simplicity congruently, using it to express God's simultaneous distinction from and intimacy to creation, the unity of the three persons of the Trinity, and the diversity and unity of divine attributes. Nonetheless several differences are present between Jenson and the classical predecessors I have discussed. In the next chapter, I develop specific proposals for the doctrine of divine simplicity through more critical engagement with Jenson's doctrine of God.

---

114 'The Greeks devised the concept of being precisely to forestall any such distinction as the biblical distinction between Creator and creature; per contra, Christian theology must so wield the concept as to enforce the distinction. The great exemplar and standard of this move is Thomas Aquinas ... we will seek to follow his example and will appropriate much of his teaching. The concept of being was also to forestall any such doctrine of divine eventfulness as the doctrine of Trinity; per contra, Christian theology must devise a trinitarian concept of being itself' (*ST*, 1:212).

Part III Toward a dramatic theology of divine simplicity

5 Divine simplicity and the triune identity

> The Christian doctrine of God, the doctrine of God's Trinity, is a doctrine of 'God the unknown'. But it is, nevertheless, a doctrine of *God*, because its purpose and function, as 'summary grammar' of the pedagogy of salvation, is to enable us appropriately not only to work and think (for a 'philosophy' might have *this* as its aim) but also to worship. And if, at one level, it enables us to worship by continually correcting our propensities towards idolatry, this (given a little self-knowledge) should not unduly surprise us.
> – Nicholas Lash[1]

5.1 Introduction

The doctrine of divine simplicity is by no means a monolithic concept. It has diverse proponents (instanced in this study by Gregory of Nyssa, Augustine, Thomas Aquinas, and Robert Jenson), and its content is shaped by the metaphysical contexts within which it is used and the ends toward which it is deployed. The pagan philosopher Plotinus does not differentiate the One from the immanent plane of reality quite as sharply as Christians do the Creator from creation – a difference that David Burrell refers to as 'the distinction'. Plotinus comes close (as Lloyd Gerson ably demonstrates[2]), but he still envisions 'divinity' to be gradable insofar as *Noûs* and Soul are intermediaries of the One in the production of sensible reality.[3] By contrast, while nonetheless retrieving several insights from Neoplatonic philosophy, Christian theologians had a different use for divine simplicity. The admonition against idolatry provokes a heightened sense of the difference between what is created (and therefore not to be worshipped) and the Creator who is to be worshipped. In this sense, a nexus of issues converge: how can we express God's difference while also affirming God's all-pervasive and intimate presence, the use of multiple divine names and perfections, and the church's worship of the three persons of Father, Son, and Spirit?

As demonstrated in the previous chapter, despite his relatively infrequent use of the language of divine simplicity, Jenson nevertheless echoes and reformulates the judgments of divine simplicity in various ways. Sometimes this has clear resonances with Gregory, Augustine, and Aquinas, and at other times there are divergences from and original extensions to their logic. Comparing Jenson with these earlier and more explicit proponents of divine simplicity

---

1 'Considering the Trinity', 194.
2 Gerson, *Plotinus*, 26–36.
3 Cf. Plotinus, *Enn.*, V.1 [10].6.29–40; VI.7 [38].13.27–29.

has several immediate benefits, not least in that it demonstrates that a certain level of material continuity is present, even amidst some notable differences and formal discontinuities. In this respect, I am not convinced by the conclusions of Stephen Holmes and Lewis Ayres when they see a radical divergence from classical Nicene theology in the contemporary trinitarian revival.[4] Certainly some of the revisions proposed under the latter banner are open to challenge in light of the recent defence of the significance of divine simplicity in pro-Nicene trinitarian theology. But even in Robert Jenson – an often polemical voice within the trinitarian revival – significant continuity with the traditional judgments on divine simplicity is recognizable. These signs of continuity cut both ways: calling into question both the sharp edge of Holmes' and Ayres' assessments and the polemical attacks on simplicity from Jenson himself. The majority of Jenson's explicit references to divine simplicity have been critical, and these criticisms have been part of the argument for Jenson's alternative proposals. However, if he has more in common with the traditional conception of divine simplicity than is typically acknowledged, then some of the motivation for his more radical revisionary claims appears to be undercut.

This latter point affects not only Jenson, but to varying degrees could apply to many who have understood their own trinitarian proposals in common cause with him.[5] The degree to which this is the case will vary depending on particular authors. For instance, drawing analogous conclusions about Pannenberg's work would be more straightforward, since so much of Jenson's and Pannenberg's projects overlap and since Pannenberg is also engaged in theological metaphysics.[6] Colin Gunton, whose treatment of simplicity was discussed in chapter one, shares many judgements in common with Jenson but does not engage in the same level of metaphysical construction, so drawing conclusions about Gunton's relation to simplicity would have to follow a different approach than I have taken with Jenson. But as I argued in chapter 1, an account of the Trinity cannot succeed if it renders the divine persons as in any way standing in a part–whole relationship with the essence they have in common. This requires conceiving of

---

[4] Ayres, *Nicaea and Its Legacy*, 404–14. Holmes, *Holy Trinity*, 182–200; most pointedly with his conclusion: 'We called what we were doing a "Trinitarian revival"; future historians might want to ask us why' (200).

[5] I think especially of Paul Hinlicky (*Divine Simplicity*), whose articulation of 'weak simplicity' claims Jenson's authority but radicalizes the polemics significantly.

[6] For instance, in his *Systematic Theology*, 1:337–68, Pannenberg connects simplicity with infinity, judging that 'The concept of the infinite rules out any idea of a composition of three different essences. God's infinity implies his simplicity' (343n10; drawing on Mühlenberg's *Unendlichkeit Gottes*).

God's *ousia* as somehow 'sharable' without being susceptible to division or to greater or lesser degrees of exemplification. Much pro-Nicene theology found in the grammar of divine simplicity an ally for this cause. And in the case of Jenson, the clearer his account of God's tri*unity* becomes, the closer he comes to fully and explicitly affirming divine simplicity. While I do not intend to suggest that every orthodox account of God's triunity *entails* acceptance of divine simplicity, I would contend that the more God's indivisible unity in three persons comes into focus, the more the account will converge with the central judgments of the doctrine of divine simplicity.

In this final chapter, I will bring some of the issues that arose in chapter two into dialogue with my reconstruction of Jenson in order to develop some constructive proposals. First, I discuss once again the relationship between metaphysics and theology and the topic of 'dramatic unity'. Then I will turn directly to the doctrine of divine simplicity, continuing to discuss it under the headings of the Creator–creature distinction, the multiple divine names, and Trinity. By clarifying the meaning and regulative function of *dramatic* unity, I argue that there is greater room for continuity and creative retrieval of the traditional approaches to divine simplicity than Jenson explicitly acknowledged, while still finding fresh possibilities in Jenson's theology. In each section that follows, I show where I think Jenson is on the right track, where there are ambiguities or tensions in his thought, and where I think a different direction should be pursued.

5.2 Metaphysics, divine simplicity, and dramatic unity

At the beginning of chapter three, I argued that part of the reason divine simplicity has become optional and even completely rejected in contemporary theology is an assumed mismatch between philosophical or metaphysical language and the language of scripture. For many theologians critical of divine simplicity, I argued, they presume an 'inverse relation' between metaphysics and scripture – i.e., the more a doctrinal statement deploys metaphysical language and categories, the less compatible with scripture it is taken to be. In this light, retrieval of the doctrine of divine simplicity requires some defence of the use of metaphysics in theology. Though Jenson is not often seen as a proponent of divine simplicity, I have argued that there are significant vestiges and even creative extensions of the doctrine in Jenson's theology, and that these can be recognized when we appreciate his way of reconciling the task of metaphysics with the reading of scripture.

Jenson argues that when the church reads the Bible *as scripture*, she reads it through the narrative unity expressed in the creeds.[7] The narrative unity of the creeds themselves consist in their focus on the *tri-unity* of God, who is in one sense scripture's author. Thus, reading the books of the Bible as Christian scripture entails reflection on the unity and agency of this divine author, which will further involve us in clarification and perhaps revision of our language and categories.[8] In our postmodern critical context, for instance, Jenson argues that reading scripture entails reflection on the divine author's *agenda*. This in turn requires a 'critical lens' that may need to deconstruct particular agendas within and around the text of scripture in order to be attentive to the overall *divine* 'agenda'. The result of such reading is that we can discern a being who created all things, and whose life is such that it can in fact enable the diversity of creaturely discourses and agendas by being in itself discourse, without an eternal hegemonic collapse of discourse into the authoritarian management of all other speakers.[9] If such a reality is possible, then our ordinary notion of speech and speakers must undergo revision so that we can imagine a triune discourse that is so perfect and replete that it enables the free exchange of all other speakers. What must such transformation of imagination entail but some level of engagement in genuine metaphysics, however far the results may be from any particular metaphysical system?[10]

These arguments connect with what I have called Jenson's rule of *dramatic unity*. There are two primary motives for pursuing theology in a theodramatic mode. The first is a desire for a non-competitive, non-contrastive account of God's transcendence and involvement with creatures. A non-competitive account of God's transcendence entails that God can invite the involvement of creatures without thereby disrupting God's transcendent actuality. Because there is no

---

7 *CC*, 11–18, 79–87.

8 Concerning the clarification and revision of our language and categories, I take it that at least part of the defining task of metaphysics is to determine the most general categories and to reflect critically on their use and interrelationship (cf. Gracia, *Metaphysics and its Task*, 131–40). So, any activity which involves us in reflection on fundamental, basic, or general categories will consequently involve some degree of metaphysical thinking. For a rich discussion of the interrelation of scripture, creed, and the 'rule of faith', see Gordon, *Divine Scripture*, 1–67.

9 So cf. Jenson's delightful reflections in 'On Hegemonic Discourse', 18–22. 'This is of course a bitter pill for most who now complain of hegemonic discourse: there can be non-hegemonic discourse only if there is what they most dread, a real Hegemon' (20).

10 For similar arguments that develop more fully biblical and exegetical warrants for theological interpretation of scripture that incorporates some metaphysical reflection, see Anderson, 'Creatio ex nihilo and the Bible'; Anderson, *Christian Doctrine and the Old Testament*, esp. 50–58; Chambers, 'Divine and Creaturely Agency'; Gordon, *Divine Scripture*.

competition between the finite and infinite – between creature and Creator – the complex drama of human involvement with God should be articulated without making either God's eternal actuality or creaturely temporal development reducible to the other. By contrast, if God's transcendence were simply the contrastive opposite of creaturely finitude and temporality, then we might be inclined to think that God's eternal actuality pre-contains the entire history and actuality of creation, which would render this history and actuality within the creaturely frame a mere projection or mirroring of what is already timelessly accomplished and contained in God. Creaturely development in time, despite its semblance of genuine involvement with God, would thereby be reduced entirely to an intradivine action with no genuine inclusion of creatures according to their finite actuality.[11] In the face of this threat, Jenson's 'dramatic theology' attempts to uphold the non-contrastive transcendence of God and thereby preserve the integrity of creatures' involvement with God in history.

The second of Jenson's motives is a desire to read the complex witness of scripture without collapsing the multiple dramatic frames of references into a single privileged context but rather upholding the complex integrity of different narratives and contexts.[12] In Jenson's own account, this entails allowing the dramatic tensions of the actual narrative account of the *dramatis personae* – human and divine – to persist even in their messiness and complexity. However, this does not mean that we should assume that the character of God known through scripture must be composed of internal contradictions and processes of development and self-actualization. Rather, it means seeking the unity of the character and redemptive purposes of God in history without collapsing or blunting the complexity of dramatic locations within scripture into a religiously reassuring construal of God's timeless purposes. In the example from the previous chapter, knowledge of God's immutability in terms of God's total redemptive activity and history with creatures should not blunt for us the severity of God's wrath toward wayward Israel. Or, to reference Aristotle's definition once more, learning through the drama how the events happen 'on account of each other' should not detract from our experience of their genuine unexpectedness. What Jennifer Newsome Martin says of Balthasar is fitting here: 'Any system that privileges the universal *at the expense* of the personal and particular, flattening out individual freedom, "signals the abdication of drama in favor of a narrative philosophy of

---

[11] As Jenson fears Barth risks (*A&O*, 161–67; *GaG*, 151–56). Balthasar regards such a collapse of history into an intradivine event as 'epic' theology (*Theo-Drama*, 2:40).

[12] Along with the Jensonian basis for this claim, which I have developed in the previous two chapters, Jacob Lett shows a similar hermeneutic at play in Balthasar; 'Balthasar's Dramatic Soteriology', 172–79.

history, an epic story of the Spirit or of mankind".[13] In a non-competitive, dramatic account of God's unity and involvement with creatures, the 'universal' transcendence and creative agency of God does not come at the expense of creatures and their particularity.

There is a further reason to pursue theology in a dramatic mode, and this is the way that scripture itself can be seen to include a complex plurality of theodramatic contexts that precisely in their complexity point to a dramatically transcendent interchange of the triune persons. As Matthew Bates argues in *The Birth of the Trinity*, early Christians used 'prosopological exegesis' to interpret the plurality of theodramatic contexts within prophetic texts and psalms in order to discern their relevance for the identification of God.[14] Prosopological exegesis is a practice of reading prophetic speech as at times entailing that the prophet is speaking in a divine persona not reducible to their own and whose speech has a different theodramatic context than the prophet's own. For his purposes, Bates defines 'theodrama' as 'the dramatic world invoked by an ancient reader of Scripture as that reader construed a prophet to be speaking from or observing the person (*prosōpon*) of a divine or human character.'[15] Such exegesis might, for example, read a given passage as signaling an intradivine conversation taking place between Father and Son, as seems to be practiced by various writers of the New Testament (i.e., Acts 13:32–35 citing Ps. 2:7; Rom. 15:2–3 citing Ps. 69:10) and even in some claims of Jesus himself (i.e., Mk. 12:35–37; Matt. 22:41–46; Lk. 20:41–4; where Jesus cites Ps. 110:1). Consequently, on Bates' reading, the complexity of dramatic locations in scripture has been – and can continue to be – read fruitfully as drawing us into the theodrama of intratrinitarian exchange.[16] This reading is largely compatible with Jenson, especially by sustaining the particularity of scenes and events within the overt meaning of scripture while also discerning other theodramatic settings therein that call for consideration of the theological level of meaning and accompanying philosophical and metaphysical questions.[17]

While much more could and, in another context, should be said about the relation between metaphysics, scripture, and theology, what I have said here should clarify how theological metaphysics can engage scripture holistically

---

[13] Martin, *Balthasar*, 95; citing *Theo-Drama*, 2:40 (emphasis mine).
[14] Bates, *Birth of the Trinity*.
[15] *Birth of the Trinity*, 5n8, see also 34–35.
[16] Bates develops proposals for how to continue to pursue and critically retrieve early Christian prosopological exegesis, *Birth of the Trinity*, 190–202.
[17] See also von Balthasar, *Theo-Drama*, 2:55–56; Lett, 'Balthasar's Dramatic Soteriology', 260–61.

while attempting to preserve the various different dramatic contexts and aims present throughout the biblical texts.[18] So used, metaphysics is not a fixed body of knowledge intruding on Christian theology and independently governing theological judgments. Rather, it is part of the critical hermeneutical reflection that is internal to the theological interpretation of scripture and articulation of Christian dogma.[19] Insofar as common pursuit of both biblical interpretation and dogmatic theology involves attention to the coherence of the object of Christian faith and self-critical reflection on the categories that are deployed in the process, then some level of metaphysics – even if it is, as Jenson styles it, *revisionary* – is already implicated.

5.3 Jenson on divine simplicity

With Jenson, then, I take it that theology can use metaphysics self-critically toward the end of responsibly negotiating our use of categories in thinking God and creation as revealed throughout the manifold witness of scripture. I have further proposed a broad form of 'dramatic theology' through dialogue with Jenson. So, what does divine simplicity look like in this approach? In this section, I offer a condensed form of what I have reconstructed from Jenson in the previous chapter. Then, in the next section, I will develop three points of critical engagement with Jenson's form of divine simplicity, arguing that a more thoroughgoing deployment of divine simplicity accomplishes some of Jenson's explicit aims while avoiding the problems identified by critics (rightly or wrongly).

One of the most important governing lenses for Jenson's doctrine of God is his claim that God is identified *by and with* historical events, which I have argued is most adequately interpreted through his insistence on the unity of our thinking of God between *Vorstellung* and *Begriff* and God's triune involvement with history.[20] The central concern is to preserve God's intimate presence to us in and through the events by which God acts, which then, conversely, entails a unity between God as the object of our thought (*Begriff*) and the 'representation' by which we think of God (*Vorstellung*). If God is genuinely present in such

---

18 Similarly, see Schwöbel, 'Trinity Between Athens and Jerusalem', 37–41.
19 For a more extended account of how theological interpretation makes positive use of metaphysics (or requires a 'theological ontology') that is developed partly in dialogue with Jenson, see Darren Sarisky's 'Theological Interpretation', 201–16, *Scriptural Interpretation*, and *Reading the Bible Theologically.*
20 On God's identification *by and with* events, see *ST*, 1:57–60; on the unity of *Vorstellung* and *Begriff*, see *OTH*, 1n1.

events, then we cannot genuinely think of God (i.e., as 'concept') apart from the revelatory acts, the 'representation', by which God makes Godself present to us. It is in this sense that Jenson comes to affirm 'Rahner's Rule', that the economic Trinity *is* the immanent Trinity (and vice-versa).[21] The emphasis, for Jenson, is on the active initiative of God, who is so identified with divine activity that God's historical acts are in fact the gift of God's own self. As he said in the early *Story and Promise*, 'In the sentence "God is God", "is" is an active transitive verb. God *does* God; God *achieves* God; God *posits* God. ... The event that God is, is the event of his turning to us, the event of his love.'[22] So, precisely because this decision consists of being incarnate *for us*, there is no way around the content of this decision to God otherwise than *as* this decision.

As critics have noted, however, the question arises whether such a strong identification of God with divine acts results in a God whose identity is in fact *actualized* through creaturely history, which would clearly entail that God is composed (at minimum) of 'actuality' and 'potentiality' (i.e., being only potential in certain respects until God actualizes that potential within history). The most problematic result of this position would be that because Jenson identifies the Son so strongly with the human history of Jesus, the Son's identity would only be actualized historically.[23] But if the Son only *becomes* Son within history with no (logically) antecedent, eternal identity, then we are left with an Arian or adoptionist christology, which would further entail that God is only 'three' contingently and in respect of creation, but not eternally.[24] Such a God would be neither simple nor triune. However, the problem with this criticism is that it ignores the radical unity between God's eternal being and historical activity that Jenson is explicitly proposing. God could only have a 'contingent' hypostasis (Jesus, the Son) who is thereby *not* 'eternally' one with the Father if there is a

---

[21] Rahner, *Trinity*, 21–24. Jenson nods toward agreement with Rahner on the identity of the immanent and economic Trinity ('Theological Autobiography', 46–47) but suggests that his judgment on these matters was not actually informed by Rahner, being shaped instead by a mixture of influences from Kierkegaard, Luther, and Occam. Consequently, it is hasty to make too much of an 'immanent–economic' collapse in Jenson's thought (along the lines of Hart, 'Lively God of Jenson', 28–34, and Henry, *Freedom of God*, 183–96), since his own work does not explicitly develop a Rahnerian interpretation of this relationship. Pannenberg also critiques Jenson's interpretation of the immanent and economic Trinity, noting, however, that Jenson does distinguish them according to the eschatological priority of the immanent Trinity consummated in the Spirit (*Systematic Theology*, 1:330).

[22] *S&P*, 119, 120 (emphases mine). See also *GaG*, 110.

[23] Which seems to allow, as Fred Sanders labels it, for God's freedom only as a 'counterfactual hypothetical' (*Image of the Immanent Trinity*, 109–13).

[24] So Hunsinger, 'Review', 167–74.

definite distinction between God's eternal identity and God's self-presencing in creation. The critique's persuasiveness relies on a subtle misrepresentation of Jenson's actual claims, smuggling in a kind of contrastive eternal–historical distinction that Jenson denies.

By contrast, Jenson radically unites God's eternal and historical reality by centering his account of God and creation on the twin categories of *event* and *word*, making the latter metaphysically fundamental for the former. Creaturely being is itself event – i.e., structured occurrence – which is determined by its movement into the horizon of the future. This much Jenson develops from Heidegger. But his theological (and deeply Lutheran) twist is to make *word* the possibility of time, and so also more fundamental.[25] This allows Jenson to conceive of God's triune eternality and creaturely time harmoniously but without conflating them or absorbing one into the other. God's intratrinitarian life is the infinite mutuality of shared language. It is a life that is being-as-event by virtue of 'happening' in the activity of giving and receiving the word, but the shared language of God's life is not 'composed' of the givenness of language (i.e., a discrete, independent, and priorly given 'past') and actual utterance ('present' locutionary acts). Creation, on the other hand, always exists as a history encountering the future as possibility; it has being only insofar as it *receives* what precedes it. Creation, seen through the lens of Israel's historical self-consciousness through covenant with God, is itself a tradition, the handing on of words that have been received from those who came before, by which the future is opened.[26] On this basis, Jenson insists that God's creative action by word is not reducible to the initiating 'word' by which creation's history began – God is not simply 'past', not simply creation's prior givenness. Rather, God is also the freedom by which all finite words open a future that is genuinely free and liberating. God is thus the unity – the 'rhyming' – of past and present, of the givenness of history by word and the liberating freedom of being by word.

This suggests that there is some resemblance between God and creation, insofar as both are 'being' as eventful occurrence, and, in both, event 'happens' in the giving of the word. But there is clearly an analogical differentiation as well, for the 'word' by which creatures have their historical being is irreducibly *received* in respect of all temporal poles, whereas for God there is no antecedent 'word' or 'language' apart from the actual relations of Father, Son, and Spirit. This allows us to interpret Jenson's unity of *Vorstellung* and *Begriff* – the identification of God by and with events – as a doctrine of revelation that flows from

---

25 *GaG*, 188–89.
26 'What if It Were True?', 89.

an affirmation of the simplicity of God's being as unconditioned 'word' or 'event'. Because God simply *is* the complete self-communication of word *qua* triune, God's historical word(s) to creatures are not something external or extrinsic to God's 'eternal being', but they are nonetheless free and often dramatically 'unexpected' events that bring the disparate moments of creaturely history into coherence. Which, under a different aspect, is to say that God is lord of creation and is its covenant partner by virtue being a life that has 'an antecedently covenantal structure'.[27]

Jenson's 'doctrine of divine simplicity', then, can be characterized simultaneously as 'triune simplicity' and 'simple triunity'. God's simplicity is, for Jenson, not an independent attribute of God, to which triunity is appended, or vice versa. God *is* identical to the triune relations of Father, Son, and Spirit, who together share a life that Jenson insists is time-like and covenant-like by subsisting as structured relations of eventful, mutual self-communication. God's life bears, analogically, the temporal poles that structure our creaturely existence, but without these poles obtaining as bounds or limiting conditions for God. Or, we might say, the triune relations as which God subsists are the condition of the possibility of the temporal relations within which creaturely history occurs. So, God's 'temporality' – which is perhaps better expressed as the structured occurrence of existing as shared word – is nothing other than the three subsistent relations of Father, Son, and Spirit, who have no constituting, extrinsic terms but subsist *as* the relations of each to the others in the event of mutual giving, expressing, and liberating.

By explicating God's transcendence according to Jesus' historical being, Jenson's metaphysics of divine simplicity incorporates the late twentieth-century shift toward narrative, though it is not reducible to a 'narrative theology', which is why I have preferred to characterize it using the category 'drama'. From this dramatic perspective, Jenson's 'doctrine' of divine simplicity entails that God is conceived as an event, where God is identical to God's event or 'happening'.[28] If we recall Aquinas's grammatical distinction between creaturely contingency (as composed fundamentally of essence and existence) and God's necessity (as the simple identity of essence and existence), Jenson could be seen as deploying a similar grammar but in the context of historical narrative. We might characterize his dramatic/narrative construal of creaturely contingency in this way: no finite event is sufficient for its own intelligibility, insofar as no

---

[27] 'What Kind of God?', 6–9 (8).
[28] Similarly Balthasar (*Theo-Drama*, 5:66–81) develops God's being-as-event as an entailment of the 'scholastic axion' that 'creation is embraced within the Trinity, which is its inalienable precondition' (61). Cf. also his *Theology of History*.

finite being is identical to its own event; God, who is identical to the event that is God, is the final intelligibility of the historicity and drama of creation, as the self-donation of being in time who has an 'antecedently' *eventful* intratrinitarian life. From this perspective, Jenson is reaching toward an understanding of the triune God's eternity as a form of *analogical temporality,* in which the 'time' of the triune God is identical to the event of God's own divine life, and in which God grants creatures time by participation. This comparison captures something of the grammar of Jenson's historical rendering of divine transcendence. But epistemologically the logic only operates one way for Jenson, for we cannot reason *from* a bare apprehension of the contingency of creaturely events to the necessity of an eternal, simple event – or at least such a chain of reasoning would not lead us to knowledge of the Bible's God as much as to an imminent principle or potentially an alternative deity. Rather we see the contingency of creaturely being-as-event only in light of the actually achieved event of divine transcendence within our own history, which is Jesus. In other words, for Jenson the grammar does not permit of a natural theological demonstration of God's necessary existence, but it does express the advent of God's historical promise for the sake of creation's participation in God's triune life.[29]

There are several benefits that accrue to an account of divine simplicity that can incorporate an explicitly narrative and dramatic orientation, even if there might also be reason for caution. One benefit is that it offers an opportunity, as I have already considered, to re-introduce metaphysics in conversation with theologians otherwise concerned with narrative. Considering that much work in biblical theology and recent efforts toward 'theological interpretation' have a concern for the narrative of scripture, an approach like Jenson's has the potential of generating renewed attention to the function of metaphysical questions in the interpretation of scripture, which would further enable more charitable engagement with premodern exegesis.[30] Such an interpretation of Jenson also has ecumenical benefits, because it connects in a single theologian's work some 'classical' metaphysical themes and doctrines (which are often at home in Catholic Thomistic theology) with post-Barthian turns to narrative (often more at home in Protestant theology). In this light, it is significant that, despite

---

29 *ST*, 1:225–26.
30 As one recent proponent of theological interpretation proposes on Jenson's lead: Sarisky, 'Theological Interpretation', esp. 207–16; which he develops more fully in his two monographs, *Scriptural Interpretation*, and *Reading the Bible Theologically*.

Jenson's broader affinities with Barth and Bruce McCormack's actualism, Jenson judges Barth's assessment of Thomas's and Przywara's *analogia entis* mistaken.[31]

5.4 Critical engagements

I have argued that Jenson's doctrine of God is in functional agreement with much of the tradition on divine simplicity and can be formulated in a way that makes that agreement explicit. This reformulation helps to clarify how Jenson's emphasis on the unity of God plays out between the 'immanent' and 'economic' Trinity or between God's eternity and historical action. But homing in on divine simplicity in conversation with Jenson allows for more: it allows also for finding finer points for development and criticism. In this final section, I consider three ways that Jenson's doctrine of God might be developed and recast when explicitly engaged through the lens of divine simplicity. First, I consider perhaps the most contested topic in recent debates about divine simplicity, the multiplicity of divine attributes or names. My purpose here is not to resolve or even address the details of those debates but rather to consider how simplicity addresses the *practice* of naming God. Despite receiving relatively little explicit attention by Jenson, the practice of naming God in a self-critical way is of central importance to his overall program. Here I continue mostly by way of defence and clarification, arguing that more explicit retrieval of divine simplicity's way of handling divine names helps to develop Jenson's own theology in a fruitful direction. Second, I consider the Creator–creature relation by focusing on how Jenson roots this relation in divine embodiment, particular the incarnate body of the Son. This is my most critical section, where I argue that there are serious risks to this predication of embodiment, and that divine simplicity provides a way to achieve Jenson's desired ends without being vulnerable to those risks. Third, I return directly to divine simplicity and the Trinity. In this section I reconsider Jenson's use of the category of subsistent relations and evaluate his arguments for identifying the relations otherwise than as 'relations of origin' as well as his use of subsistent relations in his denial of the *logos asarkos*. Here again, I consider the risks of Jenson's arguments but claim that there are resources in Jenson's own theology that help to avoid those risks, resources that are most

---

[31] 'It must be noted that Barth did misunderstand both Thomas and Pryzwara in attributing to them the idea that the *analogia entis* locates the possibility of revelation in a relation established by creation prior to the grace enacted in Christ; here McCormack gives Barth too much credit' (*ST*, 1:225n4). For McCormack's account and assessment of the Barth–Pryzwara debate, see McCormack, *Barth's Critically Realistic Dialectical Theology*, 319–22, 383–91.

readily available when his theology is engaged through the doctrine of divine simplicity.

5.4.1 Divine simplicity and the names of God

Discussion surrounding theological predication has become one of the most philosophically contentious aspects of the doctrine of divine simplicity. For many theologians and philosophers of religion, this freighted issue is sufficient warrant to reject the doctrine altogether, if they have not already rejected it based on an assumed misfit with scripture.[32] Although Jenson does not give much dedicated space to the topic of divine names or attributes, his theology does rely on the use of specific names for God – particularly word, freedom, event, future, discourse, and love.[33] He does not give enough direct guidance concerning *how* this naming functions in respect of God, particularly in terms of specifying what kind of metaphysical relationship between God and creation makes such naming possible. And this lack is perhaps partly responsible for the mixed responses to Jenson's doctrine of God. For we might want to ask: if we can use words that connect God so closely with categories of created being – especially event and future – then what prevents the use of such names from blurring the distinction between Creator and creature, either rendering God purely immanent or drawing creatures completely into the divine identity? I offer here some brief reflections on what kind of naming and predication Jenson deploys in his theology, showing where his approach contains ambiguities, particularly through dialogue with the critique of Francesca Aran Murphy. Because the distinction between Creator and creature is central to how we name things of God, I argue that Jenson, similarly to Aquinas, inverts the relation contemporary debates often presume with respect to the divine names. But I believe the ultimate ability for Jenson (and a theology sympathetic with Jenson) to use multiple names while maintaining a doctrine of divine simplicity turns on how one articulates the Creator–creature relation (which is the theme of the next section).

---

32 The classics in this respect are: Martin, 'God, the Null Set and Divine Simplicity'; Morris, 'God and Mann'; Morris, *Our Idea of God*, 113–18; and Plantinga, *Does God Have a Nature?*. Quentin Smith claims that Aquinas' doctrine is 'plainly self-contradictory' and shows a prejudice for 'faith over intellectual coherence' ('Analysis of Holiness', 524n3). See also, more recently, Kraal, 'Logic and Simplicity'.
33 He has no dedicated section on the topic in his *ST*, though there is a brief list of what 'kind of being' God has in *ST*, 1:221–23. Otherwise, see 'Triune God', 181–92, and 'Holy Spirit', 173–78.

What seems most distinctive about the choice of names that Jenson deploys most frequently is their existential, political, and eschatological valence. Jenson uses names that evoke a particular kind of self-involvement for those who might worship God with those names, a self-involvement that draws one in particular ways into the drama of the trinitarian economy as also transformative of our own existential, political, and historical reality. This distinctiveness with respect to the selection of names, however, says nothing on its own about how the names relate speakers or worshipers to God. Jenson hints at this in one of his last essays: 'there are the places in John's gospel where the mutual verbal glorification of the Father and the Son opens to the disciples, to encompass *their* glorification and indeed that of those whom their addresses will bring into the same fellowship.'[34] This kind of relationship between God and the worshiper or contemplative has also been a central component in how the doctrine of divine simplicity negotiates the multiplicity of divine names or attributes, so that reflection on *how* God is named is important for upholding both God's unique mode of bearing that which is named and the conviction that creatures have as their end some kind of share or participation in that divine perfection. So, although Jenson only hints occasionally at agreement with analogical predication, his practice seems to require some kind of participatory relationship between creatures and God, along the lines of what analogy expresses in a linguistic mode.

However, Jenson's use of names, as I noted, leaves slightly unclear how God's names, especially those that have a direct temporal reference, are similar to their creaturely counterparts and yet still name God *as transcendent*. Several criticisms raised against Jenson's theology could be expressed in terms of this dilemma. For instance, Francesca Aran Murphy's charge of 'cinematic modalism' claims that Jenson's narrative identification or naming of God fails to transcend creaturely immanence, inadvertently entailing that God is something like an eternal movie reel that simply 'appears' or 'is projected' in history's timeline.[35] She is concerned with how Barth's privileging of Christ as God's self-description gets picked up by Jenson and ends up being 'strategically manipulated to entail that our knowledge of Christ in history controls Christ's historical acts'.[36] Consequently, Murphy finds a reason for Jenson's preference (following Barth) for naming God as 'event' over 'act': 'The metaphysical word "act" has no temporal markers; the term "event" does'.[37] This strategy is also taken as accounting for

---

34 'Choose Ye This Day', 18–19.
35 Murphy, *God is Not a Story*, 265–71.
36 *God is Not a Story*, 238.
37 *God is Not a Story*, 249.

Jenson giving the Trinity musical names like 'fugue': 'For Jenson, God moves with time, like music does. God fashions *time* as Father, Son, and Spirit: the "stuff" out of which Jenson's Trinity construct themselves is time.'[38] For Jenson, then, it seems that how we name and know God becomes so constrained by the historically concrete content of God's decision that God's eternal being becomes a hidden but purely transitive decider (or, better, *narrator*) *behind* the time and events as which this decision is performed. From Murphy's perspective, Jenson fails to name God according to God's transcendence, thereby leaving, contrary to his intentions, the specter of a hidden deity who is actually unnamable and unknowable but who controls time and history so as to construct the temporal 'triune' identities according to which we know God.[39] In this way, Murphy argues that for Jenson, the triune persons are like polytheistic gods, and 'story' takes on a higher role – like that of 'Fate' in Homeric polytheism – acting through the multiple gods in the drama of history. This shows that the question of divine names is not just an issue of how we predicate things of the divine essence but is integral to the doctrines of the Trinity and of transcendence.

There are several issues at play in Murphy's criticism (not to mention a rhetorically enjoyable and engaging presentation), but at the center seems to be a concern that Jenson's mode of naming God has become so constrained by the narrative means by which we *apprehend* God that God's own trinitarian reality hardly transcends the content of our knowledge.[40] Such a worry might find further fuel in Jenson's writing on our knowledge and speech about God in his 1969 *The Knowledge of Things Hoped For*, where he follows the contemporary demands of analytic philosophy that one supply conditions of verifiability and testability for truth claims. Toward this end, identity descriptions specify about whom one is making a truth claim, and historical and narrative-temporal confirmations at minimum render the truth of the claim *plausible*.[41] But Jenson's de-

---

38 *God is Not a Story*, 258.
39 Murphy is in sympathy with Hunsinger's review, which she cites approvingly, but her way of characterizing Jenson's errors more easily shows how this issue is relevant to divine naming, whereas Hunsinger's review is concerned more explicitly with ontological aseity and priority of the Trinity (Hunsinger, 'Review', 161–200). Further, Hunsinger charges Jenson with tritheism, whereas Murphy cries modalism (*God is Not a Story*, 261–62).
40 I have some sympathy with Murphy's point, and have expressed a related concern in my essay, 'Jesus, Trinity, and Creation', 250–51. Where we differ is that I see this issue as an unresolved tension within his account rather than as determinative for the whole of his theology.
41 Jenson does insist, contra Pannenberg, that historical investigation can only render an event like Jesus' resurrection *plausible*, which is not sufficient for the kind of knowledge the Christian claims in proclaiming Christ's resurrection (*KTHF*, 227–33). This does seem to signal a distance between divine knowledge and historical verifiability in Jenson's thinking.

mand for historical reference is not simply a concession to the epistemological demands of philosophy, for it is also related to his concern to avoid Feuerbachian projection. One of the ways, Jenson seems to be saying, that our God-talk avoids being a projection of our own anthropological ideals is by having a historical reference point that norms our speech. Jenson desires, then, that our language about God be in some manner *realist*, i.e., claiming truth in a way that is somehow demonstrable and is self-critical (not reducible to ideological projection). But does Jenson conflate this historical reference and epistemological rule with an ontological claim about how God's being is historically actualized? Can an account of God's triune simplicity pursue dramatic theology along with Jenson without falling into the kind of cinematic modalism that Murphy detects? To fully respond to these questions would require describing Jenson's theology all over again, because they pertain not just to a few worrisome sentences in Jenson's corpus but more fundamentally to how one construes his entire project.

The previous two chapters contrast enough with Murphy's treatment of Jenson to suggest some ways one might respond in Jenson's defence. But more specifically, it is clear that what is at stake here is how God, in God's triune life, is related to creaturely events while remaining transcendent, which further presses the question of what God's 'transcendence' *means*. No doubt, in Jenson's mind, the meaning of 'transcendence' is in need of specification and perhaps revision, for when Christians speak of God's transcendence we somehow also make a claim about the historical person of Jesus. Reflecting on this confluence of divine transcendence and created time is a major part – if not the center – of his theological metaphysics.[42] In the next section, I consider a potential problem for Jenson's construal of the God–world relationship, and so his general account of transcendence. Here, however, a reminder of one central aspect of Jenson's revisionary metaphysics may resolve some of the ambiguity surrounding his understanding of theological language and divine names. I have in mind here the role Jenson gives to 'word'. As I have argued, Jenson picks up Heidegger's construal of the positive determination of being according to its self-determination into the horizon of the future, but he revises this notion through giving primacy to 'word' and language. Because Jenson is working, therefore, with an ontology of word, the key for our speaking of God, and the names we have for God, is the fact

---

[42] Consider: '*How* does God transcend time's contingencies? With the proposition at last in place that the sufferer of the Gospels is, without qualification or evasion, the second identity of God, we are free to say ... the Father and the Spirit take the suffering of the creature who the Son is into the triune life and bring from it the final good of that creature, all other creatures, and of God. So and not otherwise the triune God transcends suffering' (*ST*, 1:144).

that God can be communicated to persons by proclamation, by words of promise.⁴³ Creatures are, more fundamentally than anything else, *words*.⁴⁴ Creatures speak, move, and have their being as diverse expressions of the creative utterance of God, an utterance which itself happens as the triune persons open up the dialogue as which they live for the participation of that which is not God.⁴⁵ Interpreting creatures *as words* is partly dependent on the gospel revelation that in using words to proclaim the Word's triumph over death, this very Word is given for the perfection of the creatures to whom the proclamation is addressed. Proclamation uses words to speak the Word for the perfection of the words that creatures are.⁴⁶

Jenson's principal concern, then, in reflecting on the nature of theological speech is much less constrained to the truth-function of ordinary language and the consequent need for verification-protocols than his extended dialogues with analytic philosophy might at first suggest. Rather, his concern is to think about what it means to proclaim Christ *in words*. In this light, his explicit development of a word ontology might be seen as the outworking of this orienting concern. As I argued in the previous chapter, it could also be said that Jenson develops a creative extension of the doctrine of simplicity in this light: because Jesus is, in his intratrinitarian personhood, simple – bearing the identity of doer and deed and being beyond the distinction between givenness and newness – Jesus is actively present and gives himself in Spirit-enabled acts of proclamation. In such acts of proclamation, the Spirit gives by participation what Christ simply is; and human words and lives can thereby become word-events of gospel, promises that open up the future to be the event of Jesus' unhindered love. In this context, Jenson's future orientation does some important theological work in the grammar of participation. As Jenson says, even the most intense moments of achieved union and participation in God – like Eucharist and Christ's resurrected body – are still tastes of the future; that is, they are still eschatological irruptions

---

43 *KTHF*, 235–36.
44 So Jenson can say of the human creature: 'Humans are those creatures who not only exist by words that state God's moral will, but are given to hear and reply to those words' (*ST*, 2:16). He then glosses the 'word' status of creatures musically: 'To be a creature in specific relation to the Father is to be a motif in the orchestration that occurs when God's musicality opens *ad extra*. We might say: the Father hums a music "of the spheres," the tune of the creating triune conversation, and precisely so and not otherwise there are the "spheres." Nor is it merely that there are creatures who are then harmonious with each other; to be a creature *is* to belong to the counterpoint and harmony of the triune music' (2:39).
45 *ST*, 2:6–9, 33–35, 367–69; 1:234–36.
46 See above, chapter four section ii.c, for a fuller account of this interpretation of proclamation.

that are genuine participations precisely by not foreclosing a continued movement toward the future anticipated therein.[47] Existing as creaturely words of God, we enact lives that are word-events of the gospel insofar as we participate in the Word of God, the concrete life and relations enabled in the historical life, death, and resurrection of Jesus. Consequently, our participation – receiving by gift what God is by identity – shares as well the event structure of its archetype by *being toward resurrection* as both an achieved event in our past in the person of Jesus and an anticipated event in our future.

In the last four decades, debates about ide simplicity often centered around a perceived problem concerning theological predication, one that is slightly different from what I have discussed so far in Jenson. Objections often go something like this: if all properties or perfections in God are the same, so that saying that God is 'love' and that God is 'jealous' is to refer to the same reality in God without real distinction, does this not render each utterance meaningless, thereby evacuating such locutions of their content and usefulness for praising God?[48] This objection raises several complex questions about the nature of predication in respect of God which are beyond the scope of this present discussion.[49] For present purposes, however, this formulation of the objection helpfully draws attention to doxology as the primary location of attributing to God specific names or perfections, which directs the question of the multiplicity of divine names in a more explicitly soteriological and christological direction.[50] After the discussion of Jenson's location of theological predication within proclamation in the preceding paragraph, it appears that we could actually invert the question as it is posed in recent debates. Rather than asking how our words succeed in predicat-

---

[47] Consider *ST*, 2:296–99.
[48] Ryan Mullins has partly framed his concerns with simplicity in terms of the problems simplicity seems to create for ordinary speech in praise of God, see his 'Simply Impossible', 200; and 'Analytic Response to Holmes'.
[49] I personally think that the Thomistic distinction between *res sigificata* and *modus significandi* for theological predication goes a long way toward resolving the perceived problems. For discussion, see Rocca, *Speaking the Incomprehensible God*. Consider also Rolnick, 'Realist Reference'. Teske's comments in interpretation of Augustine are also helpful ('Predicaments in *Trin.* 5', 93–111). David Bennett, without appealing explicitly or exclusively to an Augustinian or Thomistic framework, considers a similar possibility by distinguishing 'states' and 'episodes' from 'properties', so that we might be able to say that in God the *state* of wisdom and/or mercy are identical to God and hence to one another without identifying God (or God's wisdom, mercy, etc) with a property; 'Divine Simplicity', 636–37.
[50] Consider Pannenberg, 'Analogy and Doxology', 212–38. For reflections on how divine simplicity helps to read scripture's own doxological use of divine names, see Barrett, *Divine Simplicity*, 147–50.

ing of God, we might instead wonder how our words participate in God's work of turning persons into meaningful signs of God.[51]

If we think in terms of this inversion, one can see commonality between Jenson and Aquinas.[52] In this doxological and proclamatory context, as Aquinas notes, the issue is first about our reception by participation of what God alone fully is and thereby gives us through salvation. This certainly involves a judgment about 'what God is', but not in abstraction from how 'what God is' is received in creatures. Commenting on John 10:35, 'those to whom the word of God came were called "gods"' (NRSV), Aquinas writes:

> It is clear that a person by participating in the word of God becomes god by participation. But a thing does not become this or that by participation unless it participates in what is this or that by its essence: for example, a thing does not become fire by participation unless it participates in what is fire by its essence. Therefore, one does not become god by participation unless he participates in what is God by essence. Therefore, the Word of God, that is the Son, by participation in whom we become gods, is God by essence.[53]

So we come to name the Son divine because through the Word we come to partake of the divine nature (2 Peter 1:4), and we could only receive divinity from the Son if the Son is divine by nature. We might then conclude that one of the critical functions of divine simplicity is to alert us to the way that our judgments concerning God themselves occur within our relationship of participation in God. In that way, when we affirm the simple identity of all divine names in God's being, we are reflecting on the process of becoming what we receive through God's generous gift as only perfected through union with God, though genuinely received through participation now. Divine simplicity helps to prevent such

---

[51] I do not pretend that this move settles the complicated debates about predication and divine simplicity. However, I do believe that the self-involving character of language for God that appears in this 'inversion' may alter how a theologian would enter into those debates and/or what theological lessons would be drawn from them.

[52] Gregory of Nyssa is also in agreement, speaking of the Christian as one who shares in Christ name and therefore receives all Christ's perfections (cf. 'On Perfection', 112–22). For a similar 'inversion' of the question of divine unity, see Williams, 'Unity of Christian Truth', 16–28; 'the unity of Christian truth is perceivable to the extent that we can perceive a unity in Christian holiness, the unity anchored in ... the enfleshment of God's eternal act of complete response to the complete self-gift we call "God the Father"' (26).

[53] *In Ioann*, 10.35, 1460 (vol. 2:215). Basil uses the same argument against Eunomius to affirm the divinity of the Holy Spirit (*Against Eunomius*, III.5). This is similar to Dionysius, for whom the divine names, like 'being', 'life', 'light', or 'logos', are properly named of God, who is 'the transcendent hiddenness', insofar as they are 'in fact nothing other than certain activities apparent to us, activities which deify, cause being, bear life, and give wisdom' (*DN*, II.7, 645 A).

praise of God from becoming ideological projection by reminding us that we as creatures have what is only proper to God in a mode befitting our particular finite nature.[54] What we then name of God by virtue of our participation pertains to God's being in an ever greater dissimilarity (*maior dissimilitudo*), transcending the mode by which we share in it.[55] That we cannot entirely demonstrate how God's simple unity includes in perfect identity what creatures receive variously and diversely does not threaten the critical judgment that whatever we have is in a radically different mode than the way God might have it.

Finally, I want to reflect briefly on how this 'inversion' might bring the benefit of thinking about the Son's simplicity in the incarnation. Jenson makes a move like this to the extent that he insists on Jesus' perfect presence in our acts of proclamation, which is based on the judgment that *qua* divine the Word is not constituted of given language and particular utterance but is the perfect identity of language and utterance – i. e., is simple.[56] Hans Urs von Balthasar develops a grammar of the divine difference in a similar manner by speaking of the identity of person and mission in Christ, expressed in part as the identity of being-for-others and being-for-self.[57] In Christ's trinitarian personhood, he is always being-for-others (*Für-andere-Sein*) in harmonious unity with being-for-self (*Für-sich-Sein*).[58] Consequently, we can participate in the Son and thereby become more fully ourselves while being simultaneously drawn into a new form of social relations constituted by being-for-the-other. We are thereby enabled to enact and perform the Son's *self-giving glory* as also our own flourishing and the redemption of the social relations in which we live.[59] Simplicity and compositeness distinguish creatures from God while also helping to express the union Christ achieves between God and humanity. Our compositeness, then, distinguishes us from God (and so also from the divine personhood of

---

[54] '*Receptum est in recipiente per modum recipientis*' (Aquinas, *STh*, I.84.1).
[55] '*inter creatorem et creaturam non potest similitudo notari, quin inter eos maior sit dissimilitudo notanda*' (*DS*, §806).
[56] Gregory of Nyssa expresses something like this in the context of the Eucharist: 'His "flesh is food indeed" and His "blood is drink indeed." But, in connection with the thought just mentioned, there is participation in such nourishment for all, since the Logos who becomes food and drink is received and assimilated without distinction by those seeking Him' ('On Perfection', 108). This directly follows Gregory's reflections on the simplicity of God and the divinity of Christ as God's power and wisdom.
[57] von Balthasar, *Theo-Drama*, 3:149–259, 271–82. German: *Theodramatik*, 2.2:136–238, 249–59.
[58] *Theo-Drama*, 3:273, 204, respectively. *Theodramatik*, 2.2:251, 187.
[59] For suggestive reflections on Christ's self-giving in light of racialized bodies, see Copeland, *Enfleshing Freedom*, 65, 81, 107–9.

Christ) but is in no way our 'imperfection' in the ordinary sense of that word.[60] Rather, our compositeness, through union with Christ, is a condition of existing through the reception of Jesus' generosity and ourselves coming to share in Jesus' mission of love. We exist in the unity of the two poles – being-for-self and being-for-others – that are identical in Jesus.[61] By participation in Jesus, these poles can become truly united rather than in competition, so that being for others does not lead to the loss of self, and vice-versa.[62] So, here as well, speaking of 'being-for-self' and 'being-for-others' in respect of Jesus' divine person allows us to name what is identical in God's divine nature while also reflecting on the kind of life human persons receive through participation in Christ the Son, thereby becoming 'words' who communicate the Word and liberty of God.

5.4.2 Divine simplicity and the question of God's availability

While Jenson shares with previous theologians a form of divine simplicity as an expression of Burrell's 'distinction', it is nonetheless true that Jenson pursues the clarification of divine difference in an original and unique way, particularly in the way he centers his entire theological account on christology.[63] This choice represents both a continuity and discontinuity with the other theologians I have discussed. The continuity lies in the fact that the church's thinking about God has been indelibly shaped from the beginning by a sense of Jesus' unsubstitutable place in God's action and identity.[64] Jenson's particular focus on chris-

---

60 Though in a technical, metaphysical sense we might say that composition is a sign of our 'imperfection' insofar as human persons have not completely attained their *telos*. Cf. Tanner, *Christ the Key*, 38–40.
61 Cf. also von Balthasar, *Prayer*, 247.
62 Reflecting on Gal. 2:19–20, Balthasar says, 'Here, quite tangibly, we sense that while Christ, in laying hold of Paul's existence, has left him intact as a conscious subject, he has also *expropriated* him in order to *personalize* him … For Paul, this means that he must respond to Christ's personal love by surrendering to him in faith and by devoting himself to his apostolic mission. Thus *en* becomes *syn*, a participation in Christ's dying and rising and in his work (*synergoi*)' (*Theo-Drama*, 3:247).
63 A choice that is manifest in one of the last essays he wrote for publication: 'Choose Ye This Day', 14–19.
64 Three recent studies are important in substantiating this claim. Matthew Bates' study, *Birth of the Trinity*, argues that prosopological exegesis – namely, a practice of reading prophetic speech as often entailing that the prophet speaks in a divine persona not reducible to their own that has a different theodramatic context than the prophet's and signals an intradivine conversation, interpretable as taking place between Father and Son – is demonstrably present in the writers of the New Testament and even in some of the most uncontested claims of Jesus himself.

tology is distinct in that he self-consciously radicalizes certain identity claims in christology. This came up in chapter four, specifically concerning how Jenson uses the Son's embodiment to specify how God loves and knows, both of which, he argues, require the kind of objectivity and availability that embodiment provides. Jenson explicitly appeals to the *communicatio idiomatum* in this respect, arguing for the most extreme form of *communicatio*, known as the '*genus tapeinoticum*', according to which predicates made of Christ according to his human nature are communicated also to the divine nature.[65] In doing so, Jenson uses a radical identity claim to ground the specification of divine difference by arguing that God is the unique subject who transcends creaturely time by virtue of the particular life God lives *within* time. Because Jenson predicates the events of Jesus' life, like birth, death, and resurrection, to God not only according to the person of the Son in the latter's union with human nature but also according to the divine nature itself, God's difference is expressed by the particular way that God acts within historical events. For Jenson, 'the distinction', then, expresses the mode of God's freedom, 'the God identified by his establishment of such an order [as the founding of Israel] can be understood as so free as to be free even from his own past acts, to be God precisely by his freedom to initiate radical change, rather than by his ability to resist and protect from it'.[66] To interpret Jenson adequately here requires that we recall his other affirmations of the unity of 'givenness' and 'utterance' in God, so that the polemic in this quotation does not give the impression of a God who is shorn of integrity with what is 'past'. Nonetheless, the mode of transcendence Jenson is articulat-

---

Consequently, on Bates' reading, the church exhibits a pattern of reading that from the beginning displays a commitment to the Son's and Spirit's co-eternality and co-divinity with the Father. Wesley Hill's, *Paul and the Trinity*, also argues for an early sense of the relations between Father, Son, and Spirit as constitutive of the divine identity, though his study proceeds by careful attention to the Pauline corpus. Most recently, and with a different focus, Rowan Williams has argued that rigorous and uncompromising reflection on the union of divine and human in the person of Jesus has been the centre of the church's thinking about the non-competitive difference between God and creation; *Christ the Heart of Creation*.

65 Jenson, 'Christ in the Trinity'. Jenson notes that Lutheran scholastics rejected the *genus tapeinoticum*, but believes that Luther did not (66). Though Jenson does not explicitly name allegiance with this fourth and most extreme form of *communicatio*, the force of the argument of the essay suggests that this is Luther's position and that Jenson sides with Luther (and therefore, by implication, with the *genus tapeinoticum*). Consider: 'It is to the Son that the Father, by an ancient theologoumenon, looks to know himself. ... *what* does the Father hear – or see – when he attends to the Son? And the answer must be: the narrative of Jesus-in-Israel' (68). See Stephen Holmes' response in 'Radicalising the *Comunicatio*'.

66 *S&P*, 23–24.

ing contrasts with more traditional accounts of divine simplicity, insofar as transcendence *happens* vis-à-vis a particular history.

Specific aspects of Jenson's historical- and narrative-oriented construal of divine identity present difficulties and are hotly debated. In particular, Jenson's claims about the implications of Jesus' embodiment for divine ontology pose interpretive difficulties. I noted some of these in the previous chapter, where I discussed how Jenson speaks of God's embodiment in the context of God's self-knowledge. For Jenson, the Son's embodiment resolves problems concerning theological knowledge and predication. Jenson worries that traditional forms of simplicity and analogical predication, especially as he finds them in Aquinas, risk agnosticism. With this criticism, Jenson means that analogy alone does not sufficiently specify the content of our theological statements, which means in turn that such statements are ultimately lacking in meaning that can be verified against historical facts.[67] According to Jenson, analogy tells us *that* there is something that is somehow similar to created realities, but we know not how, and therefore we do not finally know anything determinate about God through analogy. If all our language and knowledge is rendered utterly empty by such agnosticism, then Christians have no adequate response to the nihilistic charge of anthropomorphic projection in our religious talk. Jenson resolves this dilemma by situating our knowledge of God within God's own self-knowledge – a *theologoumenon* with long-standing precedent. But this is a self-knowledge that is determinate because it is the knowledge God has of the Son in his corporeality.[68] Knowledge of persons requires that the object of knowledge is available bodily to the knower, and according to Jenson this is no less true in the case of God's knowledge than it is in ours. Can such quasi-bodily availability obtain for persons identified as *subsistent relations?* Jenson himself suggests it cannot when he identifies God's bodily availability with the body of Jesus, who *qua* human has a body by virtue of being an 'individual instance of humanity as such' and so, presumably, not by virtue of being a subsistent relation.[69] But if God's eternal self-knowledge is actual knowledge only by virtue of the temporal embodiment of Jesus, then is it not the case that Jesus' *humanity as such* becomes constitutive of the eternal filial relation that is the divine Son? This risks undoing the logic of subsistent relations altogether by positing a term

---

[67] Cf. *KTHF*, 85–88, 91–94; and *GaG*, 84–85.
[68] *ST*, 1:228–30. This move distances Jenson further from standard contemporary apophatic theologies. Steve Wright offers a nuanced and careful exploration of Jenson's relation to apophatic theology ('Precise Mystery', 9–28), though he does not attend to Jenson's determination of divine self-knowledge according to the Son's embodiment.
[69] Jenson, 'Once More', 124.

(Jesus' human nature) as constitutive of a relation that Jenson elsewhere defines precisely as subsisting without constitutive terms, as we have seen. And it risks confusing the divine and human natures, insofar as the divine nature would be constituted in part by the active knowledge of subsisting as a human creature.

I will develop more specific proposals concerning subsistent relations in the next section; here my concern lies more directly with the predication of embodiment to God as a necessary corollary of God's self-knowledge and self-love. There are two related issues here: Jenson's approval of the *genus tapeinoticum* and the meaning and entailments of divine embodiment. What Jenson seems concerned to express here – the complete epistemic and affective availability of God to God's own self and to creatures – is, I argue, in fact better conveyed by a more fully worked out doctrine of divine simplicity than the posit of divine embodiment. But first, what of the *genus tapeinoticum*, or the predication of attributes from the human nature of Christ to the divine nature? This is difficult to analyze fully in Jenson's thought, because he does not fully explain *how* the communication of human predicates to the divine nature would work. However, it seems to me that there are two risks, both contrary to Jenson's own explicit christological convictions. The *genus tapeinoticum* either compromises the unity of the divine nature (to the extent that the Son would come to possess properties in the divine nature by virtue of the incarnation that the other divine persons would not have) or it dissolves the difference between the human and divine natures by claiming that anything that is predicated of Jesus as a personal subject (viz., as the hypostasis of the Son) is thereby predicated both humanly and divinely. Neither comports with the Nicene Creed or Chalcedon's definition. If, per the first result, the Son's divine nature is determined by properties of the human nature, then the Son's divine nature would be distinguished from that of the Father and the Spirit, and, consequently, they could not be said to be 'of one nature' (*homoousion*). And if the Son's divine nature is no longer identified by unity with the Father and Spirit, then it becomes difficult to see how Jesus actually is one with the divine nature at all, rather than some semi-divine intermediary.[70] If, per the second alternative, the difference between the natures is dissolved (as would seem to follow if each bears all the properties of the other),

---

[70] Note that the same problems do not have to obtain when the *communicatio* works the other direction, if properties of the divine nature are communicated to the human nature (the *genus maiestaticum*). This is partly because 'human nature' as a species or communal concept is not a single concrete 'individual' in the way that the Trinity simply *is* a single, undivided, concrete nature. The early Lutheran scholastic, Martin Chemnitz argued a similar point, drawing on John of Damascus (Chemnitz, *Two Natures*, 30 – 31). For further discussion of the Lutheran scholastics on this issue, see Holmes, 'Asymmetrical Assumption', esp. 365 – 71.

then we no longer have grounds to claim that in the person of the Son *two* natures achieve union; there would rather be simply one unique nature that combined the properties of divine and human natures. This would no longer uphold two natures united 'without confusion' (ἀσυγχύτως). Neither of these alternatives cohere with Jenson's other explicit christological convictions, insofar as he follows the Cyrillian priority of the union in one person of the two natures. While Jenson's doctrine of Christ's two natures is expressed in a revisionary mode, he clearly intends to uphold two asymmetrically related natures (as discussed in the last chapter).[71] Nonetheless, it is difficult to see how the affirmation of two natures fully united in one subject can be sustained alongside the *genus tapeinoticum*.[72] That Jenson affirms these divergent claims suggests that there is a metaphysical tension in his christology.

Having registered my reservations about Jenson's sympathies with the *genus tapeinoticum*, I now turn to his argument for the necessary embodiment of the Son, which is central to his construal of the God–world relation. I have already noted the ambiguity of Jenson's attribution of embodiment to the Son, which makes evaluation rather difficult. It also creates difficulties in Jenson's discussion of the Christ–church relation, when he strongly connects the Son's embodiment with the church and distinguishes the Son's subjectivity from his objective externality, identifying the latter with the church: 'The relation between Christ as a subject and the church with her sacraments is precisely that between transcendental subjectivity and the objective self.'[73] But if embodiment is in some sense necessary for God's own self-knowledge and self-love, and if the church is *literally* the body of Christ, then it seems to follow that the church is somehow constitutive of the triune identity.[74] It would be better, I think, to simply avoid positing embodiment as the condition of the possibility of God's self-knowledge and self-love. But in order to think *with* Jenson about God's intratrinitarian self-availability and availability to creatures – principally in and as the church – it is necessary to clarify what Jenson's language of embodiment is *doing*, after which an alternative conceptuality might be offered.

Jenson's insistence on divine embodiment is not necessarily a commitment to organic, material corporeality in God. This is clear when he makes appeal to Paul for his understanding of a body:

---

[71] 'Christ's identification as one of the Trinity and his identification as one of us are not ontologically symmetrical' (*ST*, 1:138).
[72] See Holmes, 'Asymmetrical Assumption', 365–73.
[73] Jenson, *ST*, 2:215.
[74] Which also blurs the distinction between Christ and church; cf. McFarland, 'Body of Christ', 232–37.

> It seems that for Paul [citing 1 Cor. 15:35–50] my body need not always be of the organic sort I now see when I look at myself, that a 'spiritual' resurrection-body which is precisely not an organic body can nevertheless be my body, and indeed somehow the same body as the organic body that died.[75]

This tension between the organic and the spiritual seems to be Jenson's warrant for his minimalist definition of 'body'; whatever a body is, a Christian understanding must be compatible both with present organic embodiment and the unknown mode of embodiment accompanying resurrection life. And in this light, 'availability to oneself and others' is a necessary condition of embodiment that applies in both contexts. Further, Jenson identifies Jesus' sacramental, bodily presence to the church as that which constitutes the boundary between earth and heaven, specifically as heaven's presence in and availability to earth:

> sacramental events make the boundary between our world and heaven, marking it by the 'visible' objects they involve. Just so they are the embodied presence to our world of what is in heaven; in the present context, they are the embodied presence of the risen Jesus and the Kingdom he presents to the Father in the Spirit, as these are anticipated for the Father by the Spirit.[76]

In his appeal to embodiment here, Jenson is emphasizing the unity of God's self-disclosure with the sacramental means of God's presence. The sacramental language seems to provide Jenson with further warrant to continue using the language of body for the mode of personal availability that applies between humans, resurrected persons, and the Son. Jenson's concern, then, is to ensure that there is sufficient objectivity to a person's existence so that they are genuinely available to others and to themselves in ways that are continuous for pre- and post-resurrection persons, as well as for God's sacramental and incarnate presence. 'Body' is his chosen expression to speak of this kind of objectivity.

Despite Jenson's eschatological and sacramental warrants, I think there are risks to the use of the word 'body' to express such objective availability, risks that bear controversial effects in Jenson's understanding of the church as the body of Christ, as I noted above. But I am sympathetic to his emphasis on personal availability, for it is impossible to imagine a personal and mutual relationship in which either party was not somehow available to the other; availability is, it seems, a necessary condition of personal relationship. What is needed is either a more robust articulation of the various senses of 'body' as Jenson uses the word – ordinary human embodiment, resurrection embodiment, sacramental

---

75 Jenson, 'Reading the Body', 75.
76 *ST*, 2:251.

embodiment, intratrinitarian embodiment – or an alternative way to express the conditions of God's personal availability. While it does seem to me that Jenson is operating with some analogical stretching of the term 'body', I think the risks of conflating the different senses or of emptying the word 'body' of meaning are too high. Consequently, I prefer to find an alternative means of articulating God's personal availability, and here I think the doctrine of divine simplicity provides a more promising way forward.

In particular, a strong distinction between interiority and exteriority itself, which seems essential to Jenson's arguments for necessary divine embodiment, is called into question from the perspective of divine simplicity. The convergence of interiority and exteriority in God is variously depicted by theologians who advocate divine simplicity, like Katherine Sonderegger in her discussion of the identity of subject and object in God, Pseudo-Dionysius the Aereopagite on the inexhaustibility of God's ecstatic love, and Nicholas of Cusa on God as 'other' and 'not other' (*non aliud*).[77] This raises a question: could the doctrine of divine simplicity itself provide the resolution to the difficulties of Jenson's assumptions about the need for bodily availability within God's own self? In each of these accounts of divine simplicity, God's availability to God's own self and to creatures is expressed as an aspect of God's intrinsic unity and perfection, rather than a fact about God's being in addition to God's internal subjectivity.

I start with Dionysius, who improvises on the Neoplatonic articulation of divine simplicity in light of the Christian conception of God as ecstatic love. After reflecting on various Old and New Testament discussions of *eros*-love for God (notably Prov. 4:6, 8; 2 Sam. 1:26; 1 Jn. 4:16), Dionysius turns to the ecstatic character of divine love itself.[78] He launches from Paul's self-description of his state in Christ, where he claims to be no longer alive except as Christ lives *in him* (Gal. 2:20) and to be *ecstatic, outside himself* for God (2 Cor. 5:13; ἐξέστημεν) – in other words, Paul 'possess[es] not his own life but the life of the One for whom he yearned'.[79] Because Paul's own ecstatic love comes from the life of Christ in him, Dionysius proceeds to link Paul's ecstatic love with the creative, outgoing love of God:

> in truth, it must be said too that the very cause of the universe in the beautiful, good superabundance of his benign yearning for all is also carried outside of himself in the loving care he has for everything. He is, as it were, beguiled by goodness, by love, and by yearning and

---

77 Respectively: Sonderegger, *Systematic Theology 1*, 210–23; Dionysius the Areopagite, *DN*, IV.13, 712AB; and Nicholas of Cusa, *God as Not-Other*.
78 *DN*, IV.10–13, 708 A–712 A.
79 *DN*, IV.13, 712 A.

is enticed away from his transcendent dwelling place and comes to abide within all things, and he does so by virtue of his supernatural and ecstatic capacity to remain, nevertheless, within himself.[80]

Dionysius here discerns a unique character of God's generous presence to creation through considering how God's presence is itself an unconditioned act of pure, outgoing love. Expressed with a dramatic flourish, Dionysius talks of God as simultaneously completely 'outside of himself' in love, fully given away to creatures, and yet remaining entirely 'within himself'. In fact, there is a sense in which God's ecstatic dwelling within all things is *by virtue of* his 'capacity to remain, nevertheless, within himself'. Eric Perl expresses Dionysius so:

> God is pure exteriority, having no inner core of 'selfhood,' no 'interior' that could be distinguished from his 'outward' productive activity… But for precisely the same reason, because his 'self' is nothing but productive giving, it is equally true that God is pure interiority, absolutely unconditioned by any relation to beings that would be an accident or an affect additional to his inner self. In God as Love, therefore, pure interiority coincides with pure exteriority.[81]

God's act of creative self-donation is so radically unique that there is no distinction between an internal *doer* of the activity and the activity itself, and yet neither is God's being reducible to the immanent existential actuality of finite beings (*esse commune*, in later scholastic language). This entails that in God's activity of creation and redemption, God is perfectly 'available' without reserve, for God gives all that God is. This even connects with Jenson's early claim discussed above: 'The event that God is, is the event of his turning to us, the event of his love'.[82]

Though Dionysius is here speaking in a different mode than I have considered so far, his judgment relates directly to Thomas's denial of subject–essence and essence–existence composition in God.[83] If in God there is no subject distinct from the nature or essence or from the active power of *esse* by which God *is*, then there is further no basis for differentiating God's 'interiority' as isolated from God's 'exteriority'.[84] Yet, despite their identity in God, there are still

---

80 *DN*, IV.13, 712AB.
81 Perl, *Theophany*, 46.
82 S&P, 120.
83 *STh*, I.3.3–4.
84 Cf. Rosemann, *Omne agens agit sibi simile*, 279–305. Rosemann concludes, to my mind aptly, that because God is 'otherwise other' and is '*supra omnia* … precisely *insofar as* he is *in omnibus et intime*', one can say that 'Transcendence is the superlative mode of immanence' (295).

grounds to speak analogically of both exteriority and interiority, namely because we should neither deny that God's life is intrinsically replete (lacking 'interiority') nor claim that God's activity is a bestowal of some purely extrinsic and external reality (as if God were not 'exterior' in God's own being in creating or as if in creating God and creatures become coordinated within a larger, overarching shared domain), which would entail that God is contrastively related as one being alongside created beings. The unity of creation and redemption is that throughout both God gives *Godself* to creation – there is no other mediating reality by virtue of which God is 'exterior' or available to creatures. Simply *by acting creatively and redemptively*, God is 'exterior', overflowing for the good of creation. If we acknowledge that God can be meaningfully spoken of as 'exterior' in self-gift to creation, 'interior' as complete and abundant in God's eternal infinite life and bearing no subject–essence or essence–existence distinction, then it follows that God is pure exteriority and pure interiority in perfect identity.

The simplicity of God's availability to creatures is offered in a new way in the incarnation, by virtue of which God makes God available to us as a human being. Because God is simple and therefore enjoys the coincidence of interiority and exteriority, God is entirely 'exterior' in any mode by which God acts *ad extra*.[85] The paradigmatic instance of God's revelation is the incarnation, in which God performs the divine life in a human body.[86] 'For in him all the fullness of God was pleased to dwell' (Col. 1:19), in the one who is the 'true light, which enlightens everyone' (Jn. 1:9). In the incarnation, God gives the divine fullness to illuminate all; God is, out of love, 'ecstatic' and 'exterior' – completely given away.[87] And in this radical act of self-giving, God is not diminished or exhausted, for the act is a new mode of the very same presence and activity by which all creation receives existence.[88] Even while speaking of God being completely 'exterior', there is no movement *away from* God or *out of* God's eternal life when the

---

[85] Consider also Palamas, *Triads*, III.2.7: 'God subsist[s] entirely in each [divine energy] without any division at all; and ... each provide Him with a name and manifest Him entirely, thanks to indivisible and supernatural simplicity' (p. 96).

[86] With Irenaeus, we may want also to affirm that the Son is particularly apt for making God 'visible' in creation because, *qua* triune relation to the Father, the Son is eternally the 'visibility' of the Father (cf. *AH*, IV.6.6).

[87] M. Shawn Copeland has powerfully contemplated the ecstatic, 'erotic' love of Christ as the lens for critically remembering and confessing the horrendous treatment of black women in *Enfleshing Freedom*.

[88] McFarland, *From Nothing*, 102–6: 'God is *already* maximally "inside" the world: since God's sustaining presence is the one necessary and sufficient condition of every creature's existence at every moment of its existence, any degree of divine absence would result in the total and instantaneous dissolution of created being (see Ps. 104:29)' (102).

Son becomes incarnate, rather God draws creation into the divine life in a new way – a new movement *within creatures* that incorporates creation more fully into the continuous outgoing movement by which God initiates and sustains it.[89]

Though redemption is therefore in a certain respect not *ad extra* to God (as if there is anything 'outside' God), it is decidedly new in respect of creation.[90] For, through Christ's and the Spirit's economic work of redemption, our bodily humanity is brought into an intimacy with God that it does not have otherwise, so that in the sanctified body of Christ and his church God's perfect availability is tangibly displayed for our sake.[91] There is a difference in dramatic contexts: in the primary theodramatic context (i.e., redemption as an intra-divine activity) the work is effected between Father, Son, and Spirit in the plenitude of their eternal processions, while in the historical drama of redemption it is an undivided work '*ad extra*' by which creation joins in the movement of the divine processions (in their economic missions, to use the classical terminology). Ian McFarland expresses a similar idea by reference to Nicholas of Cusa: 'the fact that God, in God's transcendence, is ... "not other" than creatures means that *God can also be other than God without thereby ceasing to be God*'.[92] In the incarnation, God is 'other than God' as a body by which God is available to the created other. And in becoming 'other' than God – through uniting to creation without being creation's 'other' – God performs God's intradivine availability, which is the perfect coincidence of interiority and exteriority, as the extra-divine availability of bodily life.

Returning to Jenson's arguments for the embodiment of God as requisite for divine self-knowledge and self-love, these reflections on divine simplicity open up a different possibility – one that removes the question of embodiment from the context of God's *own* self-love and knowledge but can still affirm the Son's embodiment as of ontological and epistemological significance for *humanity's* love and knowledge of God. Where Jenson defines 'body' as availability to oneself and another, and Jesus' body (at least sacramentally) as the border between heaven and earth, could we now say that Jesus' bodily availability to creatures is the incarnate mode of God's inexhaustible exteriority, which offers *ad extra* what

---

89 Cf. McCabe, 'Aquinas on the Trinity'.
90 This is to nuance McCabe's statement that says it is inadequate 'to speak of God's redemptive act as an opus ad extra. It is precisely the act by which we cease to be extra to God and come within his own life' ('Aquinas on the Trinity', 53). Cf. also McFarland, *From Nothing*, 101n38. Also consider the compelling constructive proposals for 'new social relations' as the effect of grace in Davis, *Waiting and Being*.
91 For a developed argument along similar lines, see Kelsey, *Eccentric Existence*, 1:121–22, 2:607–24.
92 *From Nothing*, 106.

God simply is *ad intra*? While the identity of exteriority and interiority might sound like a contradiction (or at least a paradox) in this context, such a claim is appropriate to a being whose infinity is a positive entitative feature, which Jenson also affirms. Jenson himself develops infinity as God's unbounded fullness, which, epistemically speaking, is 'known in discovering that we do not catch up with him'.[93] In this case, God's availability to us is also God's inexhaustibility. Could this find its complement in the Dionysian claim that God's availability to God's own self is the perfect convergence of interiority and exteriority? That God is pure 'surface', and thus pure availability, yet without being constituted in this availability as by a limiting principle, so that God's availability is the same fact as God's interiority or inexhaustibility to anything not God?[94] In other words, could it be that in God the identity of exteriority and interiority plays out in respect of creation in such a way that, in Jenson's own words, 'God is hidden precisely by his offensive availability in our world'?[95]

In this way, God performs the difference between God and creatures as the condition of the possibility of creaturely goodness (viz., in creation) *and* as a christologically enacted difference, i.e., as the bodily availability of God to creation in Christ (in redemption). The above articulation follows Jenson in affirming that christology is central to our identification of God's distinctive reality. And yet this alternative formulation of divine availability develops more coherently the logic of divine simplicity and creation out of nothing, so that God is available to creatures in Jesus' body but not because such a union traverses any actual interval (*diastema*) between God and creation – which, as Gregory argued, would necessarily entail that God and creation were bounded and discrete entities and therefore that God is one being among many. Neither is God available in Jesus' body because for God self-knowledge and self-love require some principle of distinction or objectification like a body – which would entail that God's triune life as such were not sufficient for genuine love and knowledge. Rather, God is entirely available in Jesus' body because God's simplicity entails that in every ecstatic activity of God, God is the perfect coincidence of interiority

---

93 Jenson, 'Nyssa: *Moses*', 537.
94 In framing the identity of God's 'interiority' (and inexhaustibility) and exteriority (availability) in this way, my argument intersects with the Palamite distinction between essence and energies. Whether my argument might work with some articulations of that distinction would require further development and exploration, but it seems clear that my argument is incompatible with the extent to which Vladimir Lossky attempts to ground the distinction between apophasis and cataphasis in a real distinction within God's being between essence and energies (cf. Lossky, *Image and Likeness of God*, 53–55; Lossky, *Mystical Theology*, 80–90).
95 *ST*, 1:233.

and exteriority. We find then a convergence of themes from Gregory, Augustine, Aquinas, and Jenson, with the help of Dionysius, through which to articulate God's simplicity as the condition of the possibility of God's self-donation and availability to creatures for their perfection and redemption, with no need for Jenson's posit of the necessity of divine embodiment.

5.4.3 Divine simplicity and the relations of God

As I have insisted, to whatever extent we can reconstruct a doctrine of divine simplicity in Jenson's theology, it is a triune simplicity and a simple triunity. It is appropriate then, to culminate, as the apex of the doctrine of God, with a discussion of God's triunity, or of simplicity and relations. Insofar as simplicity is being deployed toward a Christian articulation of God, it must necessarily be construed for use in explicating the mystery of God's triunity. And in contemporary theology the onus is especially high for Christian theologians sympathetic to divine simplicity to express how simplicity functions in respect of the Trinity, in no small part because it may appear that the louder one speaks of simplicity, the softer one will necessarily speak of relations.[96] Throughout, by way of discussion of historical theologians and Jenson himself, I have tried to make the case that simplicity is in fact a powerful resource for articulating God's relationality, both *ad intra* and *ad extra*. For the doctrine of the Trinity, the operative category is 'subsistent relations'. Thomas Joseph White has recently given a helpful description of how simplicity and subsistent relations function for trinitarian theology:

> Relationality in this case is not a natural property of the persons but is 'subsistent'. Or we might say that the Father is eternally subsistent as one who is ever relational: *toward* the Son and Spirit. He does not choose to generate or spirate the persons of the Son and the Holy Spirit, but he is the personal act of generation and co-spiration. This is likewise true of the other persons of the Trinity in their inherent relationality. Due to the mystery of divine simplicity, then, we ought to speak about the trinitarian persons as 'subsistent relations', in order rightly to maintain a sense of their real personal distinctiveness and their authentic unity of being.[97]

For Thomas, developing on Augustine, as well as for Jenson, simplicity helps us to express God's relationality by identifying God's relations with God's very being and essence, so that in God relations subsist *as* the divine essence.

---

[96] As Veli-Matti Kärkkäinen put it to me in personal conversation. For similar concerns, see also Begbie, 'A Semblance More Lucid?', 29–31.
[97] White, 'Simplicity and Trinity', 71.

The concept of *subsistent relations* is integral in Jenson's trinitarian theology, and he appealed to it throughout his writings. Jenson, however, does raise a critical question concerning how the relations in God are identified that distinguishes his own use of the category from classical theologians like Gregory, Augustine, and Aquinas. In particular, Jenson critiques approaches that distinguish the three relations in God by relations of origin. This concern is shared with theologians of various stripes, which makes analyzing the import of the criticism of greater relevance than simply evaluating Jenson.[98] Linn Marie Tonstad, for instance, criticizes relations of origin for their seeming complicity in the projection of gendered and sexualized forms of difference into the divine life.[99] Though Jenson's concerns are not explicitly focused on projections of gendered relations, both of their criticisms pertain to how our conceptualization of the structure of intratrinitarian relations is reciprocally affected by political and social relations. For Tonstad, this reciprocity is framed primarily in terms of sexual difference. For Jenson, it is expressed in terms of broader projectionist tendencies and how they come to entrench the status quo. This 'status quo' could be glossed as that which is *already* established, which becomes 'religiously' bolstered by a way of thinking of eternity as simply a preservation of what always has been. Conceiving of trinitarian difference purely in terms of relations of origin, then, risks projecting this same desire to revert to the already-given status quo into the furthest dimensions of Christian God-talk (that is, the immanent personal relations of Father, Son, and Spirit). In an analogous way, it risks subordinating what comes as dramatically 'new' in the Christian story: the Son and the Spirit.[100] Consequently, Jenson argues that the persons of the Trinity should be identified not only by relations of origin but also by goal.[101]

The imminent relations among the divine persons are at the furthest reaches of theological thought, and so it pushes our language and concepts to their limits. By introducing a stricter kind of 'directionality' in terms of goal into the identification of the subsistent relations, Jenson's broader metaphysics is being carried out to its furthest reaches. As I have argued, Jenson adopts Heidegger's conception of being as the movement of self-determination into the future,

---

98 Timothy McGee argues that James Cone's trinitarian theology of liberation relies on a similar downplaying, and perhaps questioning, of 'relations of origin' in McGee, 'God's Life in and as Opening'.
99 *God and Difference*, 220–25.
100 Jenson and Tonstad then agree that relations of origin alone at least tend toward subordinationism (Jenson, *TI*, 118–38; Tonstad, *God and Difference, passim*, but esp. 222).
101 Cf. *TI*, 138–48, 170–72; *ST*, 1:96–114, 138–45, 156–60, 217–18; 'You Wonder Where the Spirit Went', 115–18.

tweaking it in important theological and more explicitly eschatological ways. Thinking of 'being' in terms of movement into the future is carried seemingly directly into the triune relations. I have also argued that 'future' and 'temporality' are analogically transformed in Jenson's use of the terms for God and do not think that Jenson has subsumed God univocally under a general metaphysic.[102] Rather, the presence of the analogous conceptual move in both Jenson's trinitarian theology and his broader metaphysics means that the coherence and fruitfulness of his concept of 'being' needs all the more to be evaluated. The presence of an analogous move in his doctrine of the Trinity as in his general metaphysics heightens the metaphysical stakes.

In this light, I raise two questions. The first concerns whether Jenson's concept of subsistent relations, while not entailing a univocal metaphysics that includes God and creatures, might still entail a kind of description of the 'how' of the Trinity by projecting certain characteristics of human personhood and relationality.[103] The second question concerns the adequacy of a future-oriented metaphysics for trinitarian theology.

First, does Jenson present a projectionist description of *how* the triune relations are achieved? The threat here is twofold: (1) there is the theological-epistemological problem of what we can and should infer about the nature of triune inter-relationality from our experience of human relationality, and (2) there is the problem of whether a move like this compromises the logic of subsistent relations by implicitly treating the persons as external to their relations. Problem (1) naturally leads to (2), and both of these threats loom in the background of some of Jenson's dialectics.[104] This is especially transparent when Jenson adapts Hegel's master-slave dialectic for trinitarian reflection, where Jenson's conclusions are seemingly taken to provide some of the warrant for defining the triune relations by 'goal' as well as 'origin'. He sums up the exigencies of human relations so:

> I have no choice but to defend myself against being your object so long as you, with whom I am paired for freedom or bondage, are the one who objectifies me. And you must defend

---

[102] So he expresses the analogical difference early on: 'To be God is to anticipate a future self by an inexhaustible interpretive relation to an other *that God himself is*; to be a creature is to anticipate a future self, by a finite interpretive relation to an other *that the creature is not*' (*TI*, 182, emphasis added).
[103] Consider the more extended consideration of projection in Jenson's thought in East, 'What is the Doctrine of Trinity For?', 414–33.
[104] In addition to the example I will discuss presently, consider the kind of inferences Jenson's makes about the character of God's 'consciousness' from the transitive character of finite human consciousness in *TI*, 170–76.

yourself in the same way. But if another, whose intention for you and me is precisely our mutual love, objectifies us by that very intention, we are free to love each other.¹⁰⁵

Problem (1), concerning inference from human relations, arises immediately in Jenson's rhetoric about the need for the Spirit to 'liberate' the Son and the Father from completely objectifying each other. Following the quotation above, Jenson concludes:

> So we must learn to think: the Spirit … is another who in his own intention liberates Father and Son to love each other. The Father begets the Son, but it is the Spirit who presents this Son to his Father as an object of the love that begot him, that is, to be actively loved. The Son adores the Father, but it is the Spirit who shows the Father to the Son not merely as ineffable Source but as the available and lovable Father.¹⁰⁶

We must learn, that is, to think of the Spirit as the third party to the I–Thou relation between Father and Son who, by being present as the unsurpassable futurity of their relatedness, objectifies each for the other as the bond of their mutual love and thereby frees them to actually love the other. Unfortunately, Jenson does not make clear in this context how he distinguishes the mode of divine interpersonal relations from the human relations from which he analogizes.

The argument as stated is structurally similar to Richard of St. Victor's demonstration of the need for three divine persons based on the notions of goodness and of human perfection in *On the Trinity*.¹⁰⁷ In chapter two of book three, Richard argues that God's goodness requires interpersonal communion because 'charity' is intrinsic to goodness and charity cannot obtain for only a single person apart from being directed to another. Consequently, God's goodness requires an interpersonal relationship in which charity obtains so that the personal goodness of God can truly be said to be perfect.¹⁰⁸ It is then taken to be a proposition demonstrated by rational argumentation that in God 'the perfection of one person requires fellowship with another'.¹⁰⁹ The danger in both Jenson's and Richard's analogies is that their appeal to how interpersonal relations fulfil human personal goodness carries connotations of a 'how', a story that centers

---

105 *ST*, 1:156.
106 *ST*, 1:156.
107 Richard of St. Victor, 'On the Trinity'. Sonderegger raises similar concerns about Barth's exposition of divine love; *Systematic Theology 1*, 477.
108 Richard of St. Victor, 'On the Trinity', Book III, chapter 2, pp. 374–75 (henceforth III.2, 374–75). In chapters three and four, Richard offers variants of the argument based on 'happiness' and 'glory'.
109 'On the Trinity', III.6, 379.

on subjects who are in some sense independent of their relations to other subjects and who are fulfilled in their personhood only through developing certain kinds of relationships with others. However, this is a kind of inference we ought not make in respect of the Trinity.[110] Such an inference ends up creating difficulties for maintaining the unity of nature among the divine persons; for if each person is only perfected through relationship with the others, then the being of each person is distinguished and not the same.[111] The being of the Father, insofar as the Father requires perfection from another, is not in itself being conceived as the fullness of God, but rather as one relational pole who through perfection by the others becomes a full person of God. The divine unity, considered as the full perfection of the divine nature, is in this sense subsequent to the persons and appears to be a 'whole' composed out of the three persons.

It appears then, that the epistemological problem (1) of inferring from human interpersonal relations to the intratrinitarian relations leads into problem (2), which conceives of the persons as external to their relations and therefore not actually of the same nature. If the being of one divine person is only perfected by virtue of a relation to the others, then the person is seemingly something *other* than their relation. This creates an internal tension in Jenson's thought insofar as he consistently deploys the concept of subsistent relations but still concludes to the necessity of three persons by inference from the imperfection of human persons apart from loving relationships between two and their third. This at minimum has the air of describing 'how' it is that God is actually triune (as if God's life might have turned out otherwise).

This leads to consideration of Jenson's future-oriented metaphysics in general, with subsistent relations as something of the final test case. For if Jenson's use of future-oriented metaphysics causes problems in his trinitarian theology, then his theological warrant for it is lost and his revisionary metaphysics are compromised. Frederick Wilhelmsen states potential risks of future-oriented metaphysics incisively:

> when 'Being' is described in terms of its direction, in the prospect of its future, in the light of the things to which it is related … The universe of being is … frozen into a mosaic of relations in which nothing truly is, but in which all these nothings are related one to another. … To describe being as otherness, to see being constituted *as being* in the light of its direc-

---

110 Cf. White, 'Simplicity and Trinity', 83–84.
111 For Gunton, by contrast, Richard is a hero of trinitarian faith because he gives primacy to 'particularity' (*One, Three and Many*, 190). While I agree with Gunton that particularity as such deserves proper acknowledgment, it is not clear to me that the way to do so is to project 'particularity' in a Victorine mode into the Trinity.

tion, to understand being as 'for-ing' rather than as an 'is-ing', is to introduce nonbeing into the structure of existence.¹¹²

This connects directly with the concern I raised immediately above, that Jenson's analogy introduced a kind of 'how' into our understanding of God's triunity. But Wilhelmsen is here claiming that this problem is endemic in all future-oriented metaphysics to the extent that the 'how' – the process of actualization – so overwhelms the *reality* of the entities supposedly being actualized that 'being' can be said just as much 'to be' as 'not to be', introducing 'nonbeing into the structure of existence'. Such a dialectic might be able to be conceived as one way of analyzing the contingency of created being *ex nihilo*, though it would need to be said that the 'is' and 'is not' are spoken of real beings according to different aspects so that the law of non-contradiction is not being violated. But if this is introduced into *God's* own being, the concept of God would collapse into pure contradiction, perhaps as an eternal *agon* of divine conflict, lapse into nonsense, or result in the necessity of creation as that *to* which God's being is directed (this possibility might actually be reducible to one of the other two).¹¹³ This could be called the problem of 'transitive metaphysics', insofar as it conceives of God's being in irreducibly transitive terms.

However, it does seem like the NT depicts the actions of the three divine persons in 'transitive' (directional) terms.¹¹⁴ Jesus is sent by the Father (Jn. 6:38, 8:42, 15:15), but he is 'driven' and *led* by the Holy Spirit (Mk. 1:12). The Spirit is given *to* Jesus from the Father as 'promise' (Acts 2:33) and it is through the Spirit that Jesus returns '*to* God' (Heb. 9:14). Acknowledging that these transitive relationships happen within the economy of salvation, these texts nonetheless suggest that the immanent relations of Father, Son, and Spirit do include something analogous to 'relations of goal'. The Thomistic distinction between the personal missions and processions conceives of the processions from the economic missions by removing any creaturely term.¹¹⁵ But the texts that show Jesus having

---

112 Wilhelmsen, *Metaphysics of Love*, 39–40. Cited in Murphy, *God is Not a Story*, 278. Wilhelmsen's original statement seems to speak in a purely metaphysical mode without reference to the persons of the Trinity, but Murphy uses the quotation to charge Herbert McCabe and Jenson with these problems in their trinitarian theology. More on the validity of Murphy's move in this respect below.
113 Notice that the contradiction between 'being' and 'non-being' is different than Cusa's positive naming of God as 'other' and 'not other'; Cusa's practice of naming is not susceptible to the same (easy) threat of contradiction (Nicholas of Cusa, *God as Not-Other*).
114 Cf. Henry, *Freedom of God*, 129–31.
115 *STh*, I.43.2. For Aquinas, the missions 'include' the processions of the persons, but the missions are distinguished from the processions by taking a creaturely term.

a kind of 'goal' relation to the Spirit are not transitive by virtue of culminating in a creaturely term, for the Spirit is God and not a creature. Without any 'creaturely term' to remove, it does then seem that the Spirit has a goal-like role vis-à-vis the Son, which would hold according to both mission and procession.

Does this mean that we are obligated to think of God's triune being as 'transitive' in the sense that Wilhelmsen criticizes and that seems to arise in Jenson's (and Richard's) interpersonal analogies? Does God's trinitarian life then consist of a contradiction of being and non-being or an unresolvable and perhaps violent metaphysical tension? First, it should be noted that if this problem of transitive metaphysics is a legitimate issue for trinitarian theology, then it would apply not only to relations of goal but also to relations of origin. Both forms of identifying the divine persons do so by reference *to another*, which is central to the idea of identifying persons according to relations. When Francesca Murphy uses Wilhelmsen's argument to arraign trinitarian theologies like Herbert McCabe's and Jenson's, she does not seem to consider that any relational identification of the divine persons could be susceptible to the same claim.[116] At very least, it is not the case that God's being is contorted into irreducible metaphysical tension simply by virtue of including a 'relation of goal' into how we specify the triune relations. Something else has to go wrong in how we conceive of God's relationality for the problem of transitive metaphysics to arise.[117]

One thing that could go wrong and make the problem of transitive metaphysics a threat to trinitarian theology would be to forget that speaking of God according to relations and speaking of God according to the one being is an irreducible distinction in the order of our language. Augustine's introduction of relations for identifying the persons was predicated on this stipulation; identifying God 'by reference to another' (*ad alterutrum*) is to predicate something of God *only* 'relation-wise' (*secundum relativum*), as Edmund Hill translates it, and consequently *not* 'substance-wise' (*secundum substantiam*).[118] If this distinction in our mode of speaking of God is forgotten, then *any* transitivity expressed of the persons would be turned into a transitivity of *being* according to God's essence (*secundum substantiam*), thereby introducing a 'transitive metaphysics' with all the problems diagnosed by Wilhelmsen (and Murphy). By contrast, if

---

116 Murphy, *God is Not a Story*, 278.
117 Murphy seems to recognize this (*God is Not a Story*, 270–80), though it is not clear to me that she clearly shows why it is that McCabe and Jenson are vulnerable to her Wilhelmsen-inspired critique where other identifications of the persons by relation – particularly Balthasar's – are not.
118 Augustine, *Trin.*, V.5.6. See Aquinas's retrieval of Augustine on this point in *STh*, I.28, esp. a. 3, *responsio*.

the distinction is remembered, then relations of origin and of goal would not presume to determine the one *being* of God by transitive directionality. In respect of the order of being, rather than the order of language and thought, we could say that the problem of transitive metaphysics would arise if the logic of subsistent relations was compromised by making the divine persons external to their relations. If the persons are external to their relations, are defined by the relational distinction, and are identical to the divine essence, then the *divine essence itself* would be defined by relation to another who is also somehow within God's own being. God's being, then, would include an 'is' and an 'is-not' at the same time and in the same respect, though the contradiction would be expressed differently according to each divine person (God 'is' essentially Father but, *qua* Father, 'is-not' essentially the Son). This would clearly create logical and metaphysical problems for the doctrine of the Trinity, but, again, they are problems that arise when 'relation' and 'being/essence' are either confused or made extrinsic to each other. The logic of subsistent relations is a formalized way of expressing the mystery of the Trinity by mediating between such problematic construals of God's relationality.

I have agreed with Jenson that there are biblical grounds for including relations of 'goal' in identifying the trinitarian processions, and I have argued that this does not create a problem of 'transitive metaphysics' for the doctrine of the Trinity (i.e., defining God's *being* by transitive directionality) so long as (1) the grammatical Augustinian distinction between substance-talk and relation-talk is maintained and (2) the concept of subsistent relations is consistently deployed (so that the persons are not turned into extrinsic terms of their relations). Jenson seems also to accept the Augustinian grammatical distinction, at least as I outlined it here, insofar as he explicitly rejects a construal of God's being-as-event in transitive terms, despite using transitive terms of the divine relations.[119] The question still remains, however, of how Jenson's addition of the 'relation of goal' affects the more classical 'relation of origin'. In response to this question, I will first clarify what I take to be the primary function of 'relations of origin'. When this function is understood, 'relations of origin' do not engender the problems Jenson, Tonstad, and others fear. And with the clarification in hand, I argue that there is in fact room for 'relations of goal', but that they serve a different purpose than that which Thomas and others have given exclusively to 'relations of origin'.

---

119 Cf. 'Some Riffs', 130.

Aquinas admits that there are several relations in God and several 'notions' that can be named of the three persons.[120] While each divine person could be spoken of according to many notions and conceptual relations, there are only three persons and likewise only three *subsistent* relations in God.[121] This raises the question of how we can continue to speak of the divine persons according to multiple notions and relations without conceiving of more than three. So, for instance, the Father has a relation to the Holy Spirit and the Son has a relation to the Holy Spirit. In one respect, 'relation to the Holy Spirit' is identical to the relations that the Father and Son are in themselves, insofar as 'relation to the Holy Spirit' specifies something about Father and Son. But, apart from using the same name, 'Holy Spirit', what prevents us from imagining *two* Spirits by virtue of which Father on the one hand and Son on the other can be said to be 'related to the Spirit'?[122] 'Relations of origin' has in this context the special function of distinguishing the subsistent relations definitionally so that when speaking of the triune persons we deploy the multiple relational configurations scripture provides without also multiplying the number of subsistent relations or divine persons.[123] Even to say that the subsistent relations are 'relations of origin' is misleading if it is taken as too ontologically descriptive, for 'strictly speaking, relations do not originate or proceed from one another'.[124] The reason for privileging 'relations of origin' is, to use a distinction somewhat alien to Thomas, regulative rather than ontological. It is not the case that, according to the order of being, the Father is 'origin without being originated' more fundamentally than the Father is 'related *to* the Spirit or *to* the Son'. The Father simply *is* the relation that has both Spirit and Son as terms, and there are many ways that relation can be meaningfully expressed. Consequently, when we speak of the Holy Spirit according to the relation of the Son and according to the relation of the Father, we can run both those claims through the (regulative) 'relations of origin' to main-

---

120 'It is not improper that there be many conceptual relations in God' (my translation): '*relationes autem rationis in Deo multiplicari non est inconveniens*' (*STh*, I.32.2). Cf. also I.28.3 on notions.
121 *STh*, I.28, I.32.3.
122 There are in fact many names we could use of the Holy Spirit, so that the problem would more easily arise. We could, for instance, say that the Father is 'related to the Holy Spirit' and the Son is 'related to the Advocate' (John 14:26).
123 Alternatively, Aquinas notes that apart from the *filioque* and 'relations of origin' it would even be difficult to keep the Son and Spirit from being conceived of as the same person (*STh*, I.36.2). So relations of origin help us not to multiply the number of persons as well as not to collapse them into one another.
124 *STh*, I.28.3, ad. 3.

tain that Father and Son are related to one and the same Spirit, the Spirit who proceeds from the Father and (or through) the Son.[125]

In this light, relations of origin are helpful for consistently deploying subsistent relations to identify the three divine persons, but they do not imply any kind of ontological ranking among the persons nor any ontological privileging of one frame of reference (as if there is a bias for the 'past' and so the already given 'status quo').[126] With Jenson, then, we can say there is a 'whither' of the persons insofar as each person subsists as the relation they are *in the act of giving to and being-toward the other two persons*.[127] By virtue of being *homoousios*, the being *as which* each person subsists is also nothing other than the term *to which* the persons are oriented, insofar as God's simple being subsists relationally in and as the other persons. 'Relations of origin' do not exhaustively 'define' the divine persons ontologically and neither are they a description of 'how' the persons originate. Rather, they are simply a way for us to consistently conceive of the threefold relational distinction in the Trinity and are, therefore, partially expressive of the divine persons' imminent inter-relationality. In this sense, the trinitarian relations are more intrinsically rich than any reduction to opposition in terms of origin – or even the addition of 'goal' – might suggest.

Part of the theological benefit of using divine simplicity and subsistent relations for trinitarian theology is that these concepts obviate any sense of a descriptive 'how' or of ontological gradation in God's life. With these categories, then, there is neither the possibility of transitive metaphysics arising in the doctrine of the Trinity nor of conceiving the divine persons as extrinsic to one another and therefore only 'perfect' if they undergo specific configurations on analogy with human inter-relationality (à la Richard). I agree, then, with Tonstad when she argues:

---

125 I include 'through' and 'and' in order to avoid associating the regulative function of 'relation of origin' exclusively with the *filioque*. For, it might seem that even in its regulative function the *filioque* is needed to distinguish Son and Spirit in their procession from the Father, but I think 'through' could do similar work and is endorsed by several Orthodox theologians.
126 Cf. Catherine Pickstock's analogous reflections in response to Derrida's critique of 'presence' in *After Writing*, 11–14. The connection between 'strong simplicity' and a bias for the already-given status quo (or 'protological simplicity') is what motivates Paul Hinlicky's 'weak' construal of simplicity (*Divine Simplicity*). But if the correlation between the 'protological' and strong simplicity is shown to be false (or at least not logically necessary), then the rhetorical pressure for his 'weak' simplicity is undercut.
127 Jenson also construes relations of goal as unsubstitutable aspects of the Bible's description of the triune persons' actions, and so not as an alternative to 'relations of origin' (*ST*, 1:159).

only persons with impermeable boundaries or who are constituted by possessive expansiveness (greed) need to be penetrated, or to make room for each other, in order to establish mutually enjoyable, good relationships. The unity of the trinitarian persons, the goodness of God's being, and the sheer gratuity of their love renders any such movements unnecessary for them.[128]

As I argued in the last section, by conceiving of interiority and exteriority as legitimately spoken analogically of God, though finally perfectly coincident, divine simplicity explodes any conception of God's interiority having boundaries or requiring an additional principle in order to be available to others. Now we can see this as first and foremost a trinitarian claim in the order of being. Within God, there are three relational identities that are each entirely 'interior' and so have full 'subjective' personhood, but whose interiority is not a distinct reality from their exteriority and availability to the others.[129] Consequently, God is not 'three' by virtue of some metaphysical principle of individuation or by means of a history that differentiates what might otherwise be an undifferentiated oneness. God is three in a way that transcends the ontological conditions that would make such metaphysical principles or narratives of individuation necessary.

God's identity is pure, unreserved gift – 'exterior' by *being* what is given and therefore ecstatically present in and as the gift; 'interior' by being the subject of the gift, by being the free agent of the act of self-giving generosity. By revelation, we know that God's life as simple gift is in fact an immanent life of threefold giving, an exchange in which the coincidence of interiority and exteriority is the complete self-donation of Father to Son in the Spirit. As Jesus says, 'I am in the Father and the Father is in me … the Father who dwells in me does his works' (Jn. 14:10; also 17:10). And when Jesus gives God's eternal life to God's people, the act of giving is itself an extension of the gift-exchange by which the Father and Jesus, the Son, are mutually related and are one (Jn. 10:27–30, 38; 5:19–27).[130] Further, Paul says that our share of existence is 'from' and 'to'

---

128 *God and Difference*, 222.
129 In this way, I can agree with Jeremy Begbie ('A Semblance More Lucid?', 29–31) about the importance of conceiving of the divine persons in a way that allows for the multiple relations depicted in scripture to be retained with all the richness by which they exposit the triune life, but I disagree that divine simplicity is in any way a hindrance in this respect. Quite the opposite, I think that simplicity may be necessary to affirm the rich relations of love and co-inherence among three persons who are of one undivided common being.
130 Cf. Thompson, *God of the Gospel of John*, 78–79. And consider Bauckham, 'Trinity and the Gospel of John', 111: 'the whole story of salvation that the Gospel tells stems from the love between the Father and the Son and has as its goal the inclusions of humans within this loving relationship'.

God the Father and 'through' the Lord Jesus (1 Cor. 8:6); the juxtaposition of prepositions giving the sense of a unity-in-relationship among the Father and Jesus by virtue of which we live and move and have our created being.

How can we conceive of such an intimate interrelationship between Father and Son that is expressed as mutual interiority and perichoresis, exchange of love and self-gift, and working in and through one another for mutual glorification and for the existence, life, and eternal (new) life of God's creatures? It seems to me that divine simplicity and the concept of subsistent relations go a long way in directing our thoughts and language toward the mystery of God's triunity, helping us to imagine God's being as the unbounded, infinite exchange of self-gift and self-exteriorization, threefold relation (without remainder) subsisting purely *as* the relations of Father, Son, and Spirit.[131] With Jenson, I argue that this mystery is properly talked about with a myriad of relational configurations, including 'goal' as well as 'origin', though there are legitimate reasons for giving a specific kind of privilege to 'relations of origin'. While there are risks in some of Jenson's analogies for God's tri-personhood, I have argued that on the whole his trinitarian theology is compatible with divine simplicity and a classical retrieval of subsistent relations.

5.5 Conclusion

In this chapter, I have defended aspects of Jenson's approach to the doctrine of God and what might be considered his conception of 'dramatic unity' for theological metaphysics. After summarizing how divine simplicity functions in his theology, I returned to the three main theological deployments of divine simplicity in Christian theology to evaluate Jenson's particular claims more closely. The cumulative argument throughout my engagement with Jenson has been that the distance between his doctrine of God and the 'classical' doctrine of divine simplicity is not so great as is often assumed, and that, in fact, Jenson explicitly affirms simplicity in certain respects and tacitly relies on its grammar in others. In this chapter, I have demonstrated how a more explicit use of divine simplicity actually assists in resolving points of tension in Jenson's theology. In this way, I have argued for the theological value of the doctrine of divine simplicity, not by defending it against all attacks, but by showing the benefits it can bring to

---

131 I borrow (and modify slightly) the phrase 'relation without remainder' from Lash, *Believing Three Ways*, 32. On the logic of thinking of God as 'threefold relation', cf. Mascall, *Triune God*, 74–86.

our understanding of God's many names, God's relation to creation, and God's immanent intratrinitarian relations.

6 Conclusion

The principal question this book has attempted to address is whether the doctrine of divine simplicity helps us to confess the trinitarian dogma of the Christian faith. My answer is yes. We speak most faithfully of God when we speak of God's life as triune simplicity and simple triunity. On the way toward this answer, I have given a fresh reading of the theology of Robert W. Jenson that conscripts elements of his provocative and creative explication of God's triunity toward a dramatic theology of simplicity.

My discussion of the continuities and discontinuities on divine simplicity in Gregory of Nyssa, Augustine, and Thomas Aquinas, enabled me to demonstrate extensive overlap among them as well as the taken-for-granted character of simplicity in these earlier theologians. It also enabled me to approach Jenson's writing with a multivalent account of divine simplicity. In what followed, I argued that divine simplicity has become optional in a new way in our present theological context and that this is bound up with an assumed inverse relation between scripture and philosophical/metaphysical concepts. It is, therefore, incumbent on contemporary advocates of simplicity to clarify the relationship between the metaphysical language of simplicity and the biblical narratives through which God is revealed.

Consequently, I introduced Jenson as a significant interlocutor, for his development of a 'revisionary metaphysics' is also a theological hermeneutic of scripture. In this sense, the *rule of dramatic unity* that I derive from Jenson is itself a biblical conviction of God's involvement with creatures for the good of the history as which creation exists. Informed by the multivalent accounts of simplicity discussed in chapter two, I was able to demonstrate various ways in which Jenson himself, despite several critical remarks, actually deploys the logic or grammar of simplicity in a way that is integral to his trinitarian theology, while I also attended to the unique metaphysics and conception of 'unity' Jenson develops. Consequently, showing Jenson's commitment to divine simplicity makes an important contribution to contemporary theology because of the way it responds to the conditions that have rendered divine simplicity problematic in the eyes of many theologians (viz., simplicity's seeming misfit with the biblical depiction of God).

My reconstruction of simplicity in Jenson also enabled a more ecumenically sympathetic rendering of his doctrine of God, neutralizing several criticisms of his work that have arisen. In particular, I considered aspects of George Hunsinger's, Francesca Murphy's, and Scott Swain's critiques, which in different ways challenge the coherence of Jenson's trinitarian theology in conjunction with his historicist metaphysics. By situating Jenson's trinitarian theology within a more comprehensive account of his revisionary metaphysics and providing an interpretation of Jenson's 'dramatic unity', I was able to show how his seemingly problematic claims could be differently rendered and thereby avoid the threat of subsuming God's own life within the immanent processes of history.

Finally, this interpretation opened the way for me to engage in three points of development on Jenson's doctrine of God that contribute to an ecumenical and trinitarian conception of divine simplicity. In particular, I isolated three points that still required further clarification or development after having presented Jenson's broader alignment with the central judgments of divine simplicity – which concern divine names, the Creator–creature relation, and the trinitarian relations. On the multiplicity of divine names, I argued that with Jenson (and to an extent Aquinas) we might rather pursue an inversion of the standard question to consider instead how Christian lives and communities are transformed into words of God by participating in the simplicity of Christ's own kenotic activity. Concerning the distinction of God from creation, I analyzed Jenson's arguments for God's immanent trinitarian embodiment, proposing instead an account of God's personal availability (*ad intra* and *ad extra*) that develops more directly from an account of divine simplicity so that God's availability happens as the perfect convergence of internality and externality. This became the basis for my trinitarian development of divine simplicity, suggesting that God's 'availability' *ad extra* is an outflow of the perfect mutual availability that obtains among the triune persons.

Reflecting on Jenson's trinitarian theology, I suggested that two potential problems arise, first in Jenson's arguments for God's tri-personality by analogy with human inter-relationality and second concerning his priority of 'relations of goal' in contrast to 'relations of origin'. In both cases I critique Jenson, first arguing that his interpersonal analogies risk narrating 'how' God's life achieves a trinitarian form. Concerning 'relations of goal', I agree with Jenson (against some of his critics) that *goal* is a biblical relational identifier for the triune persons but argue that this does not serve the same function as 'relations of origin' – the latter's priority is regulative rather than descriptive. When this function is rightly understood, there need not be conflict between origin and goal because neither is descriptively adequate to explicate the richness of the intratrinitarian relations.

There are several issues that I have not been able to address directly. For instance, while I noted in chapter one several points of debate in contemporary philosophy of religion concerning divine simplicity, I have left most of them largely unresolved and unaddressed. This raises the potential objection that my positive theological use of divine simplicity is philosophically irresponsible, or at best question-begging. This is an important concern that would deserve fuller attention in a complete systematic account of divine simplicity. Here, however, I would point to other studies that have addressed these issues and note that my constructive theological use of simplicity is compatible with a diversity of philosophical positions where there are controversies.¹ For example, by inverting the 'problem' about the multiplicity of divine names to focus on creatures' reception by gift of what God is named primarily, I leave open the matter of what kind of account of predication is adequate to the God so named. Perhaps, per Aquinas, all 'properties' in God are in fact best conceived as absolutely identical extensionally, though our words retain distinct meanings in the mode of signification. Or perhaps, with Scotus, a formal distinction is deemed necessary.² As I see it, although not compatible with all construals of theological language and predication, my use of simplicity in this context could work with both these positions and others. Consequently, while I recognize that a full account of God's simplicity would need to provide more philosophical argumentation on such contentious issues, for the theological purposes here these matters had to be left to the side.

A second area for further development would be on the metaphysics of the incarnation. While I have ventured into christological concerns at times, this has largely been guided by the kinds of christological justifications Jenson provides for his trinitarian conclusions. However, this has meant that I could neither fully analyze Jenson's christology as such nor adequately account for how a simple triune God could take flesh. On the former, the most significant question for my interpretation of Jenson's work concerns christological asymmetry, namely whether and how the divine nature of Jesus has ontological priority vis-à-vis the human nature. My own analyses head in an asymmetrical direction (which creates friction with Jenson's work), but some recent arguments that resonate with some of Jenson's christological convictions, like Jordan Daniel Wood's interpretation of Maximus the Confessor, pose sharp questions for asymmetrical christology.³ Consequently, a complete critical engagement with Jenson's doc-

---

1 Cf. Dolezal, *God without Parts*; Duby, *Divine Simplicity*; Duby, 'Simplicity, Freedom, and Contingency'; Lenow, 'Shoring Up Divine Simplicity'; Tomaszewski, 'Collapsing the Modal Collapse Argument'.
2 Or consider a synthesis of Thomas and Scotus on this point, Spencer, 'Flexibility of Simplicity', 123–39.
3 Wood, 'Creation is Incarnation', 82–102, and his review of Rowan Williams' *Christ the Heart of Creation* in 'Against Asymmetrical Christology'.

trine of God would need more fully to explore aspects that push against christological asymmetry and analyze what is at stake. On the latter concern – that a full account of triune simplicity would need to account for God's taking flesh – I also admit the necessity, but there are accounts available and the task is beyond the scope of the present project.[4]

A final area for development would concern the more 'practical' impetus in much of the writings of the twentieth century trinitarian revival. As Rahner argued, one of the reasons for critically reevaluating the dogmatic relation between *de Deo uno* and *de Deo trino* is the practical 'mere monotheism' of many Christians.[5] To fully revive divine simplicity in the wake of the trinitarian revival, an articulation is needed of how it functions in relation to worship, ecclesiology, and sanctification.[6] On sanctification or perfection, for instance, I suspect it would be fruitful to explore the mirror relationship between God's simplicity on the one hand and humanity's purity and simplicity in sanctification on the other, a relationship that appears in the writings of some early theologians.[7] If simplicity proves useful in connecting Christian practice with the kind of trinitarian theology advanced above, then its significance would be more than only philosophical and systematic. My use of Jenson lends itself to this kind of development, especially in extending the logic of divine simplicity in the Holy Spirit's action of joining human persons to the Word's kenotic expression of divine love.

Addressing these issues directly would contribute to a full, systematic and dogmatic account of the God who is perfectly simple in perichoretic triune relations. My argument as it stands has provided some hints toward the development of such an account while giving primary attention to sustaining a theological vision of God's simple triunity through dialogue with Robert Jenson.

★ ★ ★ ★ ★

I conclude, then, that divine simplicity is in fact an aid for affirming the rich relations of love and co-inherence among three persons who are of one undivided being. God's simplicity is the unconditioned and unlimited act of self-giving that

---

4 See, for instance, Gorman, *Aquinas on the Metaphysics of the Hypostatic Union*; Legge, *Trinitarian Christology of Aquinas*; McFarland, *Word Made Flesh*, esp. 71–98; Riches, *Ecce Homo*; and Williams, *Christ the Heart of Creation*, esp. 1–40, 219–54.
5 *Trinity*, 10.
6 Such discussions are rare, but see King-Farlow, 'Simplicity, Analogy', 216–29; and Wittman, 'Not a God of Confusion', 151–69.
7 For instance Gregory of Nyssa, 'On Perfection', 122, and *Life of Moses*, II.243; Gregory of Nazianzus, *Orations*, 40.8–9, 18.

happens in the completely coinherent, perichoretic relations of Father, Son, and Spirit – a gift that is 'simple' because the gift and the act of giving are themselves the inexhaustible presence of the giver. *Ad intra*, this simple being-as-gift subsists in the three relations as which Father, Son, and Spirit commune. *Ad extra*, God's being-as-gift ecstatically incorporates creatures into the triune movement of mutual celebration, love, and giving that characterizes God's own eternal life and is perfected in creatures with the coming kingdom of God. God's intra-trinitarian self-giving is a kind of self-othering of God, by virtue of which God becomes 'other' through incarnation (as always the one who is 'not other'). In incarnation, the simple triune God performs God's intradivine availability (which is simultaneously the coincidence of interiority and exteriority and the perfect mutual self-donation of the trinitarian persons) as the extra-divine availability of bodily life. And in this act, creatures are given to participate by adoption in the relational movements as which God simply subsists without confusing or separating the being of God and creatures – for 'God is one being in three persons'.

Bibliography

Adams, Nicholas. *Eclipse of Grace: Divine and Human Action in Hegel*. Oxford: Wiley Blackwell, 2013.
Anatolios, Khaled. *Retrieving Nicaea: The Development and Meaning of Trinitarian Doctrine*. Grand Rapids: Baker Academic, 2011.
Anderson, Gary A. *Christian Doctrine and the Old Testament: Theology in the Service of Biblical Exegesis*. Grand Rapids: Baker Academic, 2017.
Anderson, Gary A. 'Creatio Ex Nihilo and the Bible'. In *Creation* Ex Nihilo: *Origins, Development, Contemporary Challenges*, edited by Gary A. Anderson and Markus Bockmuehl, 15–35. Notre Dame: University of Notre Dame Press, 2018.
Aquinas, Thomas. *Compendium of Theology*. Translated by Richard J. Regan. Oxford: Oxford University Press, 2009.
Aquinas, Thomas. *De ente et essentia (On Being and Essence)*. Translated by Armand A. Maurer. Second Revised. Toronto: Pontifical Institute of Mediaeval Studies, 1968.
Aquinas, Thomas. *De potentia Dei (The Power of God)*. Translated by Richard J. Regan. Oxford: Oxford University Press, 2012.
Aquinas, Thomas. *In librum Beati Dionysii De divinis nominibus expositio*. In *Corpus Thomisticum: S. Thomae de Aquino Opera Omnia*, Ed. Enrique Alarcón, online at www.corpusthomisticum.org, 2000.
Aquinas, Thomas. *Summa contra Gentiles*. Edited by Joseph Kenny. Translated by Anton C. Pegis, James F. Anderson, Vernon J. Bourke, and Charles J. O'Neil. Notre Dame: University of Notre Dame Press, 1975.
Aquinas, Thomas. *Summa Theologiæ*. Edited by Thomas Gilby. Translated by The English Dominican Friars. Blackfriars Edition. 60 vols. London: Eyre & Spottiswoode, 1963–1981.
Aquinas, Thomas. *Super Evangelium S. Ioannis lectura (Commentary on the Gospel of John)*. Edited by Daniel Keating and Matthew Levering. Translated by Fabian Larcher and James A. Weisheipl. 3 vols. Washington, DC: Catholic University of America Press, 2010.
Aristotle. *Metaphysics*. Translated by Hugh Lawson-Tancred. London: Penguin, 1998. ———. *Posterior Analytics*. Edited and translated by Jonathan Barnes. Revised Oxford Translation. The Complete Works of Aristotle. Princeton: Princeton University Press, 1991.
Aristotle. *Topica*. Translated by E. S. Forster. Loeb Classical Library 391. Cambridge, MA: Harvard University Press, 1960.
Aspray, Silvianne. 'A Complex Legacy: Louis Bouyer and the Metaphysics of the Reformation'. *Modern Theology* 34, no. 1 (January 2018): 3–22.
Athanasius. *Orationes contra Arianos (Orations Against the Arians)*. Edited by Philip Schaff and Henry Wace. Nicene and Post-Nicene Fathers of the Christian Church, Second Series, Vol. IV. Edinburgh: T&T Clark, 1892.
Augustine. *De civitate Dei (The City of God)*. Translated by William Babcock. 2 vols. The Works of Saint Augustine: A Translation for the 21st Century. New York: New City, 2013.
Augustine. *De Trinitate (The Trinity)*. Translated by Edmund Hill. The Works of Saint Augustine: A Translation for the 21st Century. Hyde Park, NY: New City, 1991.
Augustine. *De vera Religione (True Religion)*. Translated by Edmund Hill. In *On Christian Belief*, ed Boniface Ramsey. The Works of Saint Augustine: A Translation for the 21st Century. Hyde Park, NY: New City, 2005.

Augustine. *Enarrationes in Psalmos (Expositions on the Psalms)*. Edited by Boniface Ramsey and John E. Rotelle. Translated by Maria Boulding. 6 vols. Hyde Park, NY: New City, 2000–2004.
Augustine. *In Iohannis evangelium tractatus (Homilies on the Gospel of John)*. Edited by Alan Fitzgerald. Translated by Edmund Hill. The Works of Saint Augustine: A Translation for the 21st Century. Hyde Park, NY: New City, 2009.
Augustine. *The Confessions*. Translated by Maria Boulding. The Works of Saint Augustine: A Translation for the 21st Century. Hyde Park, NY: New City, 1997.
Austin, J. L. *How to Do Things with Words*. Oxford: Clarendon, 1962.
Ayres, Lewis. *Augustine and the Trinity*. Cambridge: Cambridge University Press, 2010.
Ayres, Lewis. *Nicaea and Its Legacy: An Approach to Fourth-Century Trinitarian Theology*. Oxford: Oxford University Press, 2006.
Balthasar, Hans Urs von. *A Theology of History*. London: Sheed and Ward, 1964.
Balthasar, Hans Urs von. *Prayer*. Translated by Graham Harrison. San Francisco: Ignatius, 1986.
Balthasar, Hans Urs von. *Presence and Thought: An Essay on the Religious Philosophy of Gregory of Nyssa*. Translated by Mark Sebanc. San Francisco: Ignatius, 1995.
Balthasar, Hans Urs von. *Theo-Drama: Theological Dramatic Theory*. Translated by Graham Harrison. 5 vols. San Francisco: Ignatius, 1988–1998.
Balthasar, Hans Urs von. *Theodramatik, 2. Band, Die Personen Des Spiels,* Teil 2: *Die Personen in Christus*. Einsiedeln: Johannes Verlag, 1978.
Balthasar, Hans Urs von. *Theo-Logic: Theological Logical Theory*, Vol 1: *Truth of the World*. Translated by Adrian J. Walker. San Francisco: Ignatius, 2000.
Barnes, Michel René. 'Latin Trinitarian Theology'. In *The Cambridge Companion to the Trinity*, edited by Peter C. Phan, 70–84. Cambridge: Cambridge University Press, 2011.
Barrett, Jordan P. *Divine Simplicity: A Biblical and Trinitarian Account*. Minneapolis: Fortress, 2017.
Barth, Karl. *Church Dogmatics* I/1–IV/4. Edited by Geoffrey W. Bromiley and T. F. Torrance. Edinburgh: T&T Clark, 1956–1975.
Barth, Karl. *Die Kirchliche Dogmatik* I/1–IV/4. Zürich: Evangelischer Verlag, 1944–1967.
Basil of Caesarea. *Against Eunomius*. Translated by Mark DelCogliano and Andrew Radde-Gallwitz. Washington, DC: Catholic University of America Press, 2011.
Bates, Matthew W. *The Birth of the Trinity: Jesus, God, and Spirit in New Testament and Early Christian Interpretations of the Old Testament*. Oxford: Oxford University Press, 2015.
Bauckham, Richard. 'The Trinity and the Gospel of John'. In *The Essential Trinity: New Testament Foundations and Practical Relevance*, edited by Brandon D. Crowe and Carl R. Trueman, 91–117. Phillipsburg: P&R, 2016.
Bauerschmidt, Frederick Christian. *Thomas Aquinas: Faith, Reason, and Following Christ*. Oxford: Oxford University Press, 2013.
Begbie, Jeremy. '"A Semblance More Lucid?" An Exploration of Trinitarian Space'. In *Essays on the Trinity*, edited by Lincoln Harvey, 20–35. Eugene: Cascade, 2018.
Begbie, Jeremy. *Theology, Music and Time*. Cambridge: Cambridge University Press, 2000.
Behr, John. 'Synchronic and Diachronic Harmony: St. Irenaeus on Divine Simplicity'. *Modern Theology* 35, no. 3 (July 2019): 428–41.
Beiser, Friederick. *Hegel*. London: Routledge, 2005.

Bennett, Daniel. 'The Divine Simplicity'. *The Journal of Philosophy* 66, no. 19 (October 1969): 628–37.
Berto, Francesco, and Matteo Plebani. *Ontology and Metaontology: A Contemporary Guide*. London: Bloomsbury Academic, 2015.
Billings, J. Todd. *Calvin, Participation, and the Gift: The Activity of Believers in Union with Christ*. Oxford: Oxford University Press, 2008.
Boff, Leonardo. *Trinity and Society*. Translated by Paul Burns. Maryknoll, NY: Orbis, 1988.
Braine, David. *The Reality of Time and the Existence of God: The Project of Proving God's Existence*. Oxford: Clarendon, 1988.
Brower, Jeffrey E. 'Making Sense of Divine Simplicity'. *Faith and Philosophy* 25, no. 1 (January 2008): 3–30.
Brown, David. *The Divine Trinity*. London: Duckworth, 1985.
Brugarolas, Miguel, ed. *Gregory of Nyssa*: Contra Eunomium I: *An English Translation with Supporting Studies*. Supplements to Vigiliae Christianae. Leiden: Brill, 2018.
Brunner, Emil. *The Christian Doctrine of God: Dogmatics, Vol. 1*. Translated by Olive Wyon. London: Lutterworth, 1949.
Buckley, James J. 'Intimacy: The Character of Robert Jenson's Theology'. In *Trinity, Time, and Church: A Response to the Theology of Robert W. Jenson*, edited by Colin E. Gunton, 10–22. Grand Rapids: Wm. B. Eerdmans, 2000.
Burrell, David B. 'Analogy, Creation, and Theological Language'. In *The Theology of Thomas Aquinas*, edited by Rik Van Nieuwenhove and Joseph Wawrykow, 77–98. Notre Dame: University of Notre Dame Press, 2005.
Burrell, David B. *Aquinas: God and Action*. Edited by Mary Budde Ragan. Third Edition. Eugene, OR: Wipf and Stock, 2016.
Burrell, David B. '*Creatio Ex Nihilo* Recovered'. *Modern Theology* 29, no. 2 (April 2013): 5–21.
Burrell, David B. *Knowing the Unknowable God: Ibn-Sina, Maimonides, Aquinas*. Notre Dame: University of Notre Dame Press, 1986.
Burrell, David B. 'Metaphysics of Creation'. In *Belief and Metaphysics*, edited by Peter M. Candler Jr. and Conor Cunningham, 66–72. London: SCM, 2007.
Burrell, David B. 'The Act of Creation with Its Theological Consequences'. In *Aquinas on Doctrine: A Critical Introduction*, edited by Thomas Weinandy, Daniel A. Keating, and John P. Yocum, 27–44. London: T&T Clark International, 2004.
Bussanich, John. 'Plotinus's Metaphysics of the One'. In *The Cambridge Companion to Plotinus*, edited by Lloyd P. Gerson, 38–65. Cambridge: Cambridge University Press, 1996.
Chambers, Nathan. 'Divine and Creaturely Agency in Genesis 1'. *Scottish Journal of Theology* 72, no. 1 (2019): 1–19.
Chemnitz, Martin. *The Two Natures in Christ*. Translated by J. A. O. Preuss. St. Louis: Concordia, 1971.
Chesterton, G. K. *St. Thomas Aquinas*. London: Hodder & Stoughton, 1933.
Clarke, W. Norris. 'Action as the Self-Revelation of Being: A Central Theme in the Thought of St Thomas'. In *Explorations in Metaphysics: Being—God—Person*, 45–64. Notre Dame: University of Notre Dame Press, 1994.
Clarke, W. Norris. 'The Limitation of Act by Potency in St. Thomas: Aristotelianism or Neoplatonism?' In *Explorations in Theology: Being—God—Person*, 65–88. Notre Dame: University of Notre Dame Press, 1994.

Clarke, W. Norris. 'The Meaning of Participation in St. Thomas Aquinas'. In *Explorations in Theology: Being—God—Person*, 89–101. Notre Dame: University of Notre Dame Press, 1994.
Clarke, W. Norris. *The Philosophical Approach to God: A New Thomistic Perspective*. Second Revised Edition. New York: Fordham University Press, 2007.
Coakley, Sarah. 'Afterword: "Relational Ontology", Trinity, and Science'. In *The Trinity and an Entangled World: Relationality in Physical Science and Theology*, edited by John Polkinghorne, 184–99. Grand Rapids: Wm. B. Eerdmans, 2010.
Coakley, Sarah. *God, Sexuality, and the Self: An Essay 'On the Trinity'*. Cambridge: Cambridge University Press, 2013.
Copeland, M. Shawn. *Enfleshing Freedom: Body, Race, and Being*. Minneapolis: Fortress, 2010.
Crisp, Oliver D. 'A Parsimonious Model of Divine Simplicity'. *Modern Theology* 35, no. 3 (July 2019): 558–73.
Crisp, Oliver D. 'Robert Jenson on the Pre-Existence of Christ'. *Modern Theology* 23, no. 1 (January 2007): 27–45.
Crocker, James. 'Robert Jenson and Contemporary Metaphysics'. *Journal of Analytic Theology* 4 (May 2016): 332–46.
Cross, Richard. 'Divine Simplicity and the Doctrine of the Trinity: Gregory of Nyssa and Augustine'. In *Philosophical Theology and the Christian Tradition: Russian and Western Perspectives*, edited by David Bradshaw, 53–65. Washington, DC: The Council for Research in Values and Philosophy, 2012.
Cross, Richard. 'Duns Scotus on Divine Substance and the Trinity'. *Medieval Philosophy and Theology* 11 (2003): 181–201.
Cross, Richard. *Duns Scotus on God*. Aldershot: Ashgate, 2005.
Dalferth, Ingolf U. *Radical Theology: An Essay on Faith and Theology in the Twenty-First Century*. Minneapolis: Fortress, 2016.
Dauphinais, Michael, Barry David, and Matthew Levering, eds. *Aquinas the Augustinian*. Washington, DC: Catholic University of America Press, 2007.
Davis, Joshua B. *Waiting and Being: Creation, Freedom, and Grace in Western Theology*. Minneapolis: Fortress, 2013.
Denzinger. *Enchiridion Symbolorum*. In lingua latina. Accessed 18 September 2019. http://catho.org/9.php?d=g1.
Dionysius the Areopagite. *The Divine Names*. Translated by Colm Luibheid. In *The Complete Works*. Mahwah, NJ: Paulist, 1987.
Dionysius the Areopagite. *The Mystical Theology*. Translated by Colm Luibheid. In *The Complete Works*. Mahwah, NJ: Paulist, 1987.
Dolezal, James E. *God without Parts: Divine Simplicity and the Metaphysics of God's Absoluteness*. Eugene, OR: Pickwick, 2011.
Dolezal, James E. 'Trinity, Simplicity and the Status of God's Personal Relations'. *International Journal of Systematic Theology* 16, no. 1 (January 2014): 79–98.
Dorner, Isaak August. *Divine Immutability: A Critical Reconsideration*. Translated by Robert R. Williams and Claude Welch. Minneapolis: Fortress, 1994.
Dorner, J. A. *A System of Christian Doctrine*, Vol. 1. Translated by Alfred Cave. Edinburgh: T&T Clark, 1883.
Duby, Steven J. *Divine Simplicity: A Dogmatic Account*. London: Bloomsbury T&T Clark, 2016.

Duby, Steven J. 'Divine Simplicity, Divine Freedom, and the Contingency of Creation: Dogmatic Responses to Some Analytic Questions'. *Journal of Reformed Theology* 6 (2012): 115–42.

East, Brad. 'What Is the Doctrine of the Trinity For? Practicality and Projection in Robert Jenson's Theology'. *Modern Theology* 33, no. 3 (July 2017): 414–33.

Emery, Gilles. *The Trinitarian Theology of Saint Thomas Aquinas*. Translated by Francesca Aran Murphy. Oxford: Oxford University Press, 2007.

Evans, Donald D. *The Logic of Self-Involvement: A Philosophical Study of Everyday Language with Special Reference to the Christian Use of Language about God as Creator*. London: SCM, 1963.

Fackre, Gabriel. 'The Lutheran *Capax* Lives'. In *Trinity, Time, and Church: A Response to the Theology of Robert W. Jenson*, edited by Colin E. Gunton, 94–102. Grand Rapids: Wm. B. Eerdmans, 2000.

Feser, Edward. *Scholastic Metaphysics: A Contemporary Introduction*. Heusenstamm: Editiones Scholasticae, 2014.

Fiddes, Paul S. *Participating in God: A Pastoral Doctrine of the Trinity*. London: Darton, Longman, and Todd, 2000.

Franks, Christopher A. 'The Simplicity of the Living God: Aquinas, Barth, and Some Philosophers'. *Modern Theology* 21, no. 2 (April 2005): 275–300.

Frege, Gottlob. 'Dialogue with Pünjer over Existence'. In *Posthumous Writings*, edited by P. Long and R. White, 53–67. Oxford: Blackwell, 1979.

Friedman, Russell L. 'Medieval Trinitarian Theology from the Late Thirteenth to the Fifteenth Centuries'. In *The Oxford Handbook of the Trinity*, edited by Gilles Emery and Matthew Levering, 197–209. Oxford: Oxford University Press, 2011.

Gaghan, Josh. 'Reason, Metaphysics, and Their Relationship in the Theologies of Jenson and Aquinas'. *New Blackfriars* 99, no. 1082 (July 2018): 520–40.

Gale, Richard M. *On the Nature and Existence of God*. Cambridge: Cambridge University Press, 1991.

Gavrilyuk, Paul. 'Plotinus on Divine Simplicity'. *Modern Theology* 35, no. 3 (July 2019): 442–51.

Gerson, L. P. *God and Greek Philosophy: Studies in the Early History of Natural Theology*. London: Routledge, 1990.

Gerson, Lloyd P. *Plotinus*. London: Routledge, 1994.

Gilson, Etienne. *God and Philosophy*. New Haven: Yale Nota Bene, 1954.

Gilson, Etienne. 'Quasi Definitio Substantiae'. In *St. Thomas Aquinas 1274–1974: Commemorative Studies*, edited by Armand A. Maurer, 1:111–29. Toronto: Pontifical Institute of Mediaeval Studies, 1974.

Gordon, Joseph K. *Divine Scripture in Human Understanding: A Systematic Theology of the Christian Bible*. Notre Dame: University of Notre Dame Press, 2019.

Gorman, Michael. *Aquinas on the Metaphysics of the Hypostatic Union*. Cambridge: Cambridge University Press, 2017.

Gracia, Jorge J. E. *Metaphysics and its Task: The Search for the Categorial Foundation of Knowledge*. Albany: State University of New York Press, 1999.

Grant, W. Matthews. 'Aquinas, Divine Simplicity, and Divine Freedom'. *Proceedings of the American Catholic Philosophical Association* 77 (2004): 129–44.

Green, Bradley G. *Colin Gunton and the Failure of Augustine: The Theology of Colin Gunton in Light of Augustine*. Eugene, OR: Pickwick, 2011.

Gregory of Nazianzus. *Festal Orations*. Translated by Nonna Verna Harrison. Crestwood: St. Vladimir's Seminary Press, 2008.
Gregory of Nyssa. *Against Eunomius*. Edited by Philip Schaff and Henry Wace. Translated by William Moore and Henry Austin Wilson. Nicene and Post-Nicene Fathers of the Christian Church, Second Series, Vol. V. Edinburgh: T&T Clark, 1892.
Gregory of Nyssa. *Catechetical Discourse*. Translated by Ignatius Green. Yonkers, NY: St. Vladimir's Seminary Press, 2019.
Gregory of Nyssa. *Contra Eunomium I–III*. Translated by Stuart George Hall. 3 vols. Leiden: Brill, 2007–2018.
Gregory of Nyssa. *Gregorii Nysseni Opera*. Edited by Wernerus Jaeger. Leiden: Brill, 1960.
Gregory of Nyssa. *Homilies on Ecclesiastes*. Translated by Stuart George Hall and Rachel Moriarty. Berlin: Walter de Gruyter, 1993.
Gregory of Nyssa. 'On Perfection'. In *Ascetical Works*, translated by Virginia Woods Callahan, 91–122. Washington, DC: Catholic University of America Press, 1967.
Gregory of Nyssa. 'On the Holy Spirit against the Macedonian Spirit–Fighters'. In *The Cambridge Edition of Early Christian Writings*, Vol. 1: *God*, edited and translated by Andrew Radde-Gallwitz. Cambridge: Cambridge University Press, 2017.
Gregory of Nyssa. *The Life of Moses*. Translated by Abraham J. Malherbe and Everett Ferguson. The Classics of Western Spirituality. Mahwah, NJ: Paulist, 1978.
Gunton, Colin E. *Act and Being: Towards a Theology of the Divine Attributes*. Grand Rapids: Wm. B. Eerdmans, 2002.
Gunton, Colin E. *Becoming and Being: The Doctrine of God in Charles Hartshorne and Karl Barth*. Second Edition. London: SCM, 2001.
Gunton, Colin E. 'Creation and Mediation in the Theology of Robert W. Jenson: An Encounter and a Convergence'. In *Trinity, Time, and Church: A Response to the Theology of Robert W. Jenson*, edited by Colin E. Gunton, 80–93. Grand Rapids: Wm. B. Eerdmans, 2000.
Gunton, Colin E. *The One, the Three, and the Many: God, Creation and the Culture of Modernity*. Cambridge: Cambridge University Press, 1993.
Hadot, Pierre. *Plotinus or the Simplicity of Vision*. Translated by Michael Chase. Chicago: University of Chicago Press, 1988.
Halfwassen, Jens. *Der Aufstieg zum Einen: Untersuchungen zu Platon und Plotin*. 2nd ed. München und Leipzig: K.G. Saur, 2006.
Hanby, Michael. *Augustine and Modernity*. London: Routledge, 2003.
Harris, Steven Edward. '"We Keep Our Eyes Fixed Upon Christ": An Anti-Speculative Doctrine of Final Resurrection in Bullinger and Turretin'. *Scottish Journal of Theology* 72, no. 3 (August 2019): 253–64.
Hart, David Bentley. *The Beauty of the Infinite: On the Aesthetics of Christian Truth*. Grand Rapids: Wm. B. Eerdmans, 2003.
Hart, David Bentley. *The Experience of God: Being, Consciousness, Bliss*. New Haven: Yale University Press, 2013.
Hart, David Bentley. 'The Lively God of Robert Jenson'. *First Things*, October 2005, 28–34.
Hart, David Bentley. 'The Mirror of the Infinite: Gregory of Nyssa on the *Vestigia Trinitatis*'. *Modern Theology* 18, no. 4 (2002): 541–61.
Hart, David Bentley. 'The Offering of Names: Metaphysics, Nihilism, and Analogy'. In *The Hidden and the Manifest: Essays in Theology and Metaphysics*, 1–44. Grand Rapids: Wm. B. Eerdmans, 2017.

Hasker, William. *Metaphysics and the Tri-Personal God*. Oxford: Oxford University Press, 2013.
Hasker, William. 'Simplicity and Freedom: A Response to Stump and Kretzmann'. *Faith and Philosophy* 3, no. 2 (April 1986): 192–201.
Hauerwas, Stanley. 'How to Write a Theological Sentence'. In *The Work of Theology*, 122–46. Grand Rapids: Wm. B. Eerdmans, 2015.
Hector, Kevin W. *Theology without Metaphysics: God, Language, and the Spirit of Recognition*. Cambridge: Cambridge University Press, 2012.
Heidegger, Martin. *Being and Time: A Translation of* Sein und Zeit. Translated by Joan Stambaugh. Albany: State University of New York Press, 1996.
Heidegger, Martin. *Introduction to Metaphysics*. Translated by Gregory Fried and Richard Polt. Second Edition. New Haven: Yale Nota Bene, 2014.
Heidegger, Martin. *On Time and Being*. Translated by Joan Stambaugh. London: Harper & Row, 1972.
Heidegger, Martin. *The Phenomenology of Religious Life*. Translated by Matthias Fritsch and Jennifer Anna Gosetti-Ferencei. Bloomington: Indiana University Press, 2004.
Henry, James Daryn. *The Freedom of God: A Study in the Pneumatology of Robert Jenson*. Minneapolis: Fortress Academic, 2018.
Hermann, Wilhelm. *Systematic Theology*. Translated by Nathaniel Micklem and Kenneth A. Saunders. New York: Macmillan, 1927.
Hill, Wesley. *Paul and the Trinity: Persons, Relations, and the Pauline Letters*. Grand Rapids: Wm. B. Eerdmans, 2015.
Hinlicky, Paul R. *Divine Complexity: The Rise of Creedal Christianity*. Minneapolis: Fortress, 2011.
Hinlicky, Paul R. *Divine Simplicity: Christ the Crisis of Metaphysics*. Grand Rapids: Baker Academic, 2016.
Hodgson, Leonard. *The Doctrine of the Trinity*. New York: Charles Scribner's Sons, 1944.
Holmes, Stephen R. 'Asymmetrical Assumption: Why Lutheran Christology Does Not Lead to Kenoticism or Divine Passibility'. *Scottish Journal of Theology* 72, no. 4 (November 2019): 357–74.
Holmes, Stephen R. 'Radicalising the *Communicatio:* Jenson's Theology in Confessional Lutheran Perspective'. In *The Promise of Robert W. Jenson's Theology: Constructive Engagements*, edited by Stephen John Wright and Chris E. W. Green, 131–40. Minneapolis: Fortress, 2017.
Holmes, Stephen R. *The Holy Trinity: Understanding God's Life*. Milton Keynes: Paternoster, 2012.
Hughes, Christopher. *On a Complex Theory of a Simple God: An Investigation in Aquinas' Philosophical Theology*. Ithaca: Cornell University Press, 1989.
Hunsinger, George. *Reading Barth with Charity: A Hermeneutical Proposal*. Grand Rapids: Baker Academic, 2015.
Hunsinger, George. 'Robert Jenson's Systematic Theology: A Review Essay'. *Scottish Journal of Theology* 55, no. 2 (2002): 161–200.
Inwagen, Peter van. 'Being, Existence, and Ontological Commitment'. In *Existence: Essays in Ontology*, 50–86. Cambridge: Cambridge University Press, 2014.
Inwagen, Peter van. 'Meta-Ontology'. In *Ontology, Identity, and Modality: Essays in Metaphysics*, 13–31. Cambridge: Cambridge University Press, 2001.

Irenaeus. *Against Heresies*. Edited by Alexander Roberts and James Donaldson. Ante-Nicene Fathers of the Church, Vol. I. Edinburgh: T&T Clark, 1885.
Isaac, Shirley Mae. 'The Unity of the Triune God in the Theologies of Jürgen Moltmann and Robert Jenson: A Dialectical Approach'. PhD dissertation, Toronto School of Theology, 2009.
Jenson, Robert W. *A Religion Against Itself*. Richmond: John Knox, 1967.
Jenson, Robert W. 'A Theological Autobiography, to Date'. *Dialog: A Journal of Theology* 46, no. 1 (Spring 2007): 46–54.
Jenson, Robert W. *Alpha and Omega: A Study in the Theology of Karl Barth*. New York: Thomas Nelson & Sons, 1963.
Jenson, Robert W. *America's Theologian: A Recommendation of Jonathan Edwards*. Oxford: Oxford University Press, 1988.
Jenson, Robert W. 'An Ontology of Freedom in the *De Servo Arbitrio* of Luther'. *Modern Theology* 10, no. 3 (July 1994): 247–52.
Jenson, Robert W. 'Aspects of a Doctrine of Creation'. In *The Doctrine of Creation: Essays in Dogmatics, History, and Philosophy*, edited by Colin E. Gunton, 17–28. Edinburgh: T&T Clark, 1997.
Jenson, Robert W. *Canon and Creed*. Louisville: Westminster John Knox, 2010.
Jenson, Robert W. 'Choose Ye This Day Whom Ye Will Serve'. In *Essays on the Trinity*, edited by Lincoln Harvey, 14–19. Eugene: Cascade, 2018.
Jenson, Robert W. 'Christ in the Trinity: The *Communicatio Idiomatum*'. In *The Person of Christ*, edited by Stephen R. Holmes and Murray A. Rae, 61–69. London: T&T Clark International, 2005.
Jenson, Robert W. '*Conceptus ... De Spiritu Sancto*'. *Pro Ecclesia* 15, no. 1 (Winter 2006): 100–107.
Jenson, Robert W. 'Creator and Creature'. In *Theology as Revisionary Metaphysics: Essays on God and Creation*, edited by Stephen John Wright, 155–61. Eugene, OR: Cascade, 2014.
Jenson, Robert W. 'Cur Deus Homo? The Election of Christ in the Theology of Karl Barth'. PhD dissertation, Heidelberg University, 1959.
Jenson, Robert W. '*Deus Est Ipsa Pulchritudo*'. In *Theology as Revisionary Metaphysics: Essays on God and Creation*, edited by Stephen John Wright, 207–15. Eugene, OR: Cascade, 2014.
Jenson, Robert W. *Ezekiel*. Grand Rapids: Brazos, 2009.
Jenson, Robert W. *God After God: The God of the Past and the God of the Future, Seen in the Work of Karl Barth*. New York: Bobbs-Merrill, 1969.
Jenson, Robert W. 'Gregory of Nyssa: *The Life of Moses*'. *Theology Today* 62 (2006): 533–37.
Jenson, Robert W. '*Ipse Pater Non Est Impassibilis*'. In *Theology as Revisionary Metaphysics: Essays on God and Creation*, edited by Stephen John Wright, 93–101. Eugene, OR: Cascade, 2014.
Jenson, Robert W. 'Jesus in the Trinity'. *Pro Ecclesia* 8, no. 3 (Summer 1999): 308–18.
Jenson, Robert W. 'Karl Barth on the Being of God'. In *Thomas Aquinas and Karl Barth: An Unofficial Catholic–Protestant Dialogue*, edited by Bruce L. McCormack and Thomas Joseph White, 43–51. Grand Rapids: Wm. B. Eerdmans, 2013.
Jenson, Robert W. 'On Dogmatic/Systematic Appropriateion of Paul-According-to-Martyn'. In *Apocalyptic and the Future of Theology: With and beyond J. Louis Martyn*, edited by Joshua B. Davis and Douglas Harink, 154–62. Eugene, OR: Cascade, 2012.

Jenson, Robert W. 'On Hegemonic Discourse'. In *Theology as Revisionary Metaphysics: Essays on God and Creation*, edited by Stephen John Wright, 18–22. Eugene: Cascade, 2014.

Jenson, Robert W. *On Thinking the Human: Resolutions of Difficult Notions*. Grand Rapids: Wm. B. Eerdmans, 2003.

Jenson, Robert W. 'Once More on the *Logos Asarkos*'. In *Theology as Revisionary Metaphysics: Essays on God and Creation*, edited by Stephen John Wright, 119–24. Eugene, OR: Cascade, 2014.

Jenson, Robert W. 'Parting Ways?: Review of *Systematic Theology: Volume 2*, by Wolfhart Pannenberg'. *First Things* 53 (May 1995): 60–62.

Jenson, Robert W. 'Preface'. In *Theology as Revisionary Metaphysics: Essays on God and Creation*, edited by Stephen John Wright, vii–viii. Eugene, OR: Cascade, 2014.

Jenson, Robert W. 'Proclamation without Metaphysics'. In *Theology as Revisionary Metaphysics: Essays on God and Creation*, edited by Stephen John Wright, 4–17. Eugene, OR: Cascade, 2014.

Jenson, Robert W. 'Reading the Body'. *The New Atlantis* 9 (Summer 2005): 73–82.

Jenson, Robert W. 'Response to Timo Tavast'. *Pro Ecclesia* 19, no. 4 (Fall 2010): 369–70.

Jenson, Robert W. 'Scripture's Authority in the Church'. In *The Art of Reading Scripture*, edited by Ellen F. Davis and Richard B. Hays, 27–37. Grand Rapids: Wm. B. Eerdmans, 2003.

Jenson, Robert W. 'Some Riffs on Thomas Aquinas's *De Ente et Essentia*'. In *Theological Theology: Essays in Honor of John Webster*, edited by R. David Nelson, Darren Sarisky, and Justin Stratis, 125–30. London: Bloomsbury T&T Clark, 2015.

Jenson, Robert W. *Song of Songs*. Louisville: John Knox, 2005.

Jenson, Robert W. *Story and Promise: A Brief Theology of the Gospel About Jesus*. Philadelphia: Fortress, 1973.

Jenson, Robert W. *Systematic Theology*, 2 Vols. Oxford: Oxford University Press, 1997–1999.

Jenson, Robert W. 'The Bible and the Trinity'. *Pro Ecclesia* 11, no. 3 (Summer 2002): 329–39.

Jenson, Robert W. 'The Body of God's Presence: A Trinitarian Theory'. In *Creation, Christ, and Culture: Studies in Honour of T. F. Torrance*, edited by Richard W. A. McKinney, 82–91. Edinburgh: T&T Clark, 1976.

Jenson, Robert W. 'The Holy Spirit'. In *Christian Dogmatics*, edited by Carl E. Braaten and Robert W. Jenson, 2:102–78. Minneapolis: Fortress, 1984.

Jenson, Robert W. *The Knowledge of Things Hoped For: The Sense of Theological Discourse*. Oxford: Oxford University Press, 1969.

Jenson, Robert W. 'The Strange New World of the Bible'. In *Theology as Revisionary Metaphysics: Essays on God and Creation*, edited by Stephen John Wright, 146–54. Eugene, OR: Cascade, 2011.

Jenson, Robert W. 'The Triune God'. In *Christian Dogmatics*, edited by Carl E. Braaten and Robert W. Jenson, 1:79–191. Minneapolis: Fortress, 1984.

Jenson, Robert W. *The Triune Identity: God According to the Gospel*. Philadelphia: Fortress, 1982.

Jenson, Robert W. 'The Triunity of Truth'. In *Essays in Theology of Culture*, 84–94. Grand Rapids: Wm. B. Eerdmans, 1995.

Jenson, Robert W. *Theology as Revisionary Metaphysics: Essays on God and Creation*. Edited by Stephen John Wright. Eugene, OR: Cascade, 2014.

Jenson, Robert W. 'Three Identities of One Action'. *Scottish Journal of Theology* 28, no. 1 (February 1975): 1–15.
Jenson, Robert W. 'Toward a Christian Theology of Israel'. *Pro Ecclesia* 9, no. 1 (Winter 2000): 43–56.
Jenson, Robert W. *Unbaptized God: The Basic Flaw in Ecumenical Theology*. Minneapolis: Augsburg Fortress, 1992.
Jenson, Robert W. *Visible Words: The Interpretation and Practice of Christian Sacraments*. Philadelphia: Fortress, 1978.
Jenson, Robert W. 'What If It Were True?' In *Theology as Revisionary Metaphysics: Essays on God and Creation*, edited by Stephen John Wright, 23–37. Eugene, OR: Cascade, 2014.
Jenson, Robert W. 'What Kind of God Can Make a Covenant?' In *Covenant and Hope: Christian and Jewish Reflections*, edited by Robert W. Jenson and Eugene B. Korn, 3–18. Grand Rapids: Wm. B. Eerdmans, 2012.
Jenson, Robert W. 'You Wonder Where the Spirit Went'. In *Theology as Revisionary Metaphysics: Essays on God and Creation*, edited by Stephen John Wright, 110–18. Eugene, OR: Cascade, 2014.
Jüngel, Eberhard. *God as the Mystery of the World: On the Foundation of the Theology of the Crucified One in the Dispute between Theism and Atheism*. Translated by Darrell L. Guder. Grand Rapids: Wm. B. Eerdmans, 1983.
Karfíková, Lenka, Scot Douglass, and Johannes Zachhuber, eds. *Gregory of Nyssa: Contra Eunomium II: An English Version with Supporting Studies*. Supplements to Vigiliae Christianae. Leiden: Brill, 2007.
Keller, Catherine. *Face of the Deep: A Theology of Becoming*. London: Routledge, 2003.
Kelsey, David H. *Eccentric Existence: A Theological Anthropology*. 2 vols. Louisville: Westminster John Knox, 2009.
Kerr, Fergus. *After Aquinas: Versions of Thomism*. Oxford: Blackwell, 2002.
Kilby, Karen. 'Perichoresis and Projection: Problems with Social Doctrines of the Trinity'. *New Blackfriars* 81 (November 2000): 432–45.
King-Farlow, John. 'Simplicity, Analogy and Plain Religious Lives'. *Faith and Philosophy* 1, no. 2 (April 1984): 216–29.
Kraal, Anders. 'Logic and Divine Simplicity'. *Philosophy Compass* 6, no. 4 (2011): 282–94.
Kripke, Saul. *Naming and Necessity*. Cambridge, MA: Harvard University Press, 1980.
Lacugna, Catherine Mowry. *God For Us: The Trinity and Christian Life*. New York: HarperCollins, 1991.
Langdon, Adrian. *God the Eternal Contemporary: Trinity, Eternity, and Time in Karl Barth*. Eugene: Wipf and Stock, 2012.
Lash, Nicholas. *Believing Three Ways in One God: A Reading of the Apostles' Creed*. London: SCM, 1992.
Lash, Nicholas. 'Considering the Trinity'. *Modern Theology* 2, no. 3 (1986): 183–96.
Lee, Sang Hoon. 'The Preexistence and Transcendence of the Risen One in Robert Jenson's Theology'. *Pro Ecclesia* 26, no. 4 (Fall 2017): 401–14.
Lee, Sang Hoon. *Trinitarian Ontology and Israel in Robert W Jenson's Theology*. Eugene, OR: Pickwick, 2016.
Leemans, Johan, and Mathieu Cassin, eds. *Gregory of Nyssa: Contra Eunomium III: An English Translation with Commentary and Supporting Studies*. Supplements to Vigiliae Christianae. Leiden: Brill, 2014.

Leftow, Brian. 'Divine Simplicity and Divine Freedom'. *Proceedings of the American Catholic Philosophical Association* 89 (2016): 45–56.
Legge, Dominic. *The Trinitarian Christology of St. Thomas Aquinas*. Oxford: Oxford University Press, 2017.
Leithart, Peter J. 'Jenson as Theological Interpreter'. In *The Promise of Robert W. Jenson's Theology: Constructive Engagements*, edited by Stephen John Wright and Chris E. W. Green, 45–57. Minneapolis: Fortress, 2017.
Lenow, Joseph E. 'Shoring Up Divine Simplicity against Modal Collapse: A Powers Account'. *Religious Studies*, forthcoming, 1–20.
Lett, Jacob. 'Divine Roominess: Spatial and Music Analogies in Hans Urs von Balthasar and Robert Jenson'. *Pro Ecclesia* 28, no. 3 (August 2019): 267–77.
Lett, Jacob. 'Hans Urs von Balthasar's Dramatic Soteriology: A Theology of Representation'. PhD dissertation, University of Manchester, 2018.
Levering, Matthew. *Engaging the Doctrine of Creation: Cosmos, Creatures, and the Wise and Good Creator*. Grand Rapids: Baker Academic, 2017.
Levering, Matthew, and George Kalantzis. 'Introduction: Why Think about Divine Simplicity?' *Modern Theology* 35, no. 3 (July 2019): 1–7.
Lindbeck, George A. *The Nature of Doctrine: Religion and Theology in a Postliberal Age*. 25th Anniversary Edition. Louisville: Westminster John Knox, 2009.
Long, D. Stephen. *The Perfectly Simple Triune God: Aquinas and His Legacy*. Minneapolis: Fortress, 2016.
Lossky, Vladimir. *In the Image and Likeness of God*. Edited by John H. Erickson and Thomas E. Bird. Crestwood: St. Vladimir's Seminary Press, 1974.
Lossky, Vladimir. *The Mystical Theology of the Eastern Church*. 1957. Reprint, Crestwood: St. Vladimir's Seminary Press, 1976.
Luther, Martin. *Heidelberg Disputation*. In *Martin Luther's Basic Theological Writings*, ed. Timothy F. Lull and William R. Russell. Minneapolis: Fortress, 2012.
Mann, William E. 'Divine Simplicity'. *Religious Studies* 18, no. 4 (December 1982): 451–71.
Mann, William E. 'Simplicity and Properties: A Reply to Morris'. *Religious Studies* 22, no. 3–4 (September 1986): 243–53.
Martin, C. B. 'God, the Null Set and Divine Simplicity'. In *The Challenge of Religion Today*, edited by John King-Farlow, 138–43. New York: Science History, 1976.
Martin, Jennifer Newsome. *Hans Urs von Balthasar and the Critical Appropriation of Russian Religious Thought*. Notre Dame: University of Notre Dame Press, 2015.
Mascall, E. L. *Existence and Analogy: A Sequel to 'He Who Is'*. London: Longmans, Green & Co, 1949.
Mascall, E. L. *He Who Is: A Study in Traditional Theism*. London: Longmans, Green & Co, 1943.
Mascall, E. L. *The Triune God: An Ecumenical Study*. Eugene, OR: Pickwick, 1986.
Mateo-Seco, Lucas Francisco. 'Creation'. In *The Brill Dictionary of Gregory of Nyssa*, edited by Lucas Francisco Mateo-Seco and Giulio Maspero, 183–90. Leiden: Brill, 2010.
McCabe, Herbert. 'Aquinas on the Trinity'. In *God Still Matters*, edited by Brian Davies, 46–53. London: Continuum, 2002.
McCabe, Herbert. *God Matters*. London: Geoffrey Chapman, 1987.

McCall, Thomas H. 'Trinity Doctrine, Plain and Simple'. In *Advancing Trinitarian Theology: Explorations in Constructive Dogmatics*, edited by Oliver D. Crisp and Fred Sanders, 42–59. Grand Rapids: Zondervan, 2014.

McCall, Thomas H. *Which Trinity? Whose Monotheism?: Philosophical and Theological Voices on the Metaphysics of Trinitarian Theology*. Grand Rapids: Wm. B. Eerdmans, 2010.

McCall, Thomas H., and Michael C. Rea, eds. *Philosophical and Theological Essays on the Trinity*. Oxford: Oxford University Press, 2009.

McCormack, Bruce L. *Karl Barth's Critically Realistic Dialectical Theology: Genesis and Development 1909–1936*. Oxford: Oxford University Press, 1995.

McFarland, Ian A. *From Nothing: A Theology of Creation*. Louisville: Westminster John Knox, 2014.

McFarland, Ian A. 'The Body of Christ: Rethinking a Classic Ecclesiological Model'. *International Journal of Systematic Theology* 7, no. 3 (July 2005): 225–45.

McFarland, Ian A. *The Word Made Flesh: A Theology of the Incarnation*. Louisville: Westminster John Knox, 2019.

McGee, Timothy. 'God's Life in and as Opening: James Cone, Divine Self-Determination, and the Trinitarian Politics of Sovereignty'. *Modern Theology* 32, no. 1 (January 2016): 100–117.

Meeks, M. Douglas. 'The Social Trinity and Property'. In *God's Life in Trinity*, edited by Miroslav Volf and Michael Welker. Minneapolis: Fortress, 2006.

Melanchthon, Philip. *Loci Communes Theologici*. In <i>Melanchthon and Bucer</i>, ed. Wilhelm Pauck. London: SCM, 1969.

Miller, Barry. *The Fullness of Being: A New Paradigm for Existence*. Notre Dame: University of Notre Dame Press, 2002.

Moltmann, Jürgen. *God in Creation: An Ecological Doctrine of Creation*. Translated by Margaret Kohl. London: SCM, 1985.

Moltmann, Jürgen. *The Coming of God: Christian Eschatology*. Translated by Margaret Kohl. London: SCM, 1996.

Moltmann, Jürgen. *The Trinity and the Kingdom: The Doctrine of God*. Translated by Margaret Kohl. London: SCM, 1981.

Montagnes, Bernard. *The Doctrine of the Analogy of Being according to Thomas Aquinas*. Translated by E. M. Macierowski. Milwaukee: Marquette University Press, 2004.

Moreland, J. P., and William Lane Craig. *Philosophical Foundations for a Christian Worldview*. Downers Grove: InterVarsity, 2003.

Morreall, John. 'Divine Simplicity and Divine Properties'. *The Journal of Critical Analysis* 7, no. 2 (1978): 67–70.

Morris, Thomas V. 'On God and Mann: A View of Divine Simplicity'. *Religious Studies* 21, no. 3 (September 1985): 299–318.

Morris, Thomas V. *Our Idea of God: An Introduction to Philosophical Theology*. Downers Grove: InterVarsity, 1991.

Mullins, R. T. 'An Analytic Response to Stephen R. Holmes with a Special Treatment of His Doctrine of Divine Simplicity'. In *The Holy Trinity Revisited: Essays in Response to Stephen R. Holmes*, edited by T. A. Noble and Jason S. Sexton, 82–96. London: Paternoster, 2015.

Mullins, R. T. 'Simply Impossible: A Case against Divine Simplicity'. *Journal of Reformed Theology* 7 (2013): 181–203.

Murphy, Francesca Aran. *God is Not a Story: Realism Revisited*. Oxford: Oxford University Press, 2007.
Nash, Ronald H. *The Concept of God: An Exploration of Contemporary Difficulties with the Attributes of God*. Grand Rapids: Zondervan, 1983.
Nicholas of Cusa. *On God as Not-Other: A Translation and an Appraisal of* De Li Non Aliud. Translated by Jasper Hopkins. 3rd Edition. Minneapolis: Arthur J. Banning, 1987.
Nicol, Andrew W. *Exodus and Resurrection: The God of Israel in the Theology of Robert W. Jenson*. Minneapolis: Fortress, 2016.
O'Connor, Timothy. 'Simplicity and Creation'. *Faith and Philosophy* 16, no. 3 (July 1999): 405–12.
Oderberg, David S. *Real Essentialism*. Oxon: Routledge, 2007.
O'Leary, Joseph S. 'Divine Simplicity and the Plurality of Attributes'. In *Gregory of Nyssa: Contra Eunomium II: An English Version with Supporting Studies: Proceedings of the 10th International Colloquium on Gregory of Nyssa*, edited by Lenka Karfíková, Scot Douglass, and Johannes Zachhuber, 307–37. Supplements to Vigiliae Christianae. Leiden: Brill, 2007.
Oliver, Simon. *Creation: A Guide for the Perplexed*. London: Bloomsbury T&T Clark, 2017.
O'Rourke, Fran. *Pseudo-Dionysius and the Metaphysics of Aquinas*. Notre Dame: University of Notre Dame Press, 1992.
Ortlund, Gavin. 'Divine Simplicity in Historical Perspective: Resourcing a Contemporary Discussion'. *International Journal of Systematic Theology* 16, no. 4 (October 2014): 436–53.
Osborn, Eric. *Irenaeus of Lyons*. Cambridge: Cambridge University Press, 2001.
Palamas, Gregory. *The Triads*. Edited by John Meyendorff. Translated by Nicholas Glendle. Mahwah, NJ: Paulist, 1983.
Pannenberg, Wolfhart. 'A Trinitarian Synthesis: Review of *Systematic Theology: Volumes I and II* by Robert W. Jenson'. *First Things*, May 2000, 49–53.
Pannenberg, Wolfhart. 'Analogy and Doxology'. In *Basic Questions in Theology*, translated by George H. Kehm, 1:212–38. London: SCM, 1970.
Pannenberg, Wolfhart. *Metaphysics and the Idea of God*. Translated by Philip Clayton. Grand Rapids: Wm. B. Eerdmans, 1990.
Pannenberg, Wolfhart. *Systematic Theology*, 3 Vols. Translated by Geoffrey W. Bromiley. Grand Rapids: Wm. B. Eerdmans, 1991–1993.
Pannenberg, Wolfhart. 'The Appropriation of the Philosophical Concept of God as a Dogmatic Problem of Early Christian Theology'. In *Basic Questions in Theology*, translated by George H. Kehm, 2:119–83. London: SCM, 1971.
Perl, Eric D. *Theophany: The Neoplatonic Philosophy of Dionysius the Areopagite*. Albany: State University of New York Press, 2007.
Perl, Eric D. *Thinking Being: Introduction to Metaphysics in the Classical Tradition*. Leiden: Brill, 2014.
Peters, Ted. *God as Trinity: Relationality and Temporality in the Divine Life*. Louisville: Westminster John Knox, 1993.
Peters, Ted. 'God Happens: The Timeliness of the Triune God'. *Christian Century*, April 1998, 342–44.
Peters, Ted. *God—The World's Future: Systematic Theology for a New Era*. Third Edition. Minneapolis: Fortress, 2015.

Peterson, Derrick. 'The Parting of God: Diagnosing the Fate of Divine Simplicity in Twentieth-Century Theology'. In *The Lord Is One: Reclaiming Divine Simplicity*, edited by Joseph Minich and Onsi A. Kamel, 130–73. Leesburg, VA: Davenant Institute, 2019.
Pickstock, Catherine. *After Writing: On the Liturgical Consummation of Philosophy*. Oxford: Blackwell, 1998.
Pieper, Josef. *The Silence of St. Thomas: Three Essays*. Translated by John Murray and Daniel O'Connor. South Bend: St. Augustine's, 1957.
Placher, William C. *The Domestication of Transcendence: How Modern Thinking about God Went Wrong*. Louisville: Westminster John Knox, 1996.
Plantinga, Alvin. *Does God Have a Nature?* Milwaukee: Marquette University Press, 1980.
Plantinga, Cornelius, Jr. 'Social Trinity and Tritheism'. In *Trinity, Incarnation, and Atonement: Philosophical and Theological Essay*, edited by Ronald J. Feenstra and Cornelius Plantinga Jr., 21–47. Notre Dame: University of Notre Dame Press, 1990.
Plantinga, Richard J., Thomas R. Thompson, and Matthew D. Lundberg. *An Introduction to Christian Theology*. Cambridge: Cambridge University Press, 2010.
Plato. *Parmenides*. Translated by Harold North Fowler. Loeb Classical Library 167. Cambridge, MA: Harvard University Press, 1926.
Plato. *Timaeus*. Translated by R. G. Bury. Loeb Classical Library 234. Cambridge, MA: Harvard University Press, 1929.
Platter, Jonathan M. 'Jesus, Trinity, and Creation: Divine Simplicity, the "Real" Relation, and Trinitarian Economy in Dialogue with Robert Jenson'. *Pro Ecclesia* 28, no. 3 (August 2019): 233–52.
Plotinus. *Enneads I–VI: With an English Translation by A. H. Armstrong*. 7 vols. Loeb Classical Library. Cambridge, MA: Harvard University Press, 1969–1988.
Plotinus. *The Enneads*. Edited by Lloyd P. Gerson. Translated by George Boys-Stones, John M. Dillon, Lloyd P. Gerson, R. A. H. King, Andrew Smith, and James Wilberding. Cambridge: Cambridge University Press, 2018.
Powell, Samuel M. *The Trinity in German Thought*. Cambridge: Cambridge University Press, 2001.
Preller, Victor. *Divine Science and the Science of God: A Reformulation of Thomas Aquinas*. Princeton: Princeton University Press, 1967.
Przywara, Erich. 'The Scope of Analogy as a Fundamental Catholic Form'. In *Analogia Entis: Metaphysics: Original Structure and Universal Rhythm*, translated by John R. Betz and David Bentley Hart, 348–99. Grand Rapids: Wm. B. Eerdmans, 2014.
Przywara, Erich. 'Time, Space, Eternity'. In *Analogia Entis: Metaphysics: Original Structure and Universal Rhythm*, translated by John R. Betz and David Bentley Hart, 583–95. Grand Rapids: Wm. B. Eerdmans, 2014.
Radde-Gallwitz, Andrew. *Basil of Caesarea, Gregory of Nyssa, and the Transformation of Divine Simplicity*. Oxford: Oxford University Press, 2009.
Radde-Gallwitz, Andrew. 'Gregory of Nyssa and Divine Simplicity: A Conceptualist Reading'. *Modern Theology* 35, no. 3 (July 2019): 452–66.
Radde-Gallwitz, Andrew. 'Review of Steven J. Duby, *Divine Simplicity: A Dogmatic Account*'. *International Journal of Systematic Theology* 18, no. 4 (October 2016): 480–84.
Rahner, Karl. *The Trinity*. Translated by Joseph Donceel. New York: Crossroad, 1997.
Rea, Michael, ed. *Oxford Readings in Philosophical Theology, Volume 1: Trinity Incarnation, and Atonement*. Oxford: Oxford University Press, 2009.

Rea, Michael C. 'The Trinity'. In *The Oxford Handbook of Philosophical Theology*, edited by Thomas P. Flint and Michael C. Rea, 403–23. Oxford: Oxford University Press, 2009.

Richard of St. Victor. 'On the Trinity'. In *The Twelve Patriarchs, The Mystical Ark, Book Three of The Trinity*, edited and translated by Grover A. Zinn, 371–97. New York: Paulist, 1979.

Richards, Jay Wesley. *The Untamed God: A Philosophical Exploration of Divine Perfection, Immutability, and Simplicity*. Downers Grove: InterVarsity, 2003.

Riches, Aaron. *Ecce Homo: On the Divine Unity of Christ*. Grand Rapids: Wm. B. Eerdmans, 2016.

Rist, John. 'Plotinus and Christian Philosophy'. In *The Cambridge Companion to Plotinus*, edited by Lloyd P. Gerson, 386–413. Cambridge: Cambridge University Press, 1996.

Rocca, Gregory. 'The Distinction between *Res Significata* and *Modus Significandi* in Aquinas's Theological Epistemology'. *The Thomist* 55, no. 2 (April 1991): 173–97.

Rocca, Gregory P. *Speaking the Incomprehensible God: Thomas Aquinas on the Interplay of Positive and Negative Theology*. Washington, DC: Catholic University of America Press, 2004.

Rolnick, Philip A. *Analogical Possibilities: How Words Refer to God*. Atlanta: Scholars Press, 1993.

Rolnick, Philip A. 'Realist Reference to God: Analogy or Univocity'. In *Realism & Antirealism*, edited by William P. Alston, 211–34. Ithaca: Cornell University Press, 2002.

Rook, Russell D. *Rhyming Hope and History: Theology and Culture in the Work of Robert Jenson*. Eugene, OR: Pickwick, 2012.

Rosemann, Philipp W. *Omne agens agit sibi simile: A 'Repetition' of Scholastic Metaphysics*. Leuven: Leuven University Press, 1996.

Sanders, Fred. *The Image of the Immanent Trinity: Rahner's Rule and the Theological Interpretation of Scripture*. New York: Peter Lang, 2005.

Sarisky, Darren. *Reading the Bible Theologically*. Cambridge: Cambridge University Press, 2019.

Sarisky, Darren. *Scriptural Interpretation: A Theological Exploration*. Oxford: Wiley Blackwell, 2013.

Sarisky, Darren. 'What Is Theological Interpretation? The Example of Robert W. Jenson'. *International Journal of Systematic Theology* 12, no. 2 (April 2010): 201–16.

Schindler, Alfred. *Wort und Analogie in Augustins Trinitätslehre*. Tübingen: J. C. B. Mohr (Paul Siebeck), 1965.

Schlesinger, Eugene R. 'Trinity, Incarnation and Time: A Restatement of the Doctrine of God in Conversation with Robert Jenson'. *Scottish Journal of Theology* 69, no. 2 (2016): 189–203.

Schwöbel, Christoph. 'Die Trinitätslehre Als Rahmentheorie Des Christlichen Glaubens: Vier Thesen Zur Bedeutung Der Trinität in Der Christlichen Dogmatik'. In *Gott in Beziehung: Studien Zur Dogmatik*, 25–51. Tübingen: Mohr Siebeck, 2002.

Schwöbel, Christoph. *Gott in Beziehung: Studien zur Dogmatik*. Tübingen: Mohr Siebeck, 2002.

Schwöbel, Christoph. 'The Eternity of the Triune God: Preliminary Considerations on the Relationship between the Trinity and the Time of Creation'. *Modern Theology* 34, no. 3 (July 2018): 345–55.

Schwöbel, Christoph. 'The Trinity Between Athens and Jerusalem'. *Journal of Reformed Theology* 3 (2009): 22–41.

Schwöbel, Christoph, ed. *Trinitarian Theology Today: Essays on Divine Being and Act.* London: Bloomsbury, 1995.
Schwöbel, Christoph. 'Where Do We Stand in Trinitarian Theology? Resources, Revisions, and Reappraisals'. In *Recent Developments in Trinitarian Theology: An International Symposium*, edited by Christophe Chalamet and Marc Vial, 9–71. Minneapolis: Fortress, 2014.
Scotus, John Duns. *Ordinatio.* Edited by C. Balić. *Opera Omnia.* ET by Peter Simpson: http://www.aristotelophile.com/current.htm. Civitas Vaticana: Typis Polyglottis Vaticanis, 1950.
Sholl, Brian K. 'On Robert Jenson's Trinitarian Thought'. *Modern Theology* 18, no. 1 (January 2002): 27–36.
Smith, Barry D. *The Oneness and Simplicity of God.* Eugene, OR: Pickwick, 2014.
Smith, Quentin. 'An Analysis of Holiness'. *Religious Studies* 24, no. 4 (December 1988): 511–27.
Smith, Timothy L. *Thomas Aquinas' Trinitarian Theology: A Study in Theological Method.* Washington, DC: Catholic University of America Press, 2003.
Sonderegger, Katherine. *Systematic Theology, Volume 1: The Doctrine of God.* Minneapolis: Fortress, 2015.
Soskice, Janet Martin. 'Naming God: A Study in Faith and Reason'. In *Reason and the Reasons of Faith*, edited by Paul J. Griffiths and Reinhard Hütter, 241–54. London: T&T Clark, 2005.
Soulen, R. Kendall. 'YHWH the Triune God'. *Modern Theology* 15, no. 1 (1999): 25–54.
Spencer, Mark K. 'The Flexibility of Divine Simplicity: Aquinas, Scotus, Palamas'. *International Philosophical Quarterly* 57, no. 2 (June 2017): 123–39.
Stanley, Timothy. *Protestant Metaphysics after Karl Barth and Martin Heidegger.* London: SCM, 2010.
Stump, Eleonore, and Norman Kretzmann. 'Absolute Simplicity'. *Faith and Philosophy* 2, no. 4 (October 1985): 353–82.
Swain, Scott R. *The God of the Gospel: Robert Jenson's Trinitarian Theology.* Downers Grove: InterVarsity, 2013.
Tanner, Kathryn. *Christ the Key.* Cambridge: Cambridge University Press, 2010.
Tanner, Kathryn. *God and Creation in Christian Theology: Tyranny or Empowerment?* Oxford: Basil Blackwell, 1988.
Tavast, Timo. 'Challenging the Modalism of the West: Jenson on the Trinity'. *Pro Ecclesia* 19, no. 4 (Fall 2010): 355–68.
Tavast, Timo. 'The Identification of the Triune God: Robert W. Jenson's Approach to the Doctrine of the Trinity'. *Dialog: A Journal of Theology* 51, no. 2 (Summer 2012): 155–63.
Teske, Roland J. 'Properties of God and the Predicaments in *De Trinitate* 5'. In *To Know God and the Soul: Essays on the Thought of Saint Augustine*, 93–111. Washington, DC: Catholic University of America Press, 2008.
Thiemann, Ronald F. *Revelation and Theology: The Gospel as Narrated Promise.* Notre Dame: University of Notre Dame Press, 1985.
Thompson, Marianne Meye. *The God of the Gospel of John.* Grand Rapids: Wm. B. Eerdmans, 2001.
Ticciati, Susannah. *A New Apophaticism: Augustine and the Redemption of Signs.* Leiden: Brill, 2013.

Tomaszewski, Christopher. 'Collapsing the Modal Collapse Argument: On an Invalid Argument Against Divine Simplicity'. *Analysis* 79, no. 2 (April 2019): 275–84.
Tonstad, Linn Marie. *God and Difference: Trinity, Sexuality, and the Transformation of Finitude*. London: Routledge, 2016.
Torrance, Thomas F. *Space, Time and Incarnation*. London: Oxford University Press, 1969.
Torrance, Thomas F. *The Christian Doctrine of God: One Being, Three Persons*. Second Edition. 1996. Reprint, London: Bloomsbury T&T Clark, 2016.
Torrance, Thomas F. *The Trinitarian Faith: The Evangelical Theology of the Ancient Catholic Church*. Second Edition. 1988. Reprint, London: Bloomsbury T&T Clark, 1991.
Turner, Denys. *Faith, Reason and the Existence of God*. Cambridge: Cambridge University Press, 2004.
Turner, Denys. *Thomas Aquinas: A Portrait*. Yale: Yale University Press, 2013.
Ulrich, Ferdinand. *Homo Abyssus: The Drama of the Question of Being*. Translated by D. C. Schindler. Washington, DC: Humanum, 2018.
Velde, Rudi te. *Aquinas on God: The 'Divine Science' of the Summa Theologiae*. Aldershot: Ashgate, 2006.
Verghese, T. Paul. 'Διάστημα and Διάστασις in Gregory of Nyssa: Introduction to a Concept and the Posing of a Problem'. In *Gregor von Nyssa Und Die Philosophie*, edited by Heinrich Dörrie, Margarete Altenburger, and Uta Schramm, 243–60. Leiden: Brill, 1976.
Volf, Miroslav. *After Our Likeness: The Church as the Image of the Trinity*. Grand Rapids: Wm. B. Eerdmans, 1997.
Walter, Gregory. *Being Promised: Theology, Gift, and Practice*. Grand Rapids: Wm. B. Eerdmans, 2013.
Ward, Keith. *Christ and the Cosmos: A Reformulation of Trinitarian Doctrine*. Cambridge: Cambridge University Press, 2015.
Webb, Stephen H. *Jesus Christ, Eternal God: Heavenly Flesh and the Metaphysics of Matter*. Oxford: Oxford University Press, 2012.
Weigel, Peter. *Aquinas on Simplicity: An Investigation into the Foundations of His Philosophical Theology*. Oxford: Peter Lang, 2008.
Weinandy, Thomas G. 'God and Human Suffering: His Acts of Creation and His Acts in History'. In *Divine Impassibility and the Mystery of Human Suffering*, edited by Daniel A. Keating and Thomas Joseph White, 99–116. Grand Rapids: Wm. B. Eerdmans, 2009.
Wells, Christopher. 'Aquinas and Jenson on Thinking about the Trinity'. *Anglican Theological Review* 84, no. 2 (Spring 2002): 345–82.
White, Thomas Joseph. 'Divine Simplicity and the Holy Trinity'. *International Journal of Systematic Theology* 18, no. 1 (January 2016): 66–93.
White, Thomas Joseph. 'Nicene Orthodoxy and Trinitarian Simplicity'. *American Catholic Philosophical Quarterly* 90, no. 4 (2016): 727–50.
White, Thomas Joseph. *Wisdom in the Face of Modernity: A Study in Thomistic Natural Theology*. Ave Maria: Sapientia, 2009.
Wierenga, Edward. *The Nature of God: An Inquiry into Divine Attributes*. London: Cornell University Press, 1989.
Wilhelmsen, Frederick D. *The Metaphysics of Love*. 1962. Reprint, London: Routledge, 2017.
Williams, A. N. 'The Parlement of Foules and the Communion of Saints: Jenson's Appropriation of Patristic and Medieval Theology'. In *Trinity, Time, and Church: A*

Response to the Theology of Robert W. Jenson, edited by Colin E. Gunton, 188–200. Grand Rapids: Wm. B. Eerdmans, 2000.
Williams, Rowan. *Christ the Heart of Creation*. London: Bloomsbury Continuum, 2018.
Williams, Rowan. *On Augustine*. London: Bloomsbury Continuum, 2016.
Williams, Rowan. *The Edge of Words: God and the Habits of Language*. London: Bloomsbury, 2014.
Williams, Rowan. 'The Unity of Christian Truth'. In *On Christian Theology*, 16–28. Oxford: Blackwell, 2000.
Wippel, John F. *The Metaphysical Thought of Thomas Aquinas: From Finite Being to Uncreated Being*. Washington, DC: Catholic University of America Press, 2000.
Wittman, Tyler R. '"Not a God of Confusion but of Peace": Aquinas and the Meaning of Divine Simplicity'. *Modern Theology* 32, no. 2 (April 2016): 151–69.
Wolfson, Harry A. 'The Identification of *Ex Nihilo* with Emanation in Gregory of Nyssa'. *Harvard Theological Review* 63 (1970): 53–60.
Wolterstorff, Nicholas. 'Divine Simplicity'. In *Inquiring about God: Selected Essays*, Volume I, edited by Terence Cuneo, 91–111. Cambridge: Cambridge University Press, 2010.
Wolterstorff, Nicholas. 'Is It Possible and Desirable for Theologians to Recover from Kant?' In *Inquiring about God: Selected Essays*, Volume I, edited by Terence Cuneo, 35–55. Cambridge: Cambridge University Press, 2010.
Wood, Jordan Daniel. 'Against Asymmetrical Christology: A Critical Review of Rowan Williams's "Christ the Heart of Creation"'. *Eclectic Orthodoxy* (blog), 5 August 2019. https://afkimel.wordpress.com/2019/08/04/against-asymmetrical-christology-a-critical-review-of-rowan-williamss-christ-the-heart-of-creation/.
Wood, Jordan Daniel. 'Creation Is Incarnation: The Metaphysical Peculiarity of the *Logoi* in Maximus Confessor'. *Modern Theology* 34, no. 1 (January 2018): 82–102.
Wright, Stephen John. 'A Precise Mystery'. In *The Promise of Robert W. Jenson's Theology: Constructive Engagements*, edited by Stephen John Wright and Chris E. W. Green, 9–28. Minneapolis: Fortress, 2017.
Wright, Stephen John. *Dogmatic Aesthetics: A Theology of Beauty in Dialogue with Robert W. Jenson*. Minneapolis: Fortress, 2014.
Wuellner, Bernard. *Dictionary of Scholastic Philosophy*. Milwaukee: Bruce, 1956.
Yandell, Keith. 'An Essay in Particularist Philosophy of Religion: A Metaphysical Structure for the Doctrine of the Trinity', unpublished essay.
Zizioulas, John D. *Being as Communion: Studies in Personhood and the Church*. Crestwood: St. Vladimir's Seminary Press, 1985.

Index of Names

Anatolios, Khaled   25, 34, 45
Aquinas, Thomas   4, 22, 33, 35, 37
– and Augustine   64
– and Plotinus   70
– intellectual context   54
– on analogy of being   61
– on appropriation   66
– on divine attributes   21
– on essence and existence   11, 57, 112
– on processions and missions   66
– on relations of origin   178
– on triune relations   26
Aristotle   14, 17, 33, 39, 82
– on drama   99
Athanasius   25
Augustine   4, 18, 33, 45
– and creatio ex nihilo   46
– on divine attributes   21
– and the transitivity of identity   51
– on 1 Cor 1.24   50
– on relative predication   176
– on simplicity   9
– on simplicity and Trinity   49
– on Trinity and predication   52
– on unity   2, 46
Avicenna   54
Ayres, Lewis   1, 5, 23, 25, 51, 140
– on Augustine   45

Barnes, Michel René   1, 53
Barth, Karl   1, 17, 28
– and Isaak Dorner   79
– Jenson's critique of   93
– on reformed scholasticism   79
– on supratemporality   110
Basil of Caesarea   35, 37, 157
Bates, Matthew   144, 159
Begbie, Jeremy   170
– on musical time   114
– on simplicity   180
Behr, John   1, 16
Braine, David   13 f.
Brower, Jeffrey   23

Brunner, Emil   81
Burrell, David   10, 12, 17, 55, 139
– approach to Aquinas   56

Cappadocians   22
Clarke, W. Norris   12, 14, 61
Coakley, Sarah   1, 15
Crisp, Oliver
– on Jenson   109
– on simplicity   11
Cross, Richard   27, 45

Dorner, Isaak   21, 78
Duby, Steven J.   9, 18, 23

Emery, Gilles   63
– on appropriation   66
Eunomius   33, 35, 37, 40, 43

Gilson, Etienne   28, 54
Gregory of Nyssa   4, 15, 21, 23, 33, 169
– and creatio ex nihilo   36
– and inseparable operations   122
– and non-contrastive transcendence   43
– and Plotinus   35, 41, 67
– on 1 Cor 1.24   37
– on infinity   39
– on perfection   158
– on simplicity and Trinity   42
Gunton, Colin   1, 15, 50, 140
– on simplicity   28, 81

Hart, David Bentley   9, 19, 34, 44, 104
Hasker, William   18, 21, 51
– on Augustine   50
– on simplicity   28
Hauerwas, Stanley
– on Jenson   118
Hegel, G. W. F.   18, 100, 172
Heidegger, Martin
– on Luther   77
Hinlicky, Paul   24, 50
– on protological simplicity   12, 179

– on rule-based simplicity   10
Holmes, Stephen R.   5, 23, 25, 140
Hughes, Christopher   13, 58
Hunsinger, George   10
– on Jenson   109, 146

Irenaeus of Lyons   15, 19, 167

Jenson, Robert W.   4
– and Rahner's Rule   146
– and the trinitarian revival   1
– critique of Barth   93
– dramatic unity   88, 123, 142
– early criticism of metaphysics   83
– in contemporary theology   83
– on Augustine   121
– on Barth and Przywara   150
– on being   86, 106
– on God's 'roominess'   134
– on identifying by and with events   101
– on inseparable operations   121
– on Jesus in the Trinity   119
– on law and gospel   90
– on logos asarkos   122
– on metaphysics   86
– on proclamation   127
– on relations of origin   171
– on the body of Jesus   124, 161
– on the body of the Son   163
– on the task of theology   84
– on theological metaphysics   75
– primacy of the future   95
Jesus
– and history   99, 118
– and metaphysics   92
– and the future   92
– as unity of time and eternity   93
– in the Trinity   162, 167
– prayer for unity   2
Jüngel, Eberhard   81

Kärkkäinen, Veli-Matti   170
Keller, Catherine   9
Kilby, Karen   2
Kripke, Saul   12

Lacugna, Catherine Mowry   1
– on Rahner and Aquinas   80
Lash, Nicholas   139
Lindbeck, George   85
Long, D. Stephen   56
Lossky, Vladimir   1
– on essence-energies distinction   169
Luther, Martin   77

Mann, William   22
Mascall, E. L.   3, 17, 61
McCabe, Herbert   168
McCall, Thomas
– on Jenson   101
McFarland, Ian A.   15, 123
– on incarnation   168
– on Jenson   163
Miller, Barry   13
Moltmann, Jürgen   1, 27
– on God and place   134
Mullins, Ryan   14, 18
Murphy, Francesca Aran   85, 176
– on cinematic modalism   118, 152

Nicholas of Cusa   165

O'Rourke, Fran   19

Palamas, Gregory   167
Pannenberg, Wolfhart   1, 31, 86, 140
– and Jenson on time   110
– on Jenson   125
Perl, Eric
– on Dionysius   166
Placher, William   57
Plantinga, Alvin   20
Plato   14, 42 f.
Plotinus   17, 28, 32
– and creation   67
– and Gregory of Nyssa   41, 67
– contrastive transcendence   68
– development on Plato and Aristotle   32
– on creation   139
– on simplicity   33
– on unity   70
Powell, Samuel   78
Przywara, Erich   17 f., 150

Pseudo-Dionysius the Areopagite 15
– on identity of interiority and exteriority
    165
– on names as deifying 157

Radde-Gallwitz, Andrew 9, 21, 36, 37f., 41, 68
Rahner, Karl 1, 80
relation
– of goal 175
Richard of St. Victor 173

Schwöbel, Christoph 28, 110, 145
Scotus, John Duns 26
– and Augustine 64
Sonderegger, Katherine 1, 10, 15, 165, 173
Soskice, Janet Martin 19
Soulen, R. Kendall 118
– on Jenson 115
Swain, Scott 89, 117

Tanner, Kathryn 2, 18, 43, 159
– on Plotinus 68

Tavast, Timo 117, 131
te Velde, Rudi
– on David Burrell 56
Teske, Roland 48
Tonstad, Linn Marie 171, 179

von Balthasar, Hans Urs 12, 24, 31, 42
– on persons in Christ 158
– spatial metaphors 134

Ware, Kallistos 1
Weinandy, Thomas 105
White, Thomas Joseph 3, 24, 56
– on subsistent relations 170
Whitehead, Alfred North 9
Williams, Rowan 1, 54, 101, 117, 160
Wippel, John 61
Wolterstorff, Nicholas 21, 81
Wright, Stephen John 1, 131, 161
– on simplicity in Jenson 104

Zizoulas, John 1

Index of Subjects

analogy   3, 17, 41, 46
– and agnosticism   131, 161
– and divine embodiment   161
– and participation   152
– and temporality   107, 147
– of being   61, 79, 98, 147
apophaticism   14, 38, 44, 55
– and infinity   110
– in Plotinus   33
– relation to cataphatic   55 f.
archē   31, 35
asymmetrical christology   162, 185
atemporality *see* eternity   114
Athanasian Creed   24

being
– and time   107
– as event   106, 112, 147
– for others   158

christology, *see* Jesus   160
communicatio idiomatum   162
composition
– and narrative   116
contemplation   33
creation
– and redemption   167, 169
– as diastēma   42
– as history   147
– as utterance *see* word-ontology   155
creed
– as critical theory   85

diastēma   41, 169
– and trinitarian relations   42, 69
– meaning of   42
divine names   19, 60
– and historicism   152
– infinity as name   133
– love as name   132
– roomy as name   134
– self-involving character   152

emanation   35
essence
– and definitional knowledge   38
– and existence   12, 62
– and the divine persons   52
– versus 'substance' in God   47
eternity
– and atemporality   110, 114
– and projection   93
– and religion   84, 92
– and time   127, 146, 154
– in Plotinus   42
– non-contrastive   111
event   99
– and event composition   117
existence
– as activity   12, 17, 61
– in God and in creatures   12, 46

filioque   178

generation of the Son
– and relations of origin   120
– and simplicity   25
– as motion   68
God
– as decision   93, 146, 153
– as event   149, 160, 166, 172
– as love and gift   167
– freedom of   160
gospel
– and atemporal eternity   92
– and predestination   128
– and promise   128
– and the intelligibility of history   99
– as promise   91
– confronting religion   92
Gregory of Nyssa
– on perfection   157

Holy Spirit
– and proclamation   127
– as futurity   120

identity thesis, *see* divine names 156
immutability
– as ethical constancy 79
impassibility
– and faithfulness 116
– musical metaphor 114
ineffability 48
infinity, *see* simplicity and infinity 169
inseparable operations 53, 121, 168

language
– and divine transcendence 151
– and event 106
– and proclamation 128
– and temporality 107
– and the Trinity 107
– and time 96 f.
law and gospel
– as interpretations of history 90
logos asarkos 119, 122

metaphysics
– and divine simplicity 3
– and early reformation theology 78
– and scripture 4, 77, 102, 141, 144
– and theology 9, 61, 77
– as irrelevant 83
– christological 100
– historicism in 5, 86, 95, 152
– in analytic philosophy 12, 53

Nicene Creed 24
non-contrastive 3, 18

participation 16, 19, 34, 44, 46 f., 62
– and divine names 157
– and first principles 70
– and proclamation 155
– and salvation 63
– and theological language 157
– as metaphysic 14
– in Christ 98
perichoresis 2, 27
postliberalism 85
pro-Nicene theology 23, 25, 45
– grammar of simplicity 141
process theism 9

proclamation, *see* Holy Spirit and proclamation 155
projection 161, 171
– and eternity 143
– and historical specificity 154
– and religion 92 f.
– in trinitarian theology 2
prosopological exegesis 144
Pseudo-Dionysius the Areopagite
– on divine names 19
pure act 23, 58, 113

Rahner's Rule 146
relation
– and diastēma 69
– and person 64, 173
– and predication 52, 64, 176
– of opposition 65
relations of origin
– criticism of 171
– regulative interpretation 178
relations of origin, *see* relation of opposition 171
religion
– and history 92
revelation 88, 147

scripture
– and the church 85
– as inherently metaphysical 87
– God as author 85
simplicity
– and being-itself 47
– and creatio ex nihilo 15, 46, 60
– and divine perfection(s) 36, 40, 57, 156
– and identity of essence and existence 57, 166
– and immanence 38
– and infinity 39, 44, 169
– and participation 62, 70, 159
– and temporal infinity 108
– and the trinitarian revival 140
– and theological epistemology 22, 36
– and theological language 15, 57
– and Trinity 42, 49
– and union with God 45, 54, 186
– and unity 2

– as a metaphysical doctrine   11, 47
– as a regulative doctrine   10, 55
– as ethical concept   79
– as formal feature   10
– as optional   81
– as plenitude   38, 66, 71, 134
– diagnosing its decline   76
– incompatible with scripture   82
– truth-maker account   23
social trinitarianism   28
Spirit-christology   126
subsistent relations   170
– and divine embodiment   161
– and temporality   109, 172
supersessionism   116, 118

temporal infinity   110
theological language   21
theology
– as practical and speculative   84
– as self-involving   87
time   42
– and death   90
– and metaphysics   89
– as social and political   90
transcendence
– and christology   154, 159
– and freedom   160
– and futurity   94, 98
– as event   161
– as open concept   154
– non-contrastive   43, 68, 135, 142
transitivity of identity   20, 26, 51
trinitarian revival   3, 72, 140
Trinity
– and composition   23

– and diastema   43
– and embodiment   124
– and hegemonic discourse   142
– and history   124, 148
– and motion   69, 71
– and predication   52, 131, 176
– and procession   65
– and projection   2
– and subsistent relations   26, 65, 69, 109, 170
– and temporality   148
– and transcendence   153
– appropriation   66
– as self-gift   180
– processions and missions   66
triplex via   56

unity
– and divine simplicity   4
– as event   99, 146
– hermeneutical   88
– in God and creatures   46, 71
– in God and in creatures   158
– of thought   100
– of time and eternity   93, 127
– of truth   86
– the question of   1
univocal, univocity   17, 19, 68
– and time   110

verification
– in theology   153, 155
Vorstellung and Begriff   145

word-ontology   96, 106, 129
– and divine names   154

www.ingramcontent.com/pod-product-compliance
Lightning Source LLC
Chambersburg PA
CBHW020230170426
43201CB00007B/379